To: Beau
From: Ms K

2023

MW01680274

The Newport Nightmare

Jimmy Owens

with Dave Argabright

Foreword by Mike Marlar

The Newport Nightmare

By Jimmy Owens
with Dave Argabright

ISBN 13: 978-0-9899426-8-3

Published by:
American Scene Press, LLC
P.O. Box 34
Noblesville, IN 46061
(317) 219-5716
www.daveargabright.com

Cover images:
Front cover, Rick Schwallie; back cover, Heath Lawson

Proudly written, produced and printed in the USA

Acknowledgements

As we began the process of assembling the many components needed to produce this book, a number of people stepped forward to provide a much-needed boost to our efforts.

Chris Fox went above and beyond to help us with stories of Jimmy's early career, as well as providing many of the early photos used in this book. Chris and Jimmy are more like brothers than cousins, and Chris's impact here was invaluable. He gave us lots of time and energy, and this book is better because of his help. Thank you, Chris!

Kurt Owens was helpful as we worked to identify photos, names, places, and dates. Michael Hayes was always quick to respond to our requests for information and was very generous with his feedback and time and energy.

Rick Schwallie and Heath Lawson opened up their entire photo archives to us, and their excellent images are a vital addition to this book. Working with such well-organized libraries was a blessing as we developed the illustrations throughout these pages. The quality of their work has elevated this book, and we thank them.

Among Jimmy's countless friends and fellow competitors, Mike Marlar is uniquely suited to provide insight into Jimmy and his career. As always, Mike was generous with his time and contributed a warm and insightful Foreword, which is greatly appreciated.

As we worked on building the elements of this book, Melissa Foster and Nathan Owens were welcoming and patient as we spent time in their home. Melissa was helpful as she served as proofreader and coach, as well as offering kind hospitality on our many visits. Nathan brightened the surroundings with his humor, his questions, and just generally being an all-around good kid.

Many of Jimmy's close circle of friends and crew members—past and present—offered lots of helpful input. Chris Davis of Midwest Sheet Metal is a genuine friend, and a great supporter of dirt late model racing. Cory Fostvedt, Jeff "Mullet" Strope, and Kier "Big Snack" Hoover offered insight and ongoing words of encouragement.

A number of publications and sources provided historical data, including *National Speed Sport News, Dirt on Dirt,* and the Lucas Oil Late Model Dirt Series news archives. Bob Markos is without a doubt the foremost historian of dirt late model racing and on several occasions Bob provided timely details of Jimmy's career which were both timely and helpful.

As we began the layout and production cycle a number of longtime friends and colleagues offered advice and input. Cary Stratton and Lew Boyd of Coastal 181 continue to be great friends and supporters, and Joyce Standridge stepped in with some timely advice from her enormous volume of experience. Keith Waltz and Todd Turner also provided some timely layout advices as well.

During the lengthy process of creating this book, which involved many stops and starts along the way, Jen Ashley and Bob Dillner of MAVTV offered consistent encouragement. They seemed to have an unshakeable faith that after endless talk and promise a book would eventually emerge!

Special thanks to Lisa Argabright for her patience and assistance. At various times Lisa served as proofreader, art director, marketing coach, cheerleader, counselor, and therapist. When the going got tough she urged us to keep going and her encouragement and support were crucial.

Finally, we want to thank Jimmy for opening the door and allowing us into his world. Our many hours at the shop, at the track, and rolling down the highway in the truck combined to create an experience we will forever cherish. This has been a wonderful journey and we're glad for the privilege of helping you tell your story.

Contents

Mike Marlar. (Dave Argabright photo)

Foreword

I have to admit, I smiled when they asked me to write the Foreword to this book. I wasn't sure what was expected, writing a Foreword. "Just introduce the readers to Jimmy Owens, and tell us what he's all about," they explained.

That's simple enough. And it's an honor to tell you about Jimmy, because he is one of my best friends and someone who made a huge impact on my racing career. In fact, without our first meeting by pure chance, I'm not sure I would *have* a racing career. Jimmy encouraged me, and helped me, and taught me so much.

I met Jimmy Owens on July 4, 1998, when he parked next to me at Lake Cumberland Speedway in Burnside, Kentucky. It was a typical hot and humid July night in Kentucky. I ran in the Road Hog division there, which is about as "entry level" as you can get. We had a '70 Chevelle race car, beating around the track and trying to learn how to race. Lo and behold this nice outfit rolled in the pit area and parked right next to my pit.

Jimmy had trailer problems on their way to the track, and he and Chris Fox asked if they could borrow some of my tools. Me, being the curious person I am, asked a bunch of questions about where his team had been. Jimmy and Chris told me about racing all over the country chasing UMP National Points and I was intrigued. I thought to myself, "That sounds awesome, I want to do that." At this point I was a 20-year-old kid who had primarily raced in the street stock division; however, that night I got an unexpected opportunity to drive an open-wheel modified. Jimmy loaned me a used tire and gave me a quick tutorial of what I could expect in the modified and how to handle it. He won (of course), and I ran 3rd. I was so excited to follow the same adventure as Jimmy that I bought my own modified the very next week. Our chance meeting with Jimmy not only ignited a great friendship but also my racing career.

Over the past 20-plus years, Jimmy and I have toured the country competing against one another nearly every weekend. Jimmy is probably the toughest competitor I have ever faced, and his talent behind the wheel will go down in history as one of the best ever. Jimmy has the intelligence about a racecar to match his driving ability; he really is the whole package.

Even with his personal success, Jimmy has never been one to try and hold people back. Jimmy took me under his wing and was very generous with his knowledge, and in those early years I knew nothing about a race car that he didn't teach me. And he taught me more than just the technical workings of a race car; he taught me how to *compete*.

What's it like to race with Jimmy Owens? He is fair. That's the best way I know to describe him. He finds a way to win races without leaning and pushing and shoving. He's got the talent, the skill, to do it. Jimmy is very patient and has a steady hand at the wheel. He will chip away at it, and he'll sneak in and win even when you don't think he has a chance.

Jimmy wants to beat you fair and square, and he wants both of you to have fun racing each other. Bottom line, though, he is ultra-competitive.

In the beginning I talked more with Chris, but over time Jimmy and I started talking and became good friends as well. Jimmy was still working at TRW at that time, and he and Chris were a huge help to me. As I got my own car and went out on the road, Jimmy and Chris told me what shocks to run, what setup combinations they recommend, stuff like that. They taught me a lot about a race car and really shortened my learning curve.

They started staying at my house some, and that gave us even more of a chance to get to know them better. My home track was Scenic Raceway in Oneida, Tennessee, and they'd come up and race there on Friday night. When I went to Bulls Gap, Tennessee, I'd spend the night at Jimmy's place. It worked out real well, and I can recall many nights sitting around until 4 a.m. talking about everything in the world.

As time went on we got better in the modifieds and pretty soon Jimmy and I were racing with each other often. If people watched us race each other, they'd have no idea we were close friends. We raced each other hard.

The highlight of our years together in modified racing had to be 2002, when we battled each other right down to the final race for the $100,000-to-win UMP National championship. Yet today people still mention that season, remembering the razor-close battle between Jimmy and me.

Here is the story within the story, an episode that reveals exactly who

Jimmy Owens is and what he's all about. It's a story not known to a lot of people, but it ought to be. Because, in my opinion, it's one of the coolest and finest stories you'll ever hear in racing.

Jimmy was a part of Performance Chassis at that time, along with Rick Ogle and John Weir. They wanted both of us in a Performance car that season, so they built a car for each of us. And let me clarify "we" and "us." Even though we were good friends, and running the same chassis, Jimmy and I were independent of each other. We were each doing our own thing as competitors, yet staying close as far as our friendship.

We went to Florida to start the season, a place that has never been great for either of us. But, right off, I felt like we were pretty decent. We got back home and when the weather warmed up we started winning races. Jimmy started winning, too.

There were a ton of tracks paying UMP points, so we often raced at different tracks. A perfect points night was to qualify for the pole, win your heat, and win the feature. That's the maximum points you could win. Well, we started having those nights, and so did Jimmy. Pretty soon we were both at the top of the points, nip and tuck. It was amazing. Week after week, we stayed tight at the top. I had a slight lead because I had finished 2nd in a race that paid points-and-a-half, and that same night Jimmy suffered a flat tire. That was the difference in points, that one night. Man, it was close.

And then, disaster. On a Friday night we were racing at Clinton County Speedway in Monticello, Kentucky, and got caught up in a bad crash. We completely destroyed our race car, and as I sat there after the race I felt awful. Our hopes for the $100,000 seemed shattered. We didn't have a backup car, or a spare. We needed to somehow get another car together and be ready to race again within 24 hours. Impossible!

Jimmy and I usually checked in on the phone after each night of racing, so I called him to see how they ran. He explained that they won, set fast time, won their heat…maximum points, again. As he's telling me this, I was standing there looking at the pile of scrap that used to be my race car.

"How'd you guys run?" Jimmy asked.

"Well…" It was that pause every racer has experienced. "We crashed, and my car is tore all to pieces. I'm going to try and find another car to race tomorrow, then figure out where to go from there."

It was quiet on the line for a moment, and then Jimmy spoke up.

"I have another car."

"You do? Really?"

"Yes. It's my car from last year. It's a rolling chassis, just needs a motor. Why don't you come down and put your motor in this car? That way you could keep racing."

Now, let that sink in for a minute. Here's a guy who is racing for a $100,000 championship, and his closest competitor is wrecked and basically out of commission. It's Jimmy's golden opportunity to put some distance between us, and lock up that 100 grand.

He didn't hesitate. He offered his spare car to us with no strings attached.

Ain't that the coolest thing you could ever hear? Ain't that what racing is really all about?

Jimmy is a guy who is going to do the right thing—the BEST thing—even if it means it might make life more difficult for him.

We drove through the night to get to Newport, and in the wee hours of the morning started putting our motor in the car. It was the orange-and-white No. 20, and still had the tire marks on the hood where I drove over Jimmy the year before!

After working all day we hustled back to Scenic for the Saturday night race, still putting bolts in the car when we arrived. But we were able to race, and keep going. We didn't miss a race, because Jimmy's spare car saved the day for us.

You'll read about the finale of that season here in the book. Things came right down to the final race at Eldora, when Jimmy won and we finished 7th and fell just a few points shy of the title.

That was the toughest thing I've ever had to deal with, coming so close to $100,000 but coming up short. At the same time, I was grateful for everything Jimmy had done for us. Had he not helped us, we wouldn't have been there at the finish. That's a fact.

Jimmy came up in racing the hard way: from the bottom, without any money buying his way. He earned anything he ever got. When he went modified racing, for example, in those early years he had sub-par equipment and no money in the bank. He wasn't the best driver and he got his butt handed to him—a lot.

But he didn't give up. When he found a track where he wasn't any good, or a driver he couldn't beat, he kept going to that track and raced against that driver until he figured out how to win. For example, Butch Shay won all the races at Glasgow, Kentucky, and that's a long way from Newport. But Jimmy went up there every time they had a race, because he was determined to beat Butch. He finally got it done, earning a ton of respect from Butch in the process. That says something.

Jimmy is on the Mount Rushmore of modified racing. Then he moved on to late models and he's on the Mount Rushmore there, too. When you look at his stats, and what he's accomplished, it's amazing. I don't know of anything he hasn't won, to be honest. It's been tremendous. Jimmy has set the standard for a successful racing career for generations to come.

And here is the ultimate, most meaningful compliment any racer could ever receive: other racers want to be Jimmy Owens. If you talk to younger modified racers from those years ago and younger late model racers from today and ask them who they respect the most and whose career they want to match, you'll hear "Jimmy Owens" over and over and over again.

That's probably the greatest achievement any racer could hope for: respect from our peers.

Here's the beautiful thing: None of this has changed Jimmy as a person. Not one bit. In fact, he is so humble, just by talking to him you'd never know that he is one of the greatest racers of his time.

It's been almost 25 years since Jimmy and I first met in 1998. A lot has changed in racing, and in this world. But Jimmy hasn't changed much at all.

I've been fortunate to know a number of high-achieving people, and one thing they all have in common is passion, and focus. They change in the ways they need to, but they maintain their passion and focus.

That would describe Jimmy. Being a dad and having a family changed him some, and that's to be expected. He's a good family man and, aside from racing, that's where he spends his time and his energy. But I've never seen him pick up a hobby or an interest other than racing. He's still very focused on racing and winning, and I think that's one of the keys to his success.

I am very blessed to call Jimmy my friend. That's something I realized early on, and today I feel that way more than ever. He's a great person, somebody you would do well to emulate. I am very fortunate to have him in my life.

I'm excited to read this book. Jimmy has had a heckuva life, with a ton of adventure and success. I hope you enjoy riding along as he tells his story. I know I will.

Mike Marlar
Winfield, Tennessee
July, 2022

Dave Argabright and Jimmy Owens. (Cory Fostvedt photo)

Introduction

Jimmy Owens is an extraordinary man.

He will deny this, of course. Jimmy is quick to deflect any sort of praise or adulation, anything that could distance him from his humble East Tennessee origins.

Even as he shrugs off personal praise, the fact is that Jimmy is an extraordinary *story*.

His is a story of perseverance, and triumph. A story of difficult circumstances as a child, and a young life profoundly impacted by the right mentor at the right moment. And the story of how racing can inspire and shape in all the right ways, helping a man find his place and purpose on this earth.

Many people know Jimmy Owens as the championship racer, one of the greatest dirt late model and open wheel modified racers in history. They see an easygoing man who is comfortable facing a TV camera, who easily interacts with people at the track, and a man who wins and loses with equal grace.

There's much more to Jimmy Owens. Peel back that external layer and you'll find a deeply sensitive man who is intensely loyal to his family and friends. A man who recognizes the simple joys in life, and isn't easily distracted by the next shiny object. A hard-working man who has dedicated his life to the pursuit of racing excellence, and has succeeded by every measure.

And a man with a quirky, funny sense of humor. Oh, yes.

I first met Jimmy in 2006 when I joined the SPEED TV crew televising the Lucas Oil Late Model Dirt Series. After a stellar run in open wheel modified racing, Jimmy was making the transition to dirt late models and was just about to join forces with Mike Reece, a union that would forever change the course of his career.

At first, Jimmy seemed distant, almost suspicious of me and the TV crew. He was thrust into this new world of facing the camera and microphone, and I suspect it took a while before we earned his trust. Those first few interviews seemed tense and brief, but over time Jimmy began to relax. That's when the Owens humor was allowed to surface, and his eyes would twinkle as he looked at me during an interview and say things like "Man, that was way gooder!" with the deepest Tennessee accent.

From that point I considered Jimmy my friend. I was blessed.

One day Jimmy casually mentioned that he noticed I had written several books about various racing personalities. "I think I'd like to write a book someday," he said. I have to admit; I didn't see *that one* coming. Nonetheless, we were off and running.

Well…off and *crawling* would be a better description. The book you're holding took several years to complete, because at several points either Jimmy or I were distracted by various external forces.

Looking back, those delays were the best thing that could have happened. Once we began talking about the complexities of his life, it was a cathartic experience for Jimmy. This happens often among people who write their life story. Many old emotions surfaced, and Jimmy worked through those feelings one story at a time, processing the various episodes with a perspective that was shaped by healing and the passing of time.

That's why I am excited for people to read his story. Jimmy's life has been a unique, amazing journey.

Part of my job as Jimmy's co-author is to help flesh out the person and the personality.

All humans are complex and not easily defined—you, me, everybody. But with Jimmy, it is possible to sum him up with one word: Authentic. After a great many hours together at the track and in personal one-on-one time while writing this book, I can assure you that Jimmy is absolutely authentic. The humble, self-effacing man we all know is real. With Jimmy, the old adage applies: What you see is what you get.

Jimmy is a wheel man. He can drive a race car with the best of 'em, and is intensely competitive on the track. He is hands-on with his race car, and there isn't any part of the car where he isn't proficient. His knowledge of suspension and shocks is among the best in the country. This has led him to become one of the most successful racers of his generation: four Lucas Oil Late Model championships, and he's won pretty much every dirt late model Crown Jewel worth mentioning. In the ranks of open wheel modified racing Jimmy's success is the stuff of legends, a generational talent who will be talked about long after he is finished.

He has done all of this in a quiet, confident manner. You'll never hear Jimmy boasting of his success, because that's not his way. He lets his results speak for themselves. As for the limelight, he can take it or leave it. Mostly he'd rather leave it, greatly preferring an outing with his family in their Jeep rather than listening to people talk about Owens the superstar.

Over the past four decades I have come to know hundreds of racing personalities. Racers are a unique animal, for sure. But two things about Jimmy stand out, distancing him from the crowd.

One, he has guts. Many years ago when Jimmy began racing modifieds and wanted to grow as a racer, he intentionally traveled to tracks where he wasn't very good. That meant taking a beatdown, week after week, until he improved enough to be competitive. Most racers have a fragile ego, and such humbling is beyond their capacity. But Jimmy was strong enough to take it, over and over again. Maybe that's why he is so strong today; his confidence has been heat-treated by countless humbling nights.

Two, Jimmy is a sensitive person who cares deeply for others. He has a strong sense of empathy, and seeing others struggle is troubling to him. On the other hand, he is happy for the success of others, even his fellow racers. These emotions are genuine with Jimmy, and I'll say it again: what you see is what you get.

Those are two traits I hope we have captured in this book.

Here is one more important element: Jimmy Owens is a lot of fun. He cracks jokes, he gently pokes fun at himself and those around him, and he has a way of making us laugh. Even when he's not trying! Hanging around his shop, riding with him in the hauler, sitting down at a restaurant, you never know what's coming next. Never a dull moment, that's for sure.

It's been a privilege to help Jimmy tell his story. He has touched me and my life, just like he has touched so many others. Jimmy has a way of making people comfortable, and with just a two-minute conversation he makes a new acquaintance feel like a lifelong friend.

Ready to take a ride with Jimmy? Grab hold of something and hang on…here we go!

Dave Argabright
Noblesville, Indiana
July, 2022

This book is dedicated to the dreamers; living the dream is possible, so never stop dreaming.

And...

Never give up.

- J.O.

1

Welcome to Newport

The 25-70 Highway is slick with rain this morning here in Newport, Tennessee, and it's a little foggy. When I'm driving around town I'm generally not in a hurry, so I'll roll kinda slow as I show you around a little bit. This is all real familiar to me because this is my world.

They say the pace is slow here in Tennessee. But it's our pace, and to me and my neighbors it feels normal. When I get into a big city things seem fast, and busy. I reckon this feels comfortable because this is the way it's always been here. Life moves slow, and things don't change much.

I've traveled all over the place, but I've never lived anywhere but Newport. In fact, I have lived in just two houses in my entire life. My boyhood home over on old Hwy. 411, and the home where my family and I live today. I am fierce about sticking with my roots and have never considered living anywhere but Newport.

There aren't a lot of fancy things here and that suits me. I'm not a fancy guy by any means. I'll take a pair of comfortable camo shorts over a pair of dress pants any 'ol day.

I will tell you this, right up front: There are two Jimmy Owens, and I guess that makes things kinda complicated when I try to tell my story.

Out front there is the racer Jimmy Owens, the guy you see interviewed on TV and walking around the pit area at a race track. That guy looks comfortable on TV, comfortable being around a lot of people, comfortable being in the spotlight. I had to learn how to be that guy. You might say I had to grow into that role, that person. Matter of fact, I'm *still* learning how to be that guy.

The other Jimmy Owens is the guy who drives around Newport and has hardly changed from the boy who grew up here. When I'm at the race track I've accepted that I have to be in the spotlight, and that's okay. But when I'm back here in Newport I'm able to be the normal Jimmy Owens.

The little drummer boy!

Normal. Did I just use that word? My friends would probably laugh and say I'm a lot of things, but I ain't normal. That's all right...they ain't normal either! If they were normal they wouldn't be hanging around with me.

I was an average kid who had some great things happen. My dreams came true; I dreamed of being a full-time racer and that happened.

Why did it happen? Some of it was luck, or God's will, or destiny. Take your pick. But it was also a matter of working hard and trying to make good decisions to make my dreams come true.

The luckiest thing that ever happened for me is that I realized that *you don't have to follow anybody's path but your own.* It's okay to dream of doing big things, then work toward making those dreams come true.

That is one of the biggest reasons I wanted to write this book. What I learned was very important, and I want to share it with other people. Especially younger people. I want to talk about making smart decisions, and don't be afraid to take charge of your life.

We've all heard that we learn from our mistakes. Don't make the same mistake twice, that kind of stuff. But shouldn't we also learn from the decisions that turned out to be good?

I've always got the radio playing in the truck, probably some '80s or '90s rock music or maybe something newer. I'll probably sing along with the radio when a familiar song comes on. I can't sing worth a dang but I enjoy it—in the truck where nobody can hear me.

Right here along the highway—less than a mile from my old house—they have public dumpsters, and when we were kids we'd scour those dumpsters for wheels and tires of any kind for our home-made wagons to ride down the hill. We just about killed ourselves on those wagons, and had some spectacular crashes.

Right up here is where we turn off to the road where I grew up. Old Hwy. 411 dead-ends at the 25-70 Highway, right here. It's a winding road, and you'd better be on your toes if you drive too fast.

That white house there is where my aunt Judy lived, that's Chris Fox's mother and that's where he grew up. That little gray house is where Mamaw lived.

The little house where I grew up was just a few yards away, along with my dad's body shop. My brother Kurt still lives in our old house, you can kind of tell it's a racer's place because the old race cars sitting around.

I lived in that house for most of my life, well through my mid-30s. It's a mixed bag in terms of memories. Good and bad. It's got a full basement, and we heated with wood. That little cellar window there, I'd just chuck the firewood through the window into the basement.

Across the road was our neighbor Phil Morgan and his family. They had a fine home, back a short lane. You know, we forever had their yard all marked up where we ran off the road in those wagons, and they never said a word. Very nice people.

Around the corner from us on the 25-70 Highway is the Family Inns motel. We would sneak into their swimming pool all the time, and they'd run us out. They finally got tired of chasing us off, so they called our parents and had them sign a release of liability in case we drowned or got hurt. We had lots of good times in that pool.

My buddies Stacy Phillips and Shane Maxwell were always mixed up in things like that with us. Right there in front of Clevenger Mobile Home Park we'd race our bicycles, for hours and hours and hours.

Here is Edgemont Elementary School, where I attended. It's been here just about forever and it looks just the same today. In fact, right behind the current school building was the elementary where my mother and her sisters went to school. The old building was finally torn down a few years ago.

Edgemont was probably a mile from home, and we walked there and back, most every day. We had little short cuts here and there, and all of this hasn't changed. I could walk that route today and still know every foot of it.

The school sits along Carson Springs Road, which is on a grade leading to a small mountaintop. On our ambitious days we'd ride our bicycles—dirt bikes, single speed—up the hill, which was maybe three miles. That was a hard ride. Then we'd turn around and coast off. That part was fun! Even though I didn't play a lot of sports as a kid I was in pretty good shape from all those miles on the bicycle.

My parents—Bobby Ray and Glenda Owens—were both local so they knew everybody in Newport. My brother Kurt is eight years older than me, and my sister Tammy is four years older than me. I came along on Feb. 3, 1972, and I'm the baby of the Owens bunch.

When Kurt was 16 years old he started racing street stocks around our area, and my dad and mom helped him. It came in handy that my dad was a body man, because he was making body panels for some guys racing around home.

I guess racing has been in my life since the very beginning. My Papaw raced in the long-ago days, and my dad helped some guys who raced locally and we sometimes went to the races with him. It must have made an impression on me because I was into those race cars! I can remember taking little index cards and drawing a picture of a race car and then cutting it out, gluing the pieces together. They wouldn't roll, so we'd get down and blow them across the floor. (Man, I'd love to have one of those card cars today!)

When I was maybe 10 or 11 years old Kurt was helping L.D. Ottinger, a guy from Newport who eventually raced with NASCAR. L.D. had a shop out in the country, and he took Kurt under his wing and started teaching him stuff about the race car. Eventually Kurt started keeping his street stock over at L.D.'s shop. I was allowed to go to the races some, but I wasn't able to hang around at L.D.'s shop much because it was more of a business.

Outside of my own family, there was nobody more important in my life than David and Norma Prizer. My dad passed away when I was a small kid, and David and Norma stepped up big-time in my life. It's a great story of people who were way nicer than they needed to be, just because they're good people. They kind of took me in and had a huge impact on my life.

Kurt and L.D. eventually had some sort of falling-out and Kurt took his car to David's, working out of a small garage behind his house. Somehow Kurt ended up driving for David, and I started hanging around David's little shop on New Cave Church Road.

Man, you talk about a door opening! We really hit it off. David welcomed me to hang around the shop all I wanted, and even allowed me to tag along when they went to the race track. I was young and eager and so curious…I wanted to learn to weld, and when I mentioned that to David he pointed and said, "There's the welder…try it!" He taught me the basics of welding and off it went from there. Somehow I became a halfway-decent Volkswagen mechanic and started building Baja buggies. We rode those buggies like maniacs up in the hills.

Once I got decent at welding, nobody else around the shop wanted to weld. I was the young one, I reckon, so they made me do the welding. The good thing was with the buggies you didn't have to make it pretty. We messed around with those old Volkswagen pans for many years, and later on when I finally got a chance to work with a clean piece of metal I realized I actually *could* weld.

At the time I didn't understand just how special David was to me. (And when I say "David" I mean David and Norma, because they were both a big part of it.) But David made a huge impression, and I wanted to be just like him. Even though I was young I understood that he had no obligation to treat me so nice. Like that old song goes, "I wish I could be half the man he didn't have to be." I was no kin to him, just a kid off the street.

And here's the best part: David was good to me without expecting anything in return. That's pretty cool if you think about it.

I can't imagine what might have happened to me if David hadn't stepped up at just the right time. My dad was gone, and my world was kind of in chaos. But David provided me a place to go, a place to be, a place that was fun and interesting and great. He took me in and to this day we are very close.

Big brother Kurt Owens, leading the way.

David Prizer at North Texas Motor Speedway in 1998.

We have kind of an unusual relationship, though. I would do anything that man asked me to do, but we've never spent Christmas together. David and Norma have two daughters, and I've always been careful about not imposing on their relationship in any way. There are a lot of good feelings there, too. There's a lot of bad stuff in this world and you don't usually hear about good feelings like that, but they're there.

You know, I can say these things here in the book but I can't imagine telling David how I feel about him. I'm funny like that; when it comes to bad news and difficult things, I'm a very strong person. I can stay totally together and control my emotions. But when I try to talk about happy things and good things I just get all tore up. I guess I'm just put together that way.

The dune buggies didn't kill any of us...not that we didn't try. Those were wild times, gassing up those buggies on the hills around Newport. These were inexpensive homemade buggies, and we would scout around for junk parts when we broke something. It was surprising how durable those little VW motors were. They could take a lot of abuse.

David allowed me and my friends to clutter up the shop with all our stuff, and we were forever messing around with something or other. He was very patient, and generous with his help.

I had my first major accident when I was about 15. I was on one of David's buggies and ran across my friends Steve and Gary and Buddy at the top of one of the hills. We were riding around, having fun, when we decided to race.

I was flying around the corner when I got a little out of shape, and I panicked and hit the brakes. Wrong thing to do! The front end slid into an embankment and I flipped way up in the air. It was a big-time crash, for real. It's kind of amazing I wasn't hurt. Now, the sailing through the air, that wasn't the tough part. But the hitting the ground, that was a different story. You ever hear that expression about hitting like a ton of bricks? Well, this felt like *two* tons. It tore the crap out of the buggy...mashed both front wheels all the way back into the frame and tore the right rear wheel plumb off.

It scared the other guys, and they hurried over to David's shop and brought him back "to the scene of the crime." I was sure he was going to chew my butt out for destroying his buggy, but David came walking up, his eyes wide. He took one look at the buggy and said, "You go home and take a hot bath, right now!"

"Why?"

"Just do it."

"How come?"

"Because you're gonna be so sore tomorrow morning you ain't gonna be able to walk! I've never seen a dune buggy tore up that bad."

I did what he said, and I wasn't all that sore the next day. I had a huge bruise across my stomach from the seat belt but that's about it.

I had to mow David's yard all that summer to pay for the damage. We eventually fixed the buggy, and to this day David still has it going.

On another of our buggy rides we were flying down the road, running about 50 mph. I felt a vibration and looked over, and was surprised to see our left rear wheel rolling alongside us. Right about that time a big 'mater (tomato) truck was headed our way in the oncoming lane. I've always had a way of seeing things before they happen, and I could picture that truck running into our wheel and knocking it right back on us. So I swerved left and reached my hand out and smacked the back of the wheel, turning it back into our buggy. I walked it off the road with us and luckily the truck passed by. The boy riding with me thought that was the coolest thing he'd ever seen.

Man, those were good days. Yet today David's shop has not changed a bit, and I'm able to walk right in there. It's full of good memories, and I can laugh about the crazy stuff that went on.

That's how it is in life. You laugh and enjoy the good things and keep smiling. And the bad stuff, well...you try to deal with it the best you can.

Most of all you try to learn. When you do something foolish and skin your butt up, you remember that next time and don't do it again. Better yet, you watch and learn when other people skin *their* butt.

I learned a lot in those younger years. I was pretty quiet, and I preferred to linger in the background and listen. I reckon the reason I enjoyed listening so much is that everybody hanging around the shop talked about stuff I was interested in. Dune buggies, tools, welding, building stuff...and racing.

Oh, yes. Lots of talk about racing. That suited me just fine.

2

Challenges

Hanging around David Prizer's shop during my high school years, it was natural that I eventually got involved in racing. There was always a race car sitting in the shop, and everybody had racing on their brain, all the time.

My brother Kurt was a big influence in those early years, and Kurt and I both were totally ate up with racing. We are different in a lot of ways but the one thing we've always shared is our love for racing.

It was fun going to the races to watch ol' peckerhead Kurt race. He was a good racer…I mean, *really* good. He's *still* a good racer.

There were a couple of other hobbies I had as a kid. When I was eight years old I learned to play the drums, influenced a little bit by my uncles John and Jimmy Owens who played in area bands, along with Jimmy's neighbor Billy Wise. I was a small kid, and my feet couldn't reach both the bass pedal and the cymbals. My parents took me to a bar one night and I won a talent contest by playing "Wipeout." I won an 18-carat diamond ring! Another time we traveled to Pennsylvania to visit my uncle, and I won a talent contest there also.

One night a band was playing an outdoor event at Roses, a department store here in Newport. Mom and her friends had to coax me, but I got up on stage and played a couple of songs with the band. I had to tell the drummer, "You'll have to get the cymbals, 'cause I can't reach 'em!" The guy just laughed. I might not have been any good, but I was a novelty because I was so little.

I had a drum set at home, but like any toy I lost interest over time. One day we were downstairs goofing off and an electric heater got too close to my drums and we dang near burned the house down. So I was out of the drum business, and I kinda just moved on.

You know what's funny? In recent years I have found myself walking

With my dad, Bobby Ray Owens.

Only the coolest kids had a Steve Austin "Bionic Man" action figure.

My mom, Glenda Owens.

into music stores, looking over their drum sets. I reckon I have never lost the urge to have a nice set of drums.

A little later I got into archery, and was actually pretty good at it. Somebody had a bow they wanted to sell, and my cousin Buddy Fox was an avid hunter with a bow. I paid $75 for the old, cheap bow, and started to learn. Buddy bought a bow for his brother Chris Fox, and we all started practicing together. Another cousin, Rick Gentry, was going to archery tournaments and we started tagging along with him.

Eventually Chris and me took mom's Astro van and started going to tournaments on our own. That was my first real taste of competition, I reckon. I didn't play sports, but I did enjoy competing in those tournaments. We traveled all over east Tennessee; Knoxville, Seymour, Bulls Gap. We won the East Tennessee State Championship at Morristown, and another big win came at the Expo Center in Knoxville where we won a tournament with one bullseye shot.

Chris was also very good, and sometimes if they didn't have any other juveniles he'd shoot in our class (Chris is a couple of years younger than me). Even shooting from our markers he was hard to beat.

Mom eventually bought me a Hoyt Easton bow that was nice. But, like other hobbies, archery kind of went by the wayside when I got involved with race cars.

You'll hear me mention my cousins Chris and Buddy Fox a lot. From day one we have all been very, very close. Our families lived just a few yards from each other and we spent a lot of time together. A *lot* of time together.

I have spent a good part of my adult life trying to figure out things that happened during my childhood. For many years a lot of things bothered me, and I often felt troubled about it.

I wanted life to be simple, but it wasn't. Stuff happened that messed things up and I had a hard time figuring out how I was supposed to feel about things.

This is not easy, talking about my family. We care about each other and in some ways we're close, but in other ways we're kinda distant. It's always been hard for me to open up and talk about sensitive things, even with my family.

I have to be honest, my early life was rocky at times.

I was never really mad at my parents, but as a kid I sometimes didn't understand them. As I got a little older and became a parent myself, I started to see things a little differently. I realized that my parents were human, and they weren't perfect.

Even with their mistakes I love them. And I try to be more understanding.

Look around. You see it happening over and over again, where people aren't taught the right way to do things and they go on repeating the mistakes of their parents and everybody around them. It happens everywhere.

That's the pattern Bobby Ray and Glenda Owens fell into. Their friends were still partying and having fun and when you look around and that's what everybody else is doing, it seems normal for you to do it, too. They went down some paths that created problems all around.

I can remember being confused about so many things, and a little bit upset and angry. Maybe that's why I struggled sometimes with feelings of being depressed or sad, even though my nature is happy.

It's not fun to rehash unpleasant things, but I want to understand how to be a better parent and a better person myself. Plus, I want to figure out how I'm put together and why I think and feel the way I do.

The thing that aggravated me most was that my parents were hypocritical about their lifestyle. They'd be in the front room with their friends smoking funny cigarettes, then tell us, "By God you'd better not do that!" We had lots of parties at our house, and they'd send me to my room while they partied. I could hear people yelling and hollering in the other room. They did wild stuff and the more wild it got, the stricter they were that we were not to do those things.

I was angry about that, because even as a young kid you can see how silly that is. You do this almost in front of your kids, and then you tell us not to do it ourselves? Really?

To be fair, I realize now that—in their own way—they were trying to prevent us from making those same mistakes. Deep down they didn't want us kids to go down that same path. Yet they didn't know how to avoid it themselves. It's taken me a lot of years to see this more clearly.

Everybody has a different way of looking at things. My brother and sister kind of took the position that, well, we don't talk about all that. But I don't agree. It's important to talk it through because it's part of who we are.

Most of all, at a young age I became dead set that I wasn't going down that same path myself. That's the first time I remember going against the grain. All around me people were saying, "That's just how it is." I looked around and said, "But that's not how it *has to be*."

Why can't we try to change our direction and try to do better, try to reach greater things, and try to be successful?

I knew I wanted to be different, but how do I do it? I discovered a strange thing as a young boy: people who tried to better themselves—a better job, a better home situation, a better way of living—were immediately criticized as being "snobby."

It was almost like us kids were being conditioned—programmed—to follow some of the same troublesome paths as many around us. If you spoke up and said, "Hey, it doesn't have to be that way," you were scolded for being snobby. Ain't that something? Trying to grow and have a better life is somehow *wrong*?

That was hard. How do I try and better myself without getting snobby and thinking I'm better than somebody else? I'm not a forceful person, not a powerful personality. There are a lot of people in racing who are forceful, and they have a natural ability to impose their will on the people around them. I'm not like that…I don't directly challenge people, or challenge the status quo. I'm real low-key and rather than directly challenging you and forcing you to change, I'll quietly go away and try to do things my own way.

That's the type of kid I was. In my own quiet way I had an idea that I could do things differently if I challenged myself.

My dad was a hard worker and he tried his best to give us the things we needed. We had a roof, food to eat, and all the basic things. My mom kind of kept things together on the home front, and worked some odd jobs such as mail and newspaper delivery on a part-time basis at various times. Aside from the partying they were good parents.

Some days were good, some days not so good. If they went out partying, it was probably not going to be good. For example, we had an aluminum Christmas tree that was all mangled because they came in drunk and Dad fell all over it and killed our Christmas tree. Actually, we used it for years to come, because even though it was bent it was still usable! It was silver aluminum with a spotlight and a color wheel shining on it.

It wasn't funny at the moment, but time has allowed me to look back at things like this and laugh a little bit.

One weekend they went out partying and came home and had some kind of scuffle. My sister came and woke me up—I was still just a small kid—and told me to get dressed, we're leaving. Kurt had broken up the fight, and got mom and dad separated.

I remember sitting on the bed, wondering why Mom is bleeding, wondering why Dad has a cut on his leg. I'm mad at my dad, because I figure this is somehow his fault. Mom says she's taking the kids and leaving, so we've got to go. Dad was sitting there not saying anything, just looking upset and sad. As we got up to leave, Dad spoke up and asked Kurt if he would stay with him. Kurt said yes, and sat down. Mom and me and Tammy left.

All this time later, I still wonder why Dad didn't ask *me* to stay, too. That sucks but I've always wondered.

Eventually the partying and hell-raising ended up costing Dad his life.

I was eight years old at the time. Dad went out partying with some of his friends and they ended up in a motel where my dad died. Overdose, or whatever, the exact circumstances don't matter all that much.

I can clearly remember the police coming to our door. I was outside playing with my cousin Scott, and we went to the front porch to see what was going on. The police talked to mom and explained that our dad was dead.

The details aren't all that important to me now. I don't care to know what happened. All I know is that he was gone, and our lives were immediately turned upside down.

I was too young to understand any of this. Confused. I didn't realize the gravity of what had happened, and didn't grasp the fact that I would never see my dad again. As the police drove away I said to Scott, "Okay, let's play some more!"

"Aw, man, we can't play," Scott said. "Your dad just died!"

It just made me more confused. What did all this mean?

At the funeral I saw my uncles break down and cry, and saw my mother crying. That's when I started to cry, seeing my mother so upset. It would begin a lifetime of trying to understand, trying to come to grips with what had happened and what it meant.

When I think of my dad, that's the memory that has stuck with me. The loss, the tragedy, the sadness.

Our world was different now. Mom had to go to work, and suddenly she was the sole provider for three kids. She totally stepped up, because I never did without the things I needed. She was willing to spend every dime she made to provide for her kids. Dewey's Market next door was very kind to our family and they allowed Mom to buy food on a charge account, and we never went hungry. Plus, our family nearby stepped up to help as well.

My mom had already been pushed into being an adult at a young age, and when my dad died she was pushed even further. She had to grow up fast. She worked at various jobs, including cleaning rooms at a motel. Somewhere along the line she started tending bar, and was pulling two jobs. She eventually ended up working in a town a little ways away, and it made sense for her to stay over there for several days at a time instead of driving back and forth.

I'm proud of my mom, because she worked hard to provide for us. She loved us. She was her own person and, in her own way, she encouraged me to be my own person.

In later years Mom would travel with us to the races, and we went lots of places together. On one trip we raced in Tampa and loaded up and drove straight through to Royce City, Texas, a 24-hour drive. She was a great traveling partner and rolled right along with us.

We lost Mom a few years ago, and I'm grateful for the years we had together. We were very different people, she and I, but we absolutely loved each other. And we figured out how to accept each other as we are. We didn't always agree; sometimes she would aggravate the heck out of me, and there were times when I aggravated her. But today I understand that she was thrown into a difficult situation at a young age, and it took most of her life for her to get past that and figure it all out.

One thing I wish I could change is this: I never got a chance to experience my dad's friendship as an adult. People through the years have always told me what a great guy he was, and I wish I could have got to know him at that level.

Losing my dad at such a young age, and the turmoil of the situation, stayed with me for a long time. I reckon I didn't know how to feel about it; one minute I was mad, resentful of how things went down. The next minute I was still confused about why things happened that way. Most of all I was just sad, the kind of sadness that ain't easy to shake off.

Over time I got over the mad part, and even most of the sadness. I've accepted that it was just how things played out, and I quit trying to figure out who was at fault.

What helped is that I began to realize that so many other families in this world have faced some pretty difficult things. Some years ago Melissa worked in Nathan's school, and part of her job was helping kids who were having difficulties. Man, some of this was not a pretty picture. It was heartbreaking to hear of the tough things these kids were facing at home. I immediately realized that—if I'm being honest with myself—we didn't have it all that bad at my house, not compared to other kids. Although I must say, compared to what I recognize today as a normal life, our early years were definitely tragic and a little sketchy.

I can remember playing with some neighbor kids who were so frightened of their dad that they'd run and hide when he came looking for them. Wow! What's wrong with that picture? Today somebody would look into that situation and take steps to protect the children, but back then it was considered nobody else's business what was happening in their home. (Really? Nobody else's business?)

Through most of my high school years I spent a lot of time alone. Kurt got married when I was in high school, and Tammy had left home by then, too. Mom was working in another town and often stayed over there for several days instead of driving back and forth.

I reckon that's why David Prizer had such an impact on my life. My dad was gone, and in a way my mom was gone, too. But David stepped up and was a great father figure.

One thing that helped was that I was basically a happy kid. I wasn't a worrier; I always felt that somehow everything was going to be okay. There were times that I was a little depressed, but not at anything in particular.

I didn't have nice cars, and didn't want them. Had a lot of good friends, and overall I had a good childhood.

My situation was a little unusual because, even when I was a teenager, I had a very mature relationship with my mom. The number one thing was that I was totally honest with Mom. Maybe that's why she was lenient with me. I never lied to her, and if I went to a party where there was drinking, I told her. She trusted me not to drink. I was the designated driver and took care of my friends. We'd pile into our old Astro van and it was fun.

That was one of the decisions in my life that I absolutely do not regret. I decided, after watching everything that happened around me, that I didn't need drugs or alcohol in my life. Yet to this day I have stuck with that decision and I wouldn't change a thing. Me and my friends might be hanging out and they are drinking a beer but I'll have a Mountain Dew or a cup of coffee. That works for me and we're all cool with it.

I'm not saying this to preach, or to say I'm better than anybody else. It ain't about that. It's just part of my story and part of who I am.

If you want to drink or smoke weed, that's your business. And if I choose not to do that, it's my business. I will say this, though: you look around at so many people who are struggling with all kinds of problems in their life, and it's not hard to see that their decision to drink or do drugs led to bad things happening.

I don't get it. If you know bad stuff happens when you get drunk on your ass, why do you do it? Really, I don't get it.

For me, the upside was this: once Mom realized I was serious about not drinking, she didn't have to worry about keeping a close eye on me. Therefore I was allowed to do lots more things than most kids my age.

In most ways I was a pretty normal kid during my teenage years. I hunted and fished a lot, but those hobbies disappeared pretty quick when I started racing. I went to school, got halfway decent grades, didn't get into much trouble, and was a happy kid.

I had a bunch of good friends and we had lots of fun together. I was from the wrong side of the tracks, and it was pretty much known that the kids from our end of town weren't rich.

I can remember when one of my buddies was trying to arrange for us to go swimming at a kid's pool in Newport. The boy was a little older than us, and his family was obviously doing pretty well if they had their own swimming pool. My buddy asked about us stopping in to go swimming, and the older boy kind of looked at me and then in a roundabout way said he didn't much want kids like me hanging around.

Right then I decided I didn't want to swim in that boy's pool anyhow.

Moments like that stick with you, and if you're not careful they make you think bad about yourself.

Maybe that's why I liked hanging out at David's shop, and messing with dune buggies and welding stuff and generally enjoying myself. When I was in that world I was surrounded by people who didn't care whether we were rich or poor. It didn't matter.

I enjoyed school, especially high school. I never had a problem getting out of bed in the morning and getting off to school. Now, I'm sure I missed a few days here and there, but I pretty much did okay.

My overall effort at school was fairly poor, and I regret that. Basically I put out only enough effort to get by. My grades were decent but I could have done much better had I tried a little harder. Mom was gone all the time and there wasn't anybody to put my feet to the fire, so I didn't care all that much. I remember one time when I did absolutely nothing for a six-week grading period. I still got a B, surprisingly enough.

My biggest challenge was reading, and reading comprehension. One teacher just came in, told us to read a certain story, and then gave us a test. That's all there was. The next year I had a new teacher who had a different approach. He talked to us about the story and got me interested; what a difference! Now all of a sudden I cared about what I was reading, and paid attention. It helped my confidence, and I could remember what I had read. This was way better!

While in high school I had a chance to attend vocational school. This was a game-changer because I was interested in mechanical work. They had a decent little machine shop and I learned a lot. There were several classes that you could transfer your credits and join a group that was learning CNC programming, and I learned stuff that I would use for the rest of my life.

Here's a crazy thing: when I was in high school one of my teachers lived over in Jefferson County and we became friendly enough that we went rabbit hunting together. It was cool, because instead of seeing him as "one of them" I considered him a friend and wanted to learn from him. Today guns are considered terrible, and they'd probably put a teacher in jail for going rabbit hunting with one of his students. What a change we've seen in our society.

Eventually it was time to graduate with the class of 1990. I got my overall diploma all right, but I lacked just one credit to get my certificate in CNC programming. Right away I got a job outside of school and started racing, so it didn't seem important to get my CNC certificate so I didn't bother with it. Probably should have.

I regret that I didn't continue school in some way. I got busy racing, got busy with things, and I didn't see education as all that important. I sure wish I would have continued on a little bit. Today I'm always quick to encourage anyone—young or old—to get as much education, as much training as possible. It's not just a matter of making more money; it's all about feeling good and confident and knowing you've accomplished something important with your education.

My first job was as an electrical assistant at Hodge Electric here in Newport. I was there for about a year, and I didn't like it much. It was just a job. I could pay my bills and that's about it.

The job required me to spend a lot of time at a plant in Newport that made sweeteners and various things like that. It was nasty work, being around a lot of chemicals. Most of the fixtures are outdoors, and in the winter they used steam to keep their pipes from freezing. Several rooms in the plant were exposed to the steam and were very warm, like a sauna. We'd sneak into those rooms to warm up, sitting there until we fell asleep. Then we'd wake up all sweaty and go out in the 25-degree weather. Probably not too healthy.

After my graduation Mom was living over in Bybee at the time, and I continued to live in our home on old U.S. 411. It was pretty much a run-down shack, but it was paid for and I didn't have any bills to speak of. And I do mean run down. For example, you had to balance yourself on the commode because you could see through the floor into the basement.

I didn't want to spend any money on the place because I didn't figure I would live there for long. So my mom up and gave it to me, put the old place in my name. Later on Kurt moved in with me and we fixed the old place up.

Those years when I was there by myself, I can laugh now at some of those memories. We had all kinds of critters and varmints in the house. Some years earlier—I was still a small kid—a feed mill opened maybe a quarter-mile away, and once they opened we immediately had a serious problem with rats. A SERIOUS problem!

When I pulled into the driveway I could look up through the kitchen window and see a rat walking around on the counter. I'm not kidding when I say we had a rat problem.

We tried everything to control the rats. We tried poison, but they would crawl behind something and die and get to stinking something terrible. The best method was rat traps, and I had a bunch. At night I'd lie in bed and hear a trap go off. I had learned that when you hear the trap go off you had to get out of bed and go finish the job because when you got up the next morning the rat had worked its way out and was gone.

One night I had just come home from racing when I heard the trap and ran that way. I'm gonna stomp that sucker! I rounded the corner and I swear to God, this rat was almost 18 inches long. Wow! It was walking around the kitchen with the trap on its head.

I stopped in my tracks, because this thing was just about big enough to eat me. Then I realized: It ain't a rat, it's a…*possum*!

Whew! At least it wasn't a rat. Then again, how can you feel good that a possum is walking around your kitchen with a rat trap on its head?

I wasn't sure what to do, so I called next door to Chris Fox's house. I told his dad, Buck, that he had to come over and get this possum out of my kitchen. Terry Ottinger was up there, and they laughed and laughed that I was afraid of a little ol' possum. Listen, these tough guys weren't afraid of anything!

So here they come. Buck grabbed the possum by the tail and lifted him up, then snatched the trap off his head. The possum reached back like he was gonna bite Buck, so Buck dropped him like a hot rock. When the possum hit the floor it scared Terry so bad that he jumped clear up on the kitchen counter. Tough guys! Not afraid of anything! Well, almost.

But they did get the possum out to the woods and turned him loose. All the excitement was over for the night.

I can assure you that no possums were harmed in the telling of this story. Although that critter probably had a headache for a day or two.

After about a year I quit my job at the electrical company and went to work at the TRW factory over in Seiverville. This was probably my most serious effort at having a "real job." I ended up spending almost 10 years there.

I didn't mind the TRW job. I ran a 400-ton friction screw press that made engine valves. When it was running good it was boring, but when it wasn't running good the work was hot and messy and dirty. Boring was a good thing.

By coincidence, right about the time I started the TRW job I also started racing. In fact, a couple of friends who worked there were also involved in racing. I worked there long enough that I progressed to having three weeks vacation every year. I would look at my racing schedule and see where I wanted to go, then schedule my vacation days.

In the beginning the work schedule was Monday through Friday, working a "swing shift." I worked that swing shift for what seemed like forever, and eventually they started changing things up. Sometimes I couldn't get off work on Friday night to go racing, and that wasn't cool. But overall they were good about giving the workers time off.

I drove on U.S. 411 across the way to Seiverville, and it's a winding ol' road. Today when I drive out that way I can't believe I used to ride my bike along that road. It's a miracle I didn't get ran over by a car, it really is. I wouldn't let my son Nathan ride on that road for anything in the world.

I had a Mitsubishi 3000 sports car, and while it wasn't the fastest car it would handle like crazy. I could rip through those tight curves and winding hills on 411 and it was a blast. There was a straight piece of road where I could open 'er up wide open and it was fun.

One night I wound 'er up on the straightaway and sure enough, there was a cop parked off the side of the road and I was running about 120 mph. I knew I was caught so I pulled over before he even came out to chase me. Actually, I'm pretty sure I caught him sleeping, because he didn't even get me on the radar gun. He let me go with a lecture, and I bet it was because he didn't have any idea exactly how fast I was going.

At that time I had a genuine interest in driving in Formula One. A burning interest. I would have been much more interested in Formula One than racing in NASCAR, in fact.

Over time the road courses would go away. My path was pointing toward dirt track racing, and it was only a matter of time before I got there.

3

Finding a Direction

When I was 19 years old I was sure of only one thing: I was very curious about what it would be like to drive a race car. This was only natural, because my big brother Kurt was already a heckuva racer in our area. I looked up to Kurt and if he was racing, I wanted to race too.

I reckon it was only a matter of time before I tried it. Actually, I would have tried it much earlier if I'd had the money. But it wasn't until I had been working, drawing a little bit of money, before I could pull things together to race. I was out of high school for almost a year before the racing bug finally got my butt into the seat.

In 1990 I helped Kurt and David build a super street stock car for Mitch and Ed Turner. This was to replace their existing street stock, and I started pestering Mitch and Ed to give me a chance to drive their old car.

"Why would we do that?" they asked.

"Because if you don't, I'll just build my own car and outrun you." (I didn't lack for confidence in the beginning.)

Sometime later that year they finally gave me a shot in their old car. As we were getting ready for my first race I don't remember being nervous or anything like that. The only time I felt silly was when we got to the track that first night—Kingsport Speedway in Kingsport, Tennessee—and I was walking around the pits wearing a firesuit. I remember thinking, "Man, what are you doing, walking around in a firesuit…do you think you're actually a race driver?"

It wasn't even my firesuit; it was a third-hand deal. I got it from Kurt, and he inherited it from L.D. Ottinger. This was an old suit that had been used at Daytona a bunch of years earlier. This thing was way too small for me, and the elastic at the bottom of the pant-legs hit me about three inches below my knees. Maybe that's one of the reasons I felt silly walking around the pits.

An early street stock win at Bulls Gap on March 28, 1993. (Action Attraction Photo)

David Prizer with Kurt's car at Bulls Gap in the early 1990s.

We had taken the car out for some private practice so I wouldn't be totally in the red at my first race. The previous several years I had listened as Kurt coached people, and I tried to remember all the stuff he had told them. Kurt helped a lot of drivers, and hanging around him was almost like attending a driving school. So when I finally got behind the wheel I had a general idea how the deal worked.

I rolled out for my first race…and here we go! They threw the green flag and a couple of guys messed up in front of me, and one of them spun. For an instant we are eye-to-eye on the race track. Right about then I'm wondering, "What in the hell have I got myself into here?"

But lo and behold I went on to win the race. That was pretty cool, winning the first time out. It's hard to describe what that does to your confidence. I don't care who you are, until you try something you don't really know if you can do it. So if I was questioning whether I was capable, winning sort of eased that question right away.

Things came together pretty quickly for me that first year. In addition to winning the first time out at Kingsport, I won three of my first five races. It was exciting, but it made for a fast learning curve. Not just on the track; I learned about how this business works and what happens when you win a couple of races.

The promoters decided to spice things up by putting a bounty on me. They were trying to milk some publicity out of this 19-year-old kid, and I was cool with that. That's how it works. But at the same time it was kind of frustrating because it started to feel like everyone was against me.

They beat me when they put the bounty up, but it was still kind of cool.

I could win at Kingsport, and when we traveled to Volunteer Speedway at Bulls Gap the competition was tougher. I wasn't able to win there right away, but I was a top-5 car. Eventually I did win at Bulls Gap—the final race of the season in my first year—and that meant a lot because we had watched a lot of racing over there.

My first season was pretty good overall but there were frustrations. I was racing against guys I had idolized, guys I had been watching for several years. I wanted these guys to respect me immediately but I didn't understand that respect is not given…respect is *earned.*

I guess I was learning about myself, too. I was learning who I was and what I was all about.

When you're a snot-nosed kid, you don't know anything. You're dumb, you're insecure, you're confused, and you don't even know who you are. A few young kids are good at athletics or art or something else, but the majority of kids don't find out what they're good at until much later. So you're kind of looking around, trying to find your place. It's not an easy time for kids who are trying to grow up.

So when I rolled out at age 19 and immediately started winning races it was a big, big deal. For the first time in my life—absolutely the FIRST time—I could look at myself in the mirror and feel like I was good at something.

Man, that's huge! That's part of your identity, part of what makes you who you are.

I also discovered that I have a competitive streak. I was a mellow kid, and I didn't challenge anybody or anything; just rolled with the flow. But racing tapped a vein and made me realize that deep down inside I had some fire, and a desire to be successful.

On the night of our first win, I remember riding home with Kurt. I had listened as Kurt coached a lot of guys, and of course he had coached me as well. As we rode along, I kept waiting for Kurt to speak up, but he didn't. Finally I broke the silence.

"Ain't you gonna tell me what I did wrong?" I asked him. I was ready to hear some influential and profound advice.

He just looked at me. "Well, you won. You didn't do anything wrong."

And that was it. Okay then!

The following year I bought my buddy Shane Maxwell's car and raced it for a while. Sometime later—I'm guessing it was 1993—we got busy building me a car. I was working at TRW and finally had enough money to get some of the things we wanted. We put in a four-point roll cage and bolted on 8-inch tires and wheels. This class was sometimes known as "endure" cars.

Here's something interesting about the first race car we built. David provided most of the material and when we were finished I asked him, "What do I owe you?"

"Nothin'," he said.

"C'mon, I need to pay you."

"I'll tell you what," he said. "You just put my mama's name on the car and we're even."

So we lettered "Mrs. Prizer" around the front headlight trim. David's mother lived next door, and we got her up to the shop so she could look at the car. We hadn't told her about putting her name on the car. She walked around, nodding her head, looking everything over. Then she saw her name and she smiled real big, but she didn't say anything. Man, what a smile! It was pretty cool.

Shane Maxwell raced quite a bit but hadn't won much. One day in

David's garage Shane asked me how much racing I was intending to do. I said I didn't know, and hadn't really thought about it beyond the next race. Shane looked at me and said, "Well, don't think you can ever outrun me. That ain't gonna happen."

Man, that lit the fire. The next year I bought Shane's car and won 16 races.

I didn't do it because I was mad at Shane; I did it because I wanted to prove something to myself. When somebody tells me I can't do something—even if it's a good friend—that really fires my butt up.

One of the key "facts of life" about racing is money. Even at the beginner level it takes money to race. If somebody gives you a race car you've still got to keep it running, buy pit passes, put fuel in the tow vehicle, replace stuff you break and wear out, on and on. I don't care what class you run, it takes money.

Sometime during my first racing season I quit my job at Hodge Electric and went to work at TRW. I made more money at the new job, but I was still broke. I had to borrow money from David almost every week so I could get to the races. I would borrow money, spend it to go race, make a little bit at the pay window, and give the money back to David. By Thursday I had to borrow again for the next weekend. David was my "line of credit." But I paid him back, every week.

When I bought Shane's race car I went to a finance company and borrowed $1,500. It's funny, the first major purchase of my life was a race car. Not a home or a street car, but a race car. That says something right there.

I would not recommend borrowing money to go racing. It is way risky and not a good business move. But I wanted to race, so borrowing the money made sense to me. I paid the loan back on schedule and all was okay. But I wouldn't want to do *that* again. The car did not make enough money to pay for itself, but with what I made at TRW it all worked out.

My second year was real good. We won a lot of races and that was exciting. But when you're the new kid on the block and you're winning right away, the guys you race against don't like it very much. It was a pain in the butt to not be accepted by those guys. All those guys were Kurt's age, and those cats didn't like it that Kurt's little brother was beating them. Today I understand it much better, but at the time I didn't enjoy the tension that was created.

Kurt was winning in his class almost every week, and I was winning in the street stock class. My confidence went through the roof, man. I wanted

The first street stock we built, pictured at David's garage. 1993, I reckon.

My cars honored David's mother for many years.

to win every time out. Most of all I wanted to be accepted by the guys I was racing against.

It seemed to me that they wanted to make things hard for me, but maybe that was just my imagination. Those guys were part of a clique, and I wasn't allowed inside.

Melissa's dad—Danny James—was one of those guys. We were racing one night and he came up on me—that's how I saw it—and got into me a little bit. He cut a tire and hit the wall pretty good, and afterwards he was all mad and upset. He said I needed to learn how to let off.

That bothered me. So I figured what I needed to do was become so good at driving that *nothing* would bother me. Of course it doesn't work that way; you never get so confident that criticism doesn't bother you. You might learn to take it in stride but it still bothers you.

That second year is when I started noticing the butterflies. There were times just before a race that I almost got sick in the race car because my nerves were so bad. Those guys didn't want me, but I wanted so bad to be part of their group. Maybe I was still a little wild on the track, I don't know. But I tried to always race people clean.

Just because you're winning doesn't automatically get you respect. It's still that way; you earn respect over time, and not just by winning races.

Eventually those guys accepted me. Some of them even became good friends. I'm proud of that today, and it means more than those guys will ever realize.

Later, when I progressed to race successfully at a national level, some of them were actually proud of me. Lynn Phillips was one of the toughest guys I raced against; if you tangled with Lynn you were gonna mix it up with 15 members of his family. They were a tough bunch!

A few years ago Lynn took me aside and laughed and said, "All those years ago I had to listen to the other guys razz me about you beating me every week, and boy did that piss me off. Now I tell those guys, 'Hey, look at Jimmy now, he just won the World 100! That's who I was racing against!'"

That was pretty cool.

When we won 16 races that second year people started accusing us of cheating. Now, most of the time they didn't come right out and say it; it was mostly people just hinting around.

You know how it is…if you're winning races, you must be cheating. It's the same in every class, and it's the same today as it was in 1992. A guy wins two or three races, and well, you know…

Man, that tore me up. It bothered the heck out of me, because we weren't cheating. Every racer has probably cheated at one time or another. But it sucks to be accused when you didn't cheat.

We always had junk motors, and David was a genius at making those things run. He absolutely knew how to take old, worn-out parts and put a motor together that ran good. We had Stanley Allison helping us, and Carroll Kelly. Everybody pitched in and we were all interested in trying new things. We experimented with different camshafts and things like that. That was an important time because I was learning something new almost every time out.

Our class required us to run "take-off" tires—used tires from other classes. One weekend we traveled to Beckley, West Virginia and missed our race at home. When we returned Danny James would outrun us, bad. I couldn't understand how this could happen, because we hadn't changed anything on our car. We had a suspicion that Danny was getting first dibs on the take-off tires. So we bought a brand new set of Hoosier tires and took them out on the road by our shop and scuffed 'em up real good, then grooved them. We went to the track and kicked their butt. Suddenly everybody wanted to talk about tires and wanted us thrown out! But they weren't stamping tires and there wasn't much they could say, really.

As my career progressed I was eventually able to get better motors and had other people doing our engines. But you know what? Sometimes even the great stuff wasn't as good as those junkyard motors David built. We blew up a few but they sure ran good before they blew up.

That second year I could feel some things changing. Winning races had brought me some attention, and I wasn't sure how to handle it. A couple of years earlier I was an anonymous kid living on old Hwy. 411, and only a few close friends even knew I existed. But now my picture was in the newspaper; strangers would say, "Hi, Jimmy!" when they passed.

I didn't deal with that very well, and I still don't deal with it well today. Of all the parts of racing, I've had the hardest time with that. I don't want anyone to think of me as someone special. I was still the same person, but I happened to win some races.

I didn't want to be treated differently. I didn't want my friends to hesitate to call me because they think I'm too busy.

Still, the attention was kinda fun, I must admit. And it fueled my competitive drive even more. You learn to use that part to motivate yourself, and there's nothing wrong with that.

I was very fortunate to have a fun group of friends who helped me every week. Some of those guys didn't have any racing background; they were there just to help me.

My cousins Chris and Buddy Fox, W.D. Henry, there were a bunch of guys. Shane Maxwell helped also, even though he also had his own car. Several people were right there with us in the beginning. As I got more serious many of them kind of filtered away, because they got a job or started a family and weren't ate up with it like I was. That's probably the same story with everybody in this sport; you discover a level of commitment most people just aren't willing to reach.

Looking back, I can see now that I was so consumed with this deal that I eventually started to shut those guys out. It wasn't intentional. It's like a drug, I guess. That makes me feel sad. I can't tell you the last time one of my friends came with me to the race track. I wish it wasn't like that. Some of them have said they don't want to bother me and I hate that. I never wanted racing to distance me from my friends but it happened and I don't know how you avoid it.

I've got to give a shout out to my brother Kurt. He helped build my cars, he taught me, he coached me...there's probably no way I could have ever got started without him.

Kurt is still one of the very best I've ever seen in a race car. He never went out on the road much, but in our neck of the woods he's one of the best of all time. I was proud of my big brother and I'm proud of him now. Man, he is still capable of winning races and that's cool.

Sometimes when brothers race it causes pressure between them, and I never wanted that. I sure didn't want us fussing over racing, for sure.

After I had been racing for a year or two, one night I was helping Kurt at 411 Motor Speedway. A guy stopped by our pit and I overheard him telling Kurt that he was one of the best drivers he'd ever seen. Then he said, "And you know what? You've got a brother who they say can run circles around you at Bulls Gap. Is that true?"

Kurt kind of nodded my way and said, "Well, right there he is...why don't you ask him yourself?" We kind of laughed about it, but I didn't like stuff like that. I didn't want things to be taken seriously. When I got to where I could outrun Kurt people would aggravate us about it, and I didn't like that, either. But people kept talking and it bothered me.

I liked it better when we didn't race against each other as much. I didn't like people talking crap about us.

Kurt doesn't race as much nowadays because he's on the road with our team. But you might still see him now and then at Smoky Mountain, Tazewell, 411, and Bulls Gap. Before he went out on the road with us he had a great season with his super stock car and won a lot of races. I think he's still having fun, probably more fun than I am sometimes.

When I was a real young kid, Newport Speedway used to have a lot of big races. It was dirt then, and they had NDRA there a few times. Those were big-time deals, with national racers. Larry Moore, Jerry Inman, Buck Simmons, all the big names. They'd draw such a crowd that we had to park way down the road because the track was mobbed with people. It was amazing.

I have strong memories of watching those guys. Don Seaborn ran an orange No. 74 and he was my favorite. My mom made me a t-shirt with a No. 74 on it, and one night after the races we went down to the pits and showed Don my shirt. He acknowledged me, and that made me feel like a king. So of course I was even more of a Don Seaborn fan after that.

Naturally, when I started racing the No. 74 was my favorite number. But there was another No. 74 around here—Louis Hickey—that was running well, and I didn't feel like I could take his number.

My friend Alvin Renue said, "Why don't you take the No. 20?" Alvin had a trucking company and he explained that 20 was the number of his first truck. "Nobody is running that number," Alvin reasoned. "That would be a good number for you!"

I got to thinking about it. I liked the sound of it, and he was right—nobody was using that number.

So from that point I was No. 20. Simple as that.

I wondered how the number would look on the side of the car, and was afraid it might be ugly. But I liked it right off so I stuck with it.

For the longest time I was the only No. 20 I knew of, even when I started traveling. We had to put a decal over our number one time up in Kentucky, but other than that it was rare to see another No. 20.

It's funny, I was No. 20 and Kurt always ran No. 14. This was long before Tony Stewart came along, but I can say today that the Owens boys had both his numbers covered!

4

Graduating

I raced street stocks until 1995, and had a lot of success. There is a process; once you start winning consistently you feel more confident, and when you feel more confident you win more races. It feeds on itself. Almost from the beginning a dream started forming up in my mind: What if I could somehow make a living driving a race car? I knew it was impossible to make a living running a street stock around east Tennessee, but still...what if I could progress to another class that paid better money, and provided an opportunity to travel?

In the early years that was our faraway goal. Kind of like a boy wanting to climb Mount Everest, or go to the moon. It seemed so far-fetched that if you told people about it they'd laugh.

But I was serious. I really wanted to race professionally. I started thinking about how to make the dream come true. Even if I went broke in the process, I rather go broke trying to make it happen than wonder "what if" the rest of my life.

It was right about that time when I realized that there is a certain amount of criticism and judgement out there. When I was hanging out at David Prizer's shop, building dune buggies and having fun with my friends, nobody paid any attention to me. But when I started racing—and winning—I began hearing things from people. Things I didn't like, things that bothered me.

He must be cheating.

He's real good but he ain't good enough to go anyplace.

He ought to do this, or this, or this.

He's wild on the race track.

Just who does this boy think he is, talking about racing for a living? Why, that's ridiculous! *Just who does he think he is??*

Well, I didn't think I was anybody but Jimmy Owens, the boy from

Our first real hauler...man, we were proud of this sucker.

My mom provided lots of encouragement in those early years. Thanks, mom!

over on old U.S. 411 who chased rats out of his kitchen. That said...why shouldn't I strive to be good enough to become a traveling racer?

It's easier when you're flying under the radar and nobody pays any attention to you. However, I don't believe you can accomplish anything if you stay invisible. You've got to put yourself out there. But putting yourself out there means you'll take shots from people. It's not always pleasant but there ain't no other way.

I would like to tell you that I built up a thicker skin and learned to ignore the criticism, but that's not true. Criticism and mean comments still upset me. Nobody likes to be called names, or be made fun of. I sure don't. But I don't know any way to completely avoid it.

Learning to deal with criticism and "haters" was probably one of the hardest lessons of my life. As time passed I discovered that shutting up the critics is a good, good feeling. I also discovered that if you play it right, you can use criticism as motivation.

I had been racing for a few years when the money started getting a little better for me. I had progressed to open wheel modifieds by this time, and began to travel. I was still working full-time at TRW, and spending all my off time working on the race car. It was hard work but it was starting to pay off.

The old truck we used to tow the race car was plumb wore out, and we were constantly replacing the U-joints. One day me and my buddy ran into town and I was gonna go shopping for a new pair of shoes. As we rolled past the car dealership I spotted a good-looking 1995 Ford Lariat dually pickup.

Man, that thing looked nice! So we wheeled into the lot and looked it over. It was in perfect condition, with just 15,000 miles. Diesel, had a TV, nice seats...this thing was first-class. They were asking $25,000; I looked at the new ones and they were $45k, but none were as nice as this used one. This was the truck of my dreams, and I could picture myself rolling down the highway with my race trailer right behind.

The man and I talked, and I decided to go for it. Financed that sucker! This was far and away my first major purchase as a racer.

I came out of the office and told my buddy go on, because I was driving the truck home.

When I got home, my family asked what I was doing with this truck. I explained that I just bought it from the dealership.

"Did you really buy this thing?"

"Yep. Well...I financed it."

Everybody was tickled to death. Now we can pull somewhere without replacing the U-joints every time.

And I can honestly say, I once went shopping for a pair of shoes and came home with a new tow vehicle!

What a bunch! L-R: "Possum" David Smith, Anthony "Hootie" McMahan, Alvin Renue, W.D. and Chastity Henry, Chris Fox, and Buddy Fox.

MIDWEEK Edition September 15-16, 1993

SPORTS

LOCAL AUTO RACING

Photo courtesy of Stan Johns

Kurt Owens (above) and brother Jimmy both won at Newport on Sunday night.

Kurt, Jimmy Owens double up at Newport

NEWPORT — The Owens brothers picked up a pair of wins at Newport Raceway Sunday night as Kurt won the Late Model feature, while Jimmy picked up the Street Stock victory.

It marked the first time the Owens brothers have ever won features on the same track on the same night.

Kurt Owens topped Brian Ramsey to take the Late Model victory.

Meanwhile, Jimmy Owens edged Wayne Webb.

Other winners included Pure Minis and Buzz Collins in the Dwarf Cars.

The Pure Minis will be featured Sunday night, with $1,000 going to the winner.

Gates open at 4 p.m.

Brian Ramsey; Buddy Ball; Jim McDonald; Mickey Foulks. Heat: Buddy Ball. Trophy Dash: Ball and Steven Shults of Newport.

MODIFIED STREETS: Jackie

Hurst and Michelle Owens Newport.

STREETS: Jimmy Owe Wayne Webb; Jackie Stuart; Ron Holt; Danny James. Heat: Jim Owens. Trophy Dash: Ronnie H and Katlyn Perry of Germany.

PURE MINI: Chris Helton; Jim Gorrell; Roy Leadbetter; Rich Poore; David Wines. Heat: Ma King. Trophy Dash: James Holt a Jimmy Dale Gorrell of Newport.

DWARF CARS: Buzz Colli Robert Allen; Kay Tweed; J Bowman; Garland Worley. He

There were times when Kurt and I both won races on the same day. That was a big deal for us! This was on the pavement at Newport Speedway.

Things were going pretty good for me; I was earning as much with the race car as my full-time job at TRW. Maybe even a little more! Later that year I bought a trailer that matched my truck, forest green with brown stripes and ground effects.

Well, if you've got a nice tow rig you ought to be driving a nice street car, right? So I figured I needed an upgrade there, too. I had been driving old wrecks, including an old Datsun pickup that David gave me, a $200 special. I've always loved the early Camaro's, but could never afford one. I started shopping around and came across a Mitsubishi 3000 sports car, and that thing definitely caught my eye.

I decided to go see Mama and ask her opinion. I wanted this car, but I wanted her to talk me out of it. It was a lot of money and I didn't want to do anything silly. But her talking me out of it backfired!

She walked around the car, looking it over, and she's smiling.

"What do you think, Mom? Should I get it?"

"Hell yes! You only live once, son!"

So I bought the car and drove it to work the next day. I was on Cloud Nine!

Kurt was married to Denise at the time, and I stopped by his place to visit. He was outside working on something, and I wheeled up in my new car. Denise was sitting outside watching Kurt.

I got out of the car and she said, "Well, here comes walking bankruptcy!"

Man, that hurt.

Maybe that's what motivated me to get everything paid off as soon as I could. Within a year I had everything covered: my car, my truck, my trailer. Didn't owe a dime.

Sometime later we all sat down to eat, having a nice family visit. The conversation came around to money, and Denise looked across the table at me.

"How do you afford what you've got?"

"What do you mean?"

"You know what I mean…that truck, the trailer, that sports car. How do you afford all those payments?"

"Oh, it's all paid for," I said.

"What do you mean, paid for?"

"I ain't got any payments," I said, enjoying where this conversation was going. "Everything is free and clear."

Her jaw hit the table, and that was the best moment of my life.

People have motivated me in different ways, and that's not a bad thing. In fact, I'd argue that—for me—it's been a good thing. A very good thing.

One of the great experiences was traveling outside Newport, and even outside Tennessee. Racing was the motivation to get on the road some; without racing, I'm not sure I'd have ever traveled very far from home.

From the beginning many of my friends were volunteer help on the car and in the shop, and after a while we all began piling into our truck to explore races a ways from home. We were just a bunch of young Tennessee boys who didn't have a clue, and we were as happy as could be. Shoot, sometimes we'd take off without knowing exactly where we were going. That describes our first trip to Beckley, West Virginia.

That trip was Alvin Renue's idea, and he explained that the rules up at Beckley were about the same as our rules. So we loaded the car and piled into our old three-door Suburban (this was before we bought the Ford truck) and hit the road. It was me, Chris, Buddy, and Hootie (Anthony McMahan).

Alvin gave us the directions, and Hootie rattled off the directions back to him. But some of the details must have got lost somewhere in the translation.

We headed up I-85, and Hootie said the track should be right up the road. We rode along, windows down (no A/C), joking and having a good ol' time. After about four hours we started thinking, "You know, we ought to be there by now!" We crossed over into West Virginia and started counting exit numbers. All of a sudden we were in Maryland.

We pulled off the highway and found a gas station. "How do you get to Beckley, West Virginia?"

That ol' guy looked at us like we were from another planet. "Where you boys from?"

"We're from Tennessee!"

"Well bub, you ain't gonna make it to Beckley tonight. It's six hours thataway." And he pointed in the direction we weren't going.

"Six hours??!! Are you kiddin'?"

Turns out this fellow was a racer himself. "Since you can't make it to Beckley, come with us and run up in Pennsylvania tonight! It's only an hour away!"

"Naw, we got to meet some friends in Beckley. Thanks for the directions!"

We got back on the road, and now we were starting to get tired. Man, we drove and drove and drove. We stopped and bought a map, and that was the first time we had ever read a road map.

We finally got to the track and signed in for the second night of racing. We immediately discovered they were running wider late-model tires; we had brought some 10-inch tires that were older and looked like the new "chain link 70" design, quite a bit smaller than what they were running. We also had a small motor—a 4-barrel carb with a single fuel line.

The officials looked our car over and said that it would be better if we ran their street stock class. But then the guy realized there was something-or-other on my car that wouldn't allow us to do that. So I said, "No problem, I'll just race with the modifieds. We're just here to have fun anyways."

We went out to hot lap and passed a few cars. When I got back to the pits a guy in the pit next to us said I had passed the guy who wins here just about every week. Well, it wasn't but a few minutes when the officials came running over to our pit.

We had been there all day and had hardly gotten a glance. But now the guy said we can't run our tires.

"Come on," I said. "You're going to kick us out and you're letting the other guys run late model tires?"

"Well, they can't get your tires," they said.

We went back and forth a little bit, and the Hoosier Tire truck rolled into the pits. There was a big late model race there that night, Scott Bloomquist and several other guys were there. The officials took our little tires down to the Hoosier truck, and the guy looked them over.

"Hell, anybody can get those tires," the guy said. "But I don't know why they would want to…your guys already have tires way better than these."

They agreed to let us race, but we had to start on the tail. I worked my way up to third, but the car got hot. We didn't have a screen in front of our radiator, and it got plugged up with dirt, I reckon. On my way through the field I hit several guys in the ass, and spun one guy plumb out. This was the first "new" track I had ever been to, and my corner speed was different. With my little motor I had to stay in the gas to keep up.

When I got back to my pit Buddy hurried over.

"Man, we got to get this thing loaded and get out of here!" he said, joking with me.

"How come?"

"Because somebody is probably gonna come down here lookin' to whip your ass!"

But there was no trouble, and we made our way back home.

Man, what a trip. Getting lost turned out to be fun, because I saw some of the prettiest country. Really awesome! Ever since that trip I've never minded getting lost. It kind of sucks at the time but it makes for good memories, and good stories. Same as breaking down on the highway… nobody wants to have that happen but at the same time you often meet great people and have fun. You never know what's around the next corner, but it might be a good experience and make for a good story.

I think back to the days of the old NASCAR guys, and how they ran all the way to California or New York in a pickup truck and an open trailer. Man, that must have been hard. But I also realize that I get more worn out today in our big, comfortable hauler than I did when we had that old Suburban. (Maybe it's because I was younger then.)

Hootie and Buddy did most of the driving on that first Beckley trip. We brought some candy along, and Hootie ate the last Snickers bar. Buddy started aggravating Hootie about eating all the candy, then he started getting after him for riding his foot on the clutch pedal. He finally got under Hootie's skin and Hootie jumped on the brakes and we went clear off the road.

"What's the matter?"

"Piss on you guys, I ain't never drivin' this truck again!"

Buddy had got Hootie fired up, and he threatened to buy a bus ticket back home. We laughed because he was only kidding…I think.

My years in street stocks were some of the best years of my career. In fact, there are times when I think it would be fun to go back and drive street stocks around home and enjoy myself. It would be a simple way to race.

But if you're a serious racer you want to grow, to progress. I won quite a bit with those cars, and by 1995 I had the itch for something different.

I was ready to graduate, and start a new chapter. It was a fun time, and exciting. I can truthfully say that I had no idea what I was about to get myself into.

5

New Horizons

At the end of the 1994 season we were finished with street stocks and were ready to try late models. At least I *thought* I was ready for late models; honestly, I wasn't ready but I had an opportunity.

Steve Ritchie had a good bit of money and he bought a couple of leaf-spring late model cars from Gary Myers. These were good cars, and Gary had kicked everybody's butt the past couple of seasons. Steve wanted me to drive the car, and I was eager to make that step.

As I look back I can easily see that this was not the right thing, not the right move. I wasn't ready as a driver, and Steve's expectations were too much. I had won a bunch of street stock races, and it was only natural to assume that I could win in something else, right?

I had a couple of decent outings in the car including a second-place run behind Herman Goddard, one of the fast guys in our area. That fired Steve up and he was ready to go racing, and get on the road a little bit. We decided to haul up to Gaffney, S.C. for a big race.

My experience was limited to our local tracks, and Gaffney was a very different animal. It's a big 5/8-mile track, and it draws a lot of top racers. We showed up and Mike Duvall was there, and Buck Simmons. When you're a young street stock racer and you look around and see those guys in the pits, it's an intimidating feeling.

We were fast enough to make the race, and that was the good news. But I wasn't used to that kind of speed, and it was overwhelming. Going from an 18-second car to a 13-second car is too much of a step; I know that now. I hadn't developed the instincts and the reflexes to handle that kind of speed. Things were happening really fast!

We were running along and I was thinking it was time to let off for the corner. At that instant they started wrecking in front of me, and I hit somebody. A multi-car deal! I got knocked sideways and got drilled in the door and flipped over, landing on my roof. I wasn't hurt but our car was pretty bent up.

That was the beginning of the end of my deal with Steve. He was madder than hell that I had wrecked his car. Really? I could have died and you're worried about your race car?

We got another car together, salvaging some parts from the wrecked car and adding some new stuff. We went over to Bulls Gap for a big race, and things were wrong from the time we rolled into the pits. I qualified terrible, and we had trouble with our front brakes and our day didn't amount to anything at all. They had an open practice set for the next day, and I thought it would be a good idea to work on getting the car better outside of racing conditions. But Steve was mad, and he told me to put the car in the trailer, we were going home.

Put it there yourself, I said. I'm done.

That was the end of chapter one of my late model career.

Open wheel modifieds were strong in our area, and I figured that could be the logical next step for me as a driver. I was fortunate that an opportunity came together pretty quick.

Ernie Hartzell and Tommy Morrow had raced together for a long time, and they both decided they were ready to put somebody else in the seat. That was the break I needed, at just the right time. I raced for them for a while and eventually got our own car that we kept at David's shop.

The modifieds were good for me. That's where I learned to be a racer, and got my first taste of going on the road. A lot of doors were opened for me in those cars. From 1995 to 2003 I was pretty much exclusive in the modifieds and it was an important chapter of my career.

Like most racers, everything started locally. This car was a much better transition for me than Steve's late model, much more manageable. It was definitely faster, but within reason. I adapted fairly quickly and after a little while I was very comfortable in the car.

We worked on our car, week after week, trying to get better. The class had an engine claim rule, which fit us perfectly. We were running junk motors that David put together, and he could take junk parts and make something great. He was the absolute best at taking a bunch of nothing and making something good.

The deal on the engine claim was pretty simple. For a set amount of money a guy could swap motors with anybody in the pits. We got claimed several times and we always came out better, and the other guys were probably sick when they realized what they got. When we took their motor apart we always found better parts than what we were running. However, we always had to work on it to make it run as good as David's junk stuff. That's when I started to realize just how good David was with our motors.

I remember when somebody claimed us and we ended up with a motor with angle-plug heads, and man, I was excited. It was cool to finally race with a nice set of heads.

I was always the type of guy who was patient. If you outran me I didn't lose my cool, I just kept working on my stuff until I could run with you. Plus I was learning as a driver, too. I paid attention to what the fast guys were doing, and tried to learn from them.

Danny Yanders probably taught me as much as anybody during this period. Danny was from Somerset, Kentucky, and he came down to our area and outran us all the time. Butch Shay was another top guy from that region, and I learned an awful lot from him, too.

That first year I was definitely getting better, and it came fairly quick. I could keep up with the local guys, and eventually started winning a few races. But I had the itch to travel.

One of the best things about the modified class is that you have more opportunities to go on the road, throughout Tennessee and in any direction. The cars were pretty standard and it wasn't a big deal to go 500 or even a thousand miles and find a race. It's still that way and a whole lot of guys have come up through open wheel modifieds to race late models.

When you race locally you soon realize that you're only as good as the guys you race against. That's why it's important to travel, if you can. You can only learn so much from the local guys; you have to get out and find stronger competition and learn from them, too. We were fortunate that our area had a lot of talented racers, and I was able to pick up things from just about all of them. We got to where we could outrun the local guys, but when we traveled away from home we weren't able to win as often, at least not right away.

One of my fears about traveling was that while we were away the local guys might learn something and get better and it would be much harder to win when I came back home. But it didn't happen that way. Eventually I realized something: I was the one who was learning. You don't learn a lot if you keep doing the same thing at the same track against the same people. It's harder when you travel but you've got to do it if you want to get better.

I started following Danny Yanders a little bit. He was smart, and he had figured out the money angle. Your best odds are to find a race that pays more money, and where you also have a good chance to win. Some people call this "cherry picking." Call it what you want, but it's a good strategy.

As I chased Danny around I got schooled a lot. The race format was

Hard on the gas in Danny Yanders's modified in 1996.

Modified racing really expanded our horizons. We made a trip to Eldora on October 12, 1996.

simple: qualifying and then you race the feature. I was good at qualifying, and that helped me. But in the beginning the other guys would flat outdrive me in the feature. That got tiresome, but it was good for me. Eventually I learned how to pass them back.

After a couple of years I got to where I could beat Danny, and most of the other guys in our region. Danny didn't mind it when I was running second all the time, but I don't think he figured it was all that much fun when I started beating him.

One day I was at Danny's house, not long after we raced in Huntsville, Tennessee. Danny was telling me about a big Memorial Day race up in Danville, Illinois the following weekend, and he was planning on going up to run it. He asked if I wanted to haul up there with him. This was much farther than we had ever traveled, but the idea was exciting. Right about then Danny's phone rang, and it was a promoter from up in Kentucky. He had a local guy that nobody could beat, and it was running off some of his local cars. The promoter wanted Danny to come up next week and give this guy a run for his money.

Danny agreed to run at the guy's track on the way to Danville. "Hey," he told the promoter. "I've got a buddy who is going to haul up there with me; can you let us both in for free?"

So that was our first "deal" to go on the road. We loaded our stuff and headed north with Danny.

One of our stops was Nebo, Kentucky. I took one look at that big half-mile and told Danny I'd be lucky to make the race with my little motor. Compared to most everybody else, we really *did* have a junk motor; it was a bunch of used parts and we even used hydraulic lifters. We were about 20 years behind the times with that motor.

We not only made the race; we won it. I'm still kinda amazed at that deal. Danny finished 2nd, and afterwards he said, "I don't want to hear any more bullshit about that little motor."

Danville, Illinois is Bob Pierce country. Bob is a Hall of Fame racer from that area, and he's built a ton of race cars for guys all over the Midwest. It's a super-competitive region for modified racing. It's a great late model area too, don't get me wrong, but it's seriously tough competition in modifieds. Especially at the big Memorial Day race.

There were probably a hundred cars in the pits when we rolled in, and I knew right away that making the field would be tough. Scooter May was there, Danny Swartz, Kelly Shyrock, and a whole bunch of good cars.

We were looking at a steep learning curve, because the tracks up that way were different than our local tracks. They prepared the tracks to build a tall cushion where you had to get up there and drive the snot out of your race car. It's a fun way to race, but I hadn't yet learned the technique. So we were kinda lost that first trip, trying to get a handle on a lot of new things.

Another big adjustment was drawing for heats. At home we would qualify and run the feature, with no heat races. Up north they would draw for heats, which meant a wide mix of fast cars and slow cars. Racing with slower cars was hard for me to figure out, and we ran over a lot of people. I hadn't learned yet how to race with cars of all different speeds.

I learned one thing right quick. My steering was real slow—I had to turn the wheel a bunch to make the wheels move. I was actually crossing my arms up on the cushion, wearing myself out. Those other cats, I could see they were moving their wheel just a few inches as they drove the car. At that time you couldn't yet buy a fast steering box; you bought a quickener that sped your old steering up by 2:1. Once we put a quickener on our car it helped a bunch.

We didn't make the race on our first trip, and that fired me up. This was a challenge! Back then it didn't cost an arm and a leg to travel, so I made the trip to Danville many more times over the next few years. Matter of fact, we tried for several years before we finally made the show.

One year the track promoter noticed I was from Tennessee and he came down to our pit to thank us for making the trip. I said, "Actually, I've been coming up here for several years."

"Really?" he said. "I didn't realize that."

"I'm going to keep coming up here until I make the race," I told him. "And I'm going to keep coming back until I win it."

He laughed and waved his hand, and said okay.

A year or so later I started driving a new car Danny had bought, and we were a lot more successful. It was kind of a journey, you know? My driving skills were improving, and our equipment was getting better. I was getting more confident, and everything kind of grew.

The car I drove for Danny was No. B1, and that's the only time I wasn't running the No. 20. We ran that car for two years, and we weren't half bad. We were on the verge of winning a couple of championships, so we were competitive for sure.

That car sparked a lot of ideas, things that I would eventually try on other cars. It was a fun time, learning all sorts of things with the race car.

I was fortunate to have the right people come along at the right time, people who taught me what I needed to know. After a couple of years in modifieds I started driving for Donnie Adams of Lightning Chassis, an important step for me.

Donnie is from London, Kentucky. He's a creative guy, and that appealed to me. I liked to think I was creative at that time, but it was mostly just trying crazy things with my suspension, trying to hit upon something good. Early on we ran leaf spring cars, and later everybody started running swing-arm cars, including Danny's B1 car. At the time the two main designs were swing-arm or four-bar. Modifieds were kind of following what was happening in late models, at least that's what I saw happening. Maybe it was the other way around, I don't know. But it was definitely an evolution, with things steadily changing.

When I started running for Donnie, it felt like we were starting to "get it." We were starting to understand, with some detail, what was happening with the car. I was beginning to see the total picture: what the car was doing, what we wanted it to do, how my driving could influence the car... stuff like that.

I've always been mechanically inclined, but I'm not nearly as creative as some guys I've known. In my opinion a truly creative person can make something from scratch, something nobody else has ever seen. I'm creative in my own way but I would not call myself revolutionary by any means.

Our deal with Donnie was very good. Eventually he turned the car over to me and told me to run it the way we wanted. We became their house car, you might say. It was a great setup...they gave us everything we needed to go racing and we split the money. Good motors, good chassis, definitely the things we needed to get it done.

We took what they provided and then added our sweat. We worked very hard on that car. Myself, Chris Fox, all the guys who were helping us... we busted our butt in the shop through the week, getting ready to go racing that next weekend. Maybe we'd race locally, maybe we'd haul a couple of hours away.

Running up to Danville continued to be an annual thing for us. The Danville swing eventually included stops at Paducah, Kentucky, and also Kentucky Lake Motor Speedway. The Paducah race was $3,000-to-win, Kentucky Lake was $4,000, and Danville was $5,000. At Paducah I raced my heart out and beat Kelly Shyrock, a big IMCA star. Kelly was a well-known racer, a talented guy who had been written-up in magazines.

The next night Kelly and I were at it again, racing hard. We were leading and Kelly passed me, and I got up on the wheel and passed him back and won it. It was a great race. That made two straight wins against top-notch competition!

When we got to Danville the next day people were bitching about our car. Donnie Adams had built a pull bar setup for the car, with biscuits (rubbers) with the end of the rod in a can. My aunt Judy made us a cover;

I wanted to keep mud and debris out of the can. After we won the Paducah race a guy came down and looked under our car and started raising hell. It was too late for a protest, so I told him he needed to move on. He said, "Well, we'll see about that!"

There was a spring rule with these cars: no springs smaller than five inches in diameter. I reckon this guy thought we had a small spring in the can at the end of our rod. When we got to Danville the UMP guys wanted to look at our setup, and they checked and of course found no spring in our can. We were good to go.

And we finally made the race! We were running seventh and I figured we needed to do something different. I saw a strip of moisture around the bottom, and hit that spot and stayed on the bottom and won that daggone race. Won it! Now they were *really* bitching, but at that point we didn't care.

The promoter came walking down to my pit and said, "Well, Jimmy, I guess you won't be back after this."

I was surprised when he said that.

"Why not?"

"Well, you told me last year you were coming up here until you won the race," he said. "Now you've made the race, and you won it the first time you made it!"

I was tickled that he remembered our conversation from the year before. That was cool.

Man, what a fun weekend. We brought some t-shirts—the first modified shirts we made—and I was so excited after the race that I was giving them away. Chris was about to panic—"Jimmy, you can't keep giving them away!"

"But we won!" I kept saying. "We can afford it!"

That weekend was big for me, because that's when I started getting some notice. When I called people on the phone—chassis builders, engine builders, parts builders—they recognized my name, and that helps you. The conversation is very different at that point. Doors start to open and deals come together.

It was starting to happen!

6

Progression

The best part of moving to the modifieds—and going out on the road—was the experience. Several of my friends from down home started traveling with me, and we had fun every time out. It was great to run good, but in a way it didn't matter...we were having fun.

Chris and Buddy Fox, Hootie (Anthony McMahan), W.D. Henry, Eric Gorrell, and several others...what a bunch! Nobody could have more fun than we did.

One of our Danville, Illinois trips stands out in my mind. Danville is not very far from Indianapolis, and Danville's big Memorial Day race meant you were racing the same weekend as the Indianapolis 500. You couldn't find a motel room within a hundred miles of Indianapolis, seems like. We had a makeshift hauler, and Hootie followed us in his car. We ended up sleeping in the parking lot of a Laundromat. Everybody was worn out, but we had fun!

Actually that trip was the last one for Eric, I believe. When we got home he said, "I've had enough of this, this ain't for me!"

We had fun even when stuff went wrong. When we first bought an enclosed trailer, man, we thought we were set for life. This is the setup! On our very first trip we took off for Glasgow, Kentucky, traveling across the Kentucky Parkway. Chris was driving, and we were rolling right along when he turned and gave me one of those looks.

"What's wrong?"

"The roof of the trailer just blew off!" he said, and his eyes were wide, wide open.

"What??!! No way! What do you mean, the roof blew off?"

"Jimmy, it's layin' on the side of the trailer!" he said, pulling off the road. Sure enough, the roof had blown plumb off. We took some snips and cut the roof off, then folded it up and stuck it in the trailer. We eased on

The gang's all here! Celebrating with Buddy Fox, Kenny Holt, Chris Fox, and Anthony (Hootie) McMahan in 2000.

Talking with announcer Jim Childers after a win at Kentucky Lake in 1998.
(Bailey photo)

down the road, taking it slow, and at that point we had a "semi-enclosed" trailer.

When we got back home the dealer fixed the roof up and we were like brand new again.

What a bunch. Buddy and W.D. would get to drinking and cause so much trouble. One night I was leading the race at Bulls Gap and we had a red flag. The promoter there, Mitch Turner, stuck his head in my window and said, "Jimmy, you've got to do something with your crew or I'll throw you out."

"What can I do, I'm in the race car!" But somehow we finished the race without anybody getting thrown out or arrested.

Chris was the same as those other guys, when they had a few drinks they'd get real vocal. Many times we had the officials telling us we'd better settle down or we'd get thrown out.

Man, those were fun times.

I mentioned Butch Shay a few pages back, and it got me to thinking about 'ol Butch.

When I was starting out Butch was someone I looked up to. He was one of the guys on top, and I had total respect for those guys. The idea of outrunning a guy like Butch was a little bit intimidating, but at the same time it motivated me.

I raced with Butch a lot up in Richmond, Kentucky, a hotbed for modified racing. I started traveling up to Richmond mainly because I knew it would be hard, but I would learn. Our best shot was to take them on where they were strong; Butch was definitely strong at Richmond.

Man, they took me to school. Richmond ended up being one of my best tracks, but it took a while to be able to compete, and finally win. After I was established and had good equipment, there were nights when Butch—and Danny Yanders, too—beat me with lesser equipment. That's humbling to admit but it's the truth. They were very good racers, and you had to have everything right to beat them.

It was very interesting the way things changed later on as I progressed into late models. Butch was a good example of that; when I was racing against him he was a little bit hard-nosed, tough and giving me no breaks. Whatever respect you got from Butch, you had to earn.

But when I started winning late model races at the national level, some of the older guys from the modified ranks who had once taken me to school would come by our pit to visit. When we were racing against them there was a kind of barrier there; a distance. They didn't exactly come down to my pit and encourage me, you might say. But once I moved on, they were telling me how glad they were to see me have success in late models, and that they were proud of me.

Man, that was good to hear. More than once I had to swallow real hard and keep my emotions in check when somebody like Butch game me some praise. They have no idea how much I looked up to them; to hear them say words of respect, well, that got to me sometimes.

A few years ago Butch was diagnosed with cancer, and he was very sick. We talked on the phone and he told me that he was determined to come visit my shop, and make one more trip to Florence for a big late model race. He explained that he had decided not to take any more treatment for the cancer because it was not likely to help him. He told me that he wanted to be buried in his Jimmy Owens t-shirt.

When we hung up the phone I went out on my back porch and sat down and cried. There was nothing anybody could ever tell me that would mean more than what Butch told me about being buried in my t-shirt.

As it turned out Butch was able to make the trip to Florence, and when we won the race I gave Butch a shout-out in the victory lane interview.

Butch passed away not long after. I will never forget that conversation on the phone. Those are the moments that make racing very special.

When I think back to our progression in the open wheel modified world, I can't help but think that the timing was very fortunate.

I'm not exactly sure how the class got started, but by the early 1990s it was starting to take off. UMP had organized a national championship a few years earlier, and we started running the UMP series in 1995.

Modifieds were racing all over the country, and UMP's points system pulled everybody together into one national series. Kind of like a weekly track title, except that it covered a bunch of different tracks.

It wasn't a perfect setup, but then again nothing is. You could see right away who the top guys were, and people started playing the system a little bit. Because many different tracks paid UMP points each night, some guys would specifically race at other places to avoid running against the best.

I figured the best strategy in that scenario is to race against the toughest competition you can. That's the only way you can measure your progress, and it's the only way to learn and get better. You usually don't learn much from guys you are already outrunning.

Danny Yanders was the national champion in 1995 and 1996, and after spending several years racing with Danny it was only natural that I would want to try and win the championship myself.

In 1998 things started coming together for us. We chased the UMP points and won the championship. We missed the repeat in 1999, but we were back on top of the championship in 2000 and again in 2001.

Those national titles got my name out there. That period was a game changer, you might say. I was winning races and selling t-shirts and I felt pretty doggone good.

We could win at home and we could win on the road. We would travel over to Gaffney every now and then, where they had some $2,000 or even $5,000-to-win races. We could win over there, and we got to where Chris talked about running over there all the time. I didn't want to, and I explained to him why.

Those guys over there were good, but we were faster. If we go over there all the time, we're going to beat them and they'll get motivated to get their program better and then they'll be stronger at the bigger shows. I figured it was smarter to leave them alone, not poke at them, and just come in for the better-paying shows with a better chance of winning.

I ain't sure that's right but that's how I had it figured.

Our 1999 season was very special, even though we didn't get the UMP National title. We were racing about as well as anybody, and we won 49 races in 65 starts. If you spend any time around racing you realize those are good numbers. It's hard to win, at any level or in any class. There are always lots of guys capable of beating you. So to win 49 out of 65, we were very happy with that level of success.

That's when we started to struggle with the whole idea of being somebody special. It had been there since the beginning, but now it was bothering me more and more. Having total strangers come up to you and talk to you like you're old friends, that was uncomfortable. It pushed me out of my comfort zone, and I didn't know how to deal with it.

You'd read on the computer where somebody—a total stranger—said, "Jimmy Owens likes to race at such-and-such track," or, "Jimmy doesn't like so-and-so because they got together last year and Jimmy spun out."

You learn right away that you should avoid the message boards because there is almost no chance the stuff written there will make you feel good. However, if they're talking about you—good or bad—you're probably doing something right.

People—race fans—have been awesome to me, from the very beginning. They've cheered for me, they've come back to the pits and shook my hand, they've bought my shirts, they've always been there for me. I love that part of it, because racing has helped me connect with a ton of people I would never have met otherwise. When I started traveling with the modified I met hundreds of people, maybe thousands. I enjoyed that, because I basically like people and I don't have any trouble getting along with folks.

But meeting people and making friends is a little different than having people make a big deal out of meeting you.

What was happening, I reckon, is that I had to grow into a new situation. The simple world I knew had changed; I had to learn about life in the spotlight. It was almost like racing was forcing me to change my identity, changing me from a down-home Newport boy into a well-known racer.

I resisted that, I really did. Probably more than I should have. I was aware it was happening and I tried to press against it. I kinda grabbed hold of my roots and held on as hard as I could.

I've never completely embraced the new world. Over time I figured out how to balance things somewhat, where I could fulfill the things the spotlight demanded yet not let it change me completely.

I'll tell you one thing for sure: that old saying is right. "Be careful what you wish for." I wanted to go out on the road and make a living as a race driver. I got my wish, and that's all right. All of that was good. But there were parts I didn't know about, and wasn't prepared for. Over time things got better, but it took a while.

It was almost like, "Ready or not, here we come..."

We had so many great adventures during those modified years.

Or maybe the right word is "mis-adventures."

For example, the worst I've probably ever hurt a race car didn't even happen at the track.

We'd always head to the car wash to clean our car after a weekend of racing. Chris was the designated washer, because he was so picky. Nobody could wash well enough to please Chris, so he got the job.

We had raced someplace and Chris wasn't with us, so it was just Kenny Holt and me. We had sold our enclosed trailer, and for a little bit we were back using an open trailer as a backup. You could wash on that little trailer without unloading, but you had to roll the car back and forth to get it all washed.

We finished washing and Kenny walked over to a nearby store to get something. One of our friends had seen us washing and stopped by to shoot the breeze. Kenny came back from the store and we jumped in the truck and headed for the shop.

We missed one little detail: we didn't tether the car down. The car was not in gear, and we just had a couple of wheel scotches in place. We zipped along our curvy New Cave Church Road without a care in the world.

Our shop is situated behind David Prizer's house and garage, and the driveway is plumb steep. We were about halfway up the driveway when I felt the truck lurch and shift gears, and right then I didn't even have to look back. I knew what had happened.

Our car slipped off the back of the trailer, and as it free-wheeled down the driveway it turned left and dead centered a tree in front of David's house.

Man, that thing was hurt. It knocked the fuel cell out, and basically totaled the thing. Right about that time Chris came rolling up, and when he saw the car he was hot.

"I ain't gonna help you fix it!" he hollered. "You guys done it…you fix it!"

We didn't have a spare car at the moment, so we scrambled to get the car fixed before the next weekend. And that led to another adventure. Or, once again, "mis-adventure."

Me and Kenny got the porta-power going, braced against the ceiling, trying to straighten the frame. We were banging on the car, and all of a sudden it jumped off the stand and the porta-power flew off. It was danged near a catastrophe.

We were very lucky it didn't break both our legs, no kidding. *Very* lucky.

That was another of those times when me and Kenny looked at each other and said, "Well…let's not tell anybody about this."

We had more than a few of these little adventures. One of the best involved a pontoon boat a buddy of ours owned. One of the pontoons had a big dent, so we hooked up our air hose, figuring we'd feed air into the pontoon until the pressure pushed the dent out.

What we didn't know is that there were internal baffles that divided the pontoon into sections. We kept feeding air into the pontoon, feeding it, feeding it, and then…BOOM!

One of the baffles blew out from the pressure, and I'm telling you it was as loud as any bomb. The boat jumped about a foot in the air and we thought we were all going to die. That was a good one.

Sometimes David would look at everything that was going on and just shake his head. I didn't have a clue back then, but I get it now. It's a wonder we made it through all that.

The success we had with UMP, and winning our first national title in 1998, helped me begin to understand the business process—or maybe I'd say financial process—of how sponsors and corporate support can help your team and your career.

At Bristol with Jeff Cone in 2000.

The Lightning Chassis association was an important step in my career, for sure.

Right off, I saw other racers getting help from different product sponsors. Racers will talk, naturally, and guys would mention working with so-and-so for various products and support.

A lot of those deals don't involve money directly, but products. The manufacturer will provide their products at a reduced cost—or maybe no cost at all—and you run the product and the sticker on your car. That's a great help to a team, because a deal with a shock manufacturer, for example, allows you to take the money you were spending on shocks and direct it someplace else on the car.

By the late 1990s we had lots of conversations with different manufacturers about helping us with their products. But nothing had come of it.

That's when I began to realize something: as an aspiring young racer, everything I was telling a potential product sponsor—how good we were running, how much we wanted to succeed, our goals and ideas to win races—they had heard before. Over and over again.

We got lots of encouragement from various manufacturers: "Keep in touch, Jimmy, and we'll try to find a way to get you in our program next year!" But the next year rolled around and we never made the cut.

We were just another voice, just another name. We hadn't really done much to stand out from everyone else, at least in the eyes of those manufacturers and product reps.

I can't pinpoint one event or one exact moment when we started to make some headway with manufacturers. But a couple of trips to Royse City, Texas seemed to turn the tide in elevating our image and our reputation.

The Longhorn Roundup ran for a few years at North Texas Motor Speedway, offering a big purse and attracting a bunch of top modified racers from around the country each February. It was not an easy race for us to run, because it was scheduled just a few days after we finished racing at East Bay Raceway Park in Florida. That meant a long tow—about 20 hours—from Tampa to just outside Dallas, and then the long tow back to Newport.

The 2000 Lone Star Roundup turned out to be pretty good for us.

We were amazed to see nicer modified teams at North Texas than we'd seen in super late model racing—lots of toter homes and nice trailers. We were towing with a small truck and trailer, and we looked totally outclassed.

The rules for the event were kinda loose, but the promoters said they were running IMCA modified rules. There were a couple of exceptions; teams were allowed to run Brinn or Bert transmissions, for example.

We were parked next to Mark Noble, a top modified racer from Minnesota. Even without a weight rule many guys were running lead on the rear of their car to maintain a rear percentage weight. Mark and I were standing there talking, and he wondered why we didn't run lead on the back of our car. I explained that I just couldn't see why anybody would put lead on their car if they didn't have to. A few minutes later we set fast time in qualifying, and when we got back to our pit Mark was standing there smiling.

"I guess you're right!" he laughed.

I don't know if we were right or not, but it worked.

The first thing on the schedule was a rained-out $30,000-to win feature from the previous year, as I recall. We finished second to Tim Donlinger, and then the main program got underway.

The track rubbered up pretty bad, and we were stuck mid-pack in our qualifying race. Somebody blew a motor and laid down a path of oil in the high groove almost all the way around the track and the caution came out.

All of a sudden I remembered seeing this happen at Prestonsburg, Kentucky in a late model race. Donnie Moran got up there and ran the oil in and made a lane for himself and won the race, and I figured I'd try the same trick. We didn't have anything to lose, because we were stuck mid-pack with very little hope of passing anybody. So while we circled under caution I drove through the oil, working my car back and forth, running it in.

They threw the green and I put my tires up in that oil and shot forward. Within two laps we went from 12th and were leading!

People mentioned that night to me for several years, talking about how we just blew past everybody. I reckon I was amazed, too, because it was awesome.

We drove on to win, which locked us in for one of the features on Sunday. They split the field into two groups, with a $15,000-to-win feature for each group.

After each qualifying race they ran the transfer cars through tech. That's when our trouble began.

The tech inspector looked at our brake adjuster. Most guys used an adjuster to control the bias between the front and rear brakes; we set ours up to control the right/left bias. There was nothing in the rules prohibiting this.

The tech guy shook his head.

"You can't run a brake shutoff," he said. "You're disqualified."

"It ain't a shutoff," I argued. "It's an adjuster, just like everybody else."

"But it controls right and left brakes," he said.

"Don't matter," I said. "The rules don't say anything about a right/left adjuster."

I started getting nervous, and upset. There was a lot on the line here. We were looking at a 40-hour round-trip tow, and throwing us out after we locked in for the main event would be a bitter pill to swallow.

The tech guy said, "Buddy, if you keep yelling at me, I'm going to throw you out right now!"

I explained that I wasn't yelling at him; I was only shouting so he could hear me over the cars on the track.

Finally the guy kinda threw up his hands and said, "You got to talk to the race director."

"Okay…where is he?"

"Up in the tower."

We walked up to the tower and stepped inside.

"I'm from the number 20 car," I explained. "I need to see the race director."

"Oh my gosh!" a lady spoke up. She was the scorer. "When you passed all those cars on that restart, I 'bout fell out of my chair! That's the most amazing thing I've ever seen!"

I was grateful for the compliment but I wasn't sure this was going to help our cause.

The race director didn't seem to want to budge. He kept saying, "According to IMCA rules…"

"But you're not running IMCA rules," I insisted.

"Sure we are."

"Well, if you're running IMCA rules, you've got to throw out the top five guys in the qualifier that's on the track right now."

"Why would we do that?" he said, kinda surprised.

"Because IMCA rules clearly say, 'Fiberglas roof only.' Those five guys are all running a metal roof."

"Oh," he said, looking out at the cars on the track. "Well, I don't know about that."

We went back and forth, round and round. This was a good experience for me, a good lesson. Sometimes a racer has to stand his ground, stand up for himself. I wasn't screaming or cussing, I wasn't calling him names, I wasn't nasty. I just pointed out why I felt we were right.

Finally he said, "All right…you take that adjuster off and you can come back tomorrow."

That was a fair compromise. I didn't like it, of course. Technically, we were absolutely within the rules. But sometimes you have to accept things you don't necessarily agree with because it makes good business sense.

All's well that ends well! We came back the next day for the final and won $15,000 from the pole. Randy Zimmerman was right there on us, but we held him off. The 50-lap feature went green-to-checker, and that helped. No restarts to worry us. Wayne Brooks of Arkansas won the second feature.

They paid everybody in cash, and we counted up our winnings. $15,000 for our main event win, plus $12,000 for finishing second in the rained-out feature…it was a box full of money. More cash at one time than I ever recall, before or since.

It was a fun ride home. With all that cash, we figured we were king of the world!

A lot of the big product reps were at Royse City, and they saw us have a great weekend. Within a week they were returning our e-mails and returning our calls. Now when we asked them to work with us, they were willing. We were no longer just another name, just another sales pitch.

At first I felt upset by all this. It didn't seem right, to be ignored at first until they saw us win. I was almost tempted to turn the stuff down; if we weren't good enough before, why are we good enough now?

But I was a little naïve, and didn't understand that's the way the world works. When you win, people look at you differently. It might seem unfair and not cool, but that's how it is. That's the real world of racing.

You've got to get past the idea that everything is fair, or level. It ain't. People decide to do business with you based on your performance on the track. Not because you're a nice guy.

Being nice to people is important, and it's what I always strive for. But in terms of getting sponsorship and help from manufacturers, that's not enough. You also have to win races. Hate to say it, but…it's that simple. It really is.

7

One Hundred Grand

Bob Memmer was the founder of UMP, and he was a unique guy. Racers loved him…sometimes. Other times, we didn't. Bob was an eccentric guy and he had the thankless job of trying to protect us from ourselves. I didn't always agree with Bob but he was all about the racers and the sport needs more people like him.

UMP typically had their championship banquet up in Louisville, and we made the trip up there to accept our 2001 title. That was the night when Bob made an announcement that rocked our world.

The 2002 UMP open wheel modified title would pay $100,000 to the champion.

Wow! This was big news! The point fund was typically a *total* of $100,000, with $20,000 to the winner. But this was something very different. This was $100,000 *to the winner.*

Right then and there I made up my mind: We wanted to win that $100,000. Up to that point we had set many goals, such as winning a street stock title or winning the UMP national championship. But the idea of winning $100,000 at one swoop…man, that was intriguing.

We had begun the transition to running some super late models, and I ran a few races in Jerry Weisgarber's car. But with the UMP announcement we both agreed that I needed to focus on winning the title so for 2002 I focused on our modified and ran only a few late model races.

Technically, it was possible to win the UMP title while racing locally. If your local track paid UMP points, you could contend for the championship. That wasn't my strategy; my deal was to go out on the road as much as possible. In fact, if somebody else was leading the point standings, I specifically wanted to go to his track and try to beat him. That's a tough challenge but if you can pull it off you can gain points. Otherwise,

Racing with Mike Marlar. It doesn't get much better than this!

After a win at Tri-City Speedway in August 2001, with Kenny Holt and Chris Fox. Look who joined us in victory lane! Mikey Marlar is a good ol' friend.

if you are racing at different tracks and you are both winning, you can't gain any points on him. I'm happy to say that we gained a ton of respect from modified racers by doing this.

We didn't focus on "state" championships, but we placed in the top standings in several states. I was proud of that. We weren't cherry picking; far from it. We were specifically looking to race against the other top guys in hopes of beating them and gaining points.

Part of what made modified racing so tough during this period was the many great racers who came up through the ranks. It gave us the opportunity to meet tons of new people, and make many new friends.

By the way…you can race against people and still be friends. It is competitive and intense, but it can still be fun. It surprises me sometimes when people figure because you're racing someone hard, there must be bad feelings between you. I've mentioned this elsewhere in the book, but some of the best times I've ever had was when we'd get in a really intense and close race with someone, then go down and laugh and joke with them afterwards. That's an awesome way to race!

As the 2002 season went along, the points narrowed up and it became clear that the championship was going to come down to myself and Mike Marlar. That was fun and very special, because Mikey is one of my best friends in racing—on and off the track.

I'm not sure of the exact date, but we first met Mikey when we were racing modifieds in Burnside, Kentucky and Mikey was running a street stock. Mikey and Chris Fox hit it off immediately, and pretty quick we all became good friends. We didn't share a lot of racing info or anything like that, but we just raced together and had a good time.

Mikey is from Winfield, Tennessee, right up along the state line with Kentucky. Sometimes when we raced up that way we would stay at Mikey's place. Mikey is a good guy, as good as anybody you will ever find. He is the kind of friend who is always there, and he will give you the shirt off his back if you need it. To this day, right this minute, if either of us needed anything all we'd have to do is call the other. That's how it is with me and Mikey.

There have been nights when we have raced each other really hard, beating on each other's quarter-panels just because we could. It was so much fun, we'd finish the race and climb out of the car just laughing and all excited, and discover that our crews were all worked up with each other. We'd have to settle everybody down and let them know it was all okay. Man, those were fun times.

Mikey usually has himself completely under control; he's a very calm person. However a while back I saw a video of him having a meltdown at Florence and I loved it. I aggravated him to no end about that deal. It was great.

That 2002 season was important for us a lot of ways. First of all, that's when we officially made the step toward becoming a full-time professional racer. Up to that time I had continued to work full-time at the TRW plant, running my machine every day and using my vacation time to go racing.

My co-workers didn't understand that. They'd read in the local newspaper where I won a $2,000 race the previous weekend, and they couldn't figure out why I still came to work.

"You're winning all that money," they said. "Why do you need to work?"

I tried to explain that you have a lot of costs that come out of that $2,000. Plus you don't win every weekend. No matter how good you hope to be, you aren't going to win all the races.

So I kept my "real job." Then one day, due to unforeseen circumstances, the folks at TRW fired me. Apparently they decided it was time for me to race full-time! To be honest, I sensed it was coming. If I would have said what they wanted me to say, I could have kept my job. But I wasn't upset about getting fired, because I was ready to move on at that point. No hard feelings.

So me and TRW parted ways. I'm happy to report that the company kept right on trucking and did not close down just because I was no longer there. They did just fine without me. And I did just fine without them, because now we were able to focus every minute of our time and energy on racing.

I was also able to continue my involvement at Performance Chassis, where I had partnered with Rick Ogle to build race cars. They had a shop along Hwy. 411 just down the road from my house, and it was a good setup. We built quite a few cars and did well. A lot of guys won races in our cars.

In fact, Mike Marlar was also running one of our chassis in 2002. That was another thing that kept us working closely together.

One of the neat things about the 2002 championship season was that UMP would have their season finale in October at Eldora Speedway in Ohio. That was cool because it meant the season would wrap up at a big, half-mile dirt track with a lot of history. I hadn't raced much at Eldora, and I was looking forward to October, hoping we would be in contention for that $100,000.

The idea of winning the money was big, but it wasn't the only thing that motivated me. First off, you would always like to win a championship if possible. But we also knew that this was a unique situation. We kinda figured the $100,000 top prize was like a one-off; if you fell short this time, you might not get a chance to try it again.

Bob Memmer was getting up in years (he died in 2004 at age 69) and I think the $100,000 championship fund was his idea of establishing something very special as a "final chapter" to his long career (UMP also offered $100,000 to their late model champion in 2002). From his first announcement at the banquet, we figured we might never see that kind of money again for a modified championship.

When we got to Eldora in October we were right there in the hunt for the title. The best modified guys in the country were there, including a handful of guys I had not raced against. It was a stout field and winning this race would be special, never mind the championship part of it.

Mikey and I had battled for much of the season. Although I kid him that he avoided me a lot that year—racing where I wasn't—he was definitely good enough to beat me. He was *very* good. But now it all came down to who was better on this final day, head-to-head.

As we got ready for the championship race Mikey held a very slim point lead. In order for me to win the title I had to win the race and Mikey had to finish no better than 7th.

We both qualified well and won our heat. We were starting back a ways, in the same row. We would line up side-by-side.

When the race began I really took off, on a mission. I worked my way to the front and was trying to watch my crew as they gave me signals. The track was starting to lock down in three and four, so I knew I needed to get to the bottom. I could see somebody else's crew signaling that the guy had a big lead—was this the leader? I wondered—so I was racing hard, trying to pass everybody I could.

I passed the next car but I could see the crew still giving somebody the "big lead" signal. I spotted a car running almost a straightaway ahead of us—Brian Ruhlman.

By now the track had locked down, and Brian was cruising because of the signals from his crew. I ran him down in two laps and before they could let him know I was coming, I was right there.

Brian was messing with a lapped car and I hit him in the ass, almost spinning him out. I bumped him in the front to get him straightened back out and let him have his spot back, because I wasn't going to rough him up

Chris Fox isn't big on giving a speech, but he looks proud at the 2002 UMP banquet. That's Bob Memmer looking on.

With Chris and David Prizer at an earlier UMP banquet. Those years were a huge part of my career!

just to win. A lap later he slid wide just enough, and it opened it up for me on the bottom.

I got alongside, and then pulled him coming off the corner. From that point I was counting down the laps. We took the checkered flag and I drove to the scales and climbed out of my car.

My crew was celebrating, but we had to wait and see where Mikey had finished. After a few moments we got the word: he was 7th.

We had won the UMP National championship—by a razor-thin margin.

Now we could celebrate. But I didn't get all that excited; not really. That moment was a good example of how it works for me emotionally; I tend to hurry back to the middle right quick. I don't get crazy excited when good things happen, and I don't get way down when things are tough. I'm an even-keeled guy…even when we've just won $100,000.

It *was* cool, however, to get the check at the banquet. That was a neat moment, looking down at the check and realizing everything it represented. I've always had an element of doubt about my success, and I never bragged. But here, in the form of that big check, was proof that I could actually do this. This money was actually going into the bank; you can't get much more hardcore proof of success than that.

Taking the check to the bank was also a cool moment. You know, it's not often that you fill out all six digits on the deposit ticket. A guy doesn't get to do that every day! At least *this guy* doesn't. When I handed the check and deposit ticket to the teller I was grinning like a little kid.

And I must say, it was cool standing on the stage at the banquet with Bob Memmer. That super payoff was a big part of his dream, and it was my dream, too. I am proud that we could win it in his honor. The fact that he left us within the next couple of years will forever make that banquet a very special memory for me.

I paid off a lot of things with that money. My truck and trailer, and several other smaller things.

At that point I considered it a great season if we won $100,000 in *total* money—race winnings and point money. I figured six-figures was a good target to shoot for. At that level you could actually *make* money. To get $100,000 in point money *plus* all your race winnings, that was a flat-out awesome season.

My time in open wheel modifieds was very important. It opened the door and prepared me for late model racing, but that wasn't all of it. It was also important because I truly loved racing those cars, and associating with the people involved. It was fun and I wouldn't change much from those years even if I could.

It's funny...in the beginning, I didn't figure we'd like the modifieds. My idea was to stay in fendered cars—I wanted to go from a street stock to a super stock, and then late models. But I surprised myself because I came to love racing the modifieds.

Times change, and so do we. My career path was changing, and after that 2002 season I could sense that things were about to take off in a different direction.

It was time. I needed to go late model racing.

8

Graduating, Again

Ambition has always been a struggle for me. It's been a challenging thing to get through, because as my racing career progressed I had to decide who I was and who I wanted to be.

A part of me wanted to be a regular guy, the boy who lived over on old U.S. 411. But another part of me wanted to grow, to compete, to win. And those two visions are very different things.

What makes this especially challenging is that you have internal and external elements working. Internally, we have our own self-doubts; *who do you think you are, trying to be a champion?* And then there is the external forces; other people saying the same thing.

Everybody knows you shouldn't let other people control how you feel, and how you live. You've heard this a hundred times: "I just tune that stuff out and don't pay any attention." Shoot, I've said it myself many times, in conversations and interviews.

But the fact is, I have a hard time tuning out criticism from certain people. Especially my family and friends.

When I got in the street stock and started winning races, people began to notice me. As things went along my name was in the newspaper, and even my picture.

"Say, this boy is winning races! He might even be...*something*."

Immediately people started saying stuff.

"You better not let this go to your head!"

"Don't be thinkin' you're a star!"

"Oh, now that you're somebody special, you'll probably be too busy to stay connected with all your friends and family."

That used to bother the crap out of me, and looking back I realize how much I struggled to get past all that.

Sometimes I felt like I was standing on a narrow fence, trying to keep

My confidence was growing, and I was starting to find my way. Kinda!
This is around 2001 or so.

my balance. On one side were the people staring at me, hinting that I was getting too big for my britches and shaking their head. On the other side were people encouraging me, saying I had the potential to be a professional racer.

There is nothing wrong with ambition. You shouldn't feel guilty for wanting to succeed, and wanting to grow as a racer and as a person.

I'm a down-home Tennessee boy and I always will be. No matter what happens, I'm going to be most comfortable wearing camo pants and a t-shirt. I ain't going to talk fancy and I'll never figure I'm better than anyone else.

When I got the chance to race late models in the early 2000's my career was on the upswing. We had a very successful run in open wheel modifieds and we were ready for the next step.

It wasn't just ambition; it was personal. I was genuinely curious if I could do it, and I was itching to try. It was the challenge of racing and winning; late models were obviously a higher level of competition and I wanted to see if I was good enough to win there.

Luckily, a lot of good things happened for me. The right people came along at the right time. It was exciting and even though we've had some ups and downs, I wouldn't change anything about how it all came together.

What I *would* do, I reckon, is enjoy it more while it was going on. I can't go back and change anything, but time has helped me understand why I felt so much stress and conflict when many good things were happening.

Modified racing had a downturn in our area in 2003, and racing seemed to be dwindling. The officials weren't enforcing the rules, and some expensive elements—mainly big motors—were creeping into the sport.

People who couldn't afford an expensive motor—or couldn't justify spending that kind of money—began to quit, and it felt like the class was dying out. We had to travel farther to race, and my instincts began to tell me that the time was right for a change. My plan was to continue to run the modified class while working my way into late model racing.

Right from the get-go, I knew I needed to get a ride in somebody else's car. There was no doubt; no way could we support the costs of buying and maintaining a late model on our own. That was out of the question! My job at TRW was long gone at this point, and I was working full-time building race cars for Performance Chassis.

My first real break came through Leroy Van, who helped Clay Kelly quite a bit. Leroy knew I was interested in moving on to late models, and

Making an early late model start in Jerry Weisgarber's car in 2000.
(Randall Perry photo)

he suggested I connect with Jerry Weisgarber of Oliver Springs, Tennessee. Jerry had a Rocket Chassis and was looking for a driver; Leroy gave me Jerry's phone number and encouraged me to give him a call.

I was excited and very nervous when I called Jerry. We talked on the phone, and Jerry suggested that I come by his shop and look the car over. On the phone I was trying to sound calm, cool, and collected; but man, I was wired!

I wanted to sound confident. I didn't know where Jerry lived, and I was afraid that if I asked him directions to his shop he'd think I was clueless about things. So after we hung up I called Leroy to get directions to Jerry's place.

Oliver Springs is west of Knoxville, about 90 minutes from Newport. I made my way over and met Jerry. He showed me the car, and then I was even more pumped up. This was a nice race car! I had already heard that Jerry was a good mechanic who knew how to make the car work.

Our first race together was Cleveland Speedway, at a double-header late model and modified show. We ran decent in the late model, and I was reminded that these cars are very different than a modified. We ran in the top-5 and I felt like that was pretty decent.

Jerry really helped me with the big learning curve. He knew his stuff and he still does. Being with a guy who knows what he's doing helped me a ton.

After the late model race I hustled down to get in my modified, and when the race started I was thinking, "Man…if I could make the late model handle like this modified, I could beat everybody!" The late model was way more powerful and it drove harder, like it wanted to rear up. They were much harder to drive, for sure.

This transition time—2001 through 2004 or so—was good for me. Not *easy*, but good. We were still running our modified, and many nights we'd do double-duty and run two feature races. That's a lot of laps and it's a big help in making you a better driver.

To say I was in learning mode is a huge understatement. I have always tried to pay attention, and by this time felt like we had a reasonable handle on the mechanics of a race car and how a car should be driven. But man, there is so much you have to learn. As a driver, you've got to learn it and learn it and learn it until it's instinctive. Things are a little different for a mechanic, because you've got time to process your thoughts and figure out your adjustments. But as a driver things are happening in real time, real fast.

Jerry was a great guy and he was a big part of my education. Every time I climbed into his car, it was ready. And honestly, when it came to giving Jerry good feedback I wasn't much help in the beginning.

I was hanging on for dear life in the car, because I wasn't used to the speed. I'd finish a race and Jerry would say, "What's the car doing?"

I'd kind of have this blank look and Jerry would say, "I thought you knew what you were doing!"

I'd tell him right quick, "Oh no, let's get this shit straight. I don't know yet!"

Jerry was a lot of fun to be around. He and his brother Archie were hardworking, good people. Jerry builds racing engines, and these days he's running the Phantom Race Engines shop.

Jerry was similar to Chris Fox in that he was emotional. He was normally a very easygoing guy, but when you got to the race track he could get fired up. One night I went out to qualify and we timed bad, and I drove back to our pit and hopped out of Jerry's car. I hurried down to race my modified, and when I finished my heat race I came back to Jerry's hauler. I was shocked to see they were gone!

I mean, left the premises, you know?

I called Jerry right quick on the phone and said, "Where'd you go, son? Your hauler ain't here!"

"Aw, we sucked!" he said. "Ain't no need to hang around just to run in the back!"

Another night he got mad, and he didn't actually leave but he went to hang out in somebody else's pit until he cooled off a little bit.

But you know…it's all good. Seriously. That's just stuff that happens at the race track. Everybody gets out of shape now and then, and you let it slide off and don't let it be a big deal. You cool off and move on and keep working together. Jerry and I never got bogged down when we disagreed. Whenever anybody got a little upset in the heat of the moment we were always able to forget it and move on.

One thing for sure, Jerry gave us great equipment. There was no junk, not with Jerry's deal. And he was kind enough to give me a ride at an important time in my career.

C.J. Rayburn was a giant in late model racing, a person who had a massive impact. You could probably argue that, when it comes to the design of dirt late models, he's had the biggest impact of all.

C.J. was a very intelligent man. This is the guy who put down the original base design that everyone still goes off of today. It was 40-plus years ago that C.J. designed a breakthrough car that forever changed the sport, and many of the things we're doing today are based on C.J.'s original ideas.

Everybody in dirt racing knows C.J.'s name, and knows how important he is. When I first started racing our modified I was so ate up that I thought about race cars just about every minute I was awake. More than anything I wanted to learn; I wanted to know exactly how these things worked, because knowledge is speed.

I wore people out with my questions. Somewhere along the line people suggested that I call C.J. Rayburn and talk to him. I specifically remember Jeff Cone telling me that C.J. would talk to anybody who wanted to learn.

So I tracked down his phone number up in Indiana and called him. He took my call, and after that first call I'd dial him up every so often. We'd talk about racing, what to do, what not to do. It was very helpful.

One day we took the modified up to Paducah to the Summernationals. C.J. was there, and I walked up to him like we were buddies. "Hey C.J., are you busy?"

He said, "Yep." Then he turned around and walked off.

That ticked me off. How rude!

I didn't call him after that, and a few months later we were up in Indianapolis for the PRI trade show. C.J. was hosting an open house at his shop in Whiteland, and Mikey Marlar and I rode down to the open house. On the way I was telling Mikey, "Man, this guy is hateful!"

When we got there I told Mikey I'd introduce him to C.J. "Hi C.J., I'm Jimmy and this is Mike Marlar."

C.J. says, "Yeah, yeah," or something like that and walked off.

"See Mikey," I told him. "This guy really *is* an asshole!"

That next year I was driving for Jerry, and we were doing okay locally. One day my phone rang and I was surprised to hear a familiar voice.

"Hello Jimmy, this is C.J.," he said. "I've been watching you, and you're doing good. I want us to work together…I've got a car for you. You come up here and get this car, and go race it. When you sell it, just give me the money. Are you interested?"

I was shocked. *Totally* shocked. I'm sure I dang near dropped my phone when he said that.

"Really?" was about all I could get out of my mouth.

"Yes, really," he said, and I could tell that he was smiling.

My mind was spinning. I remember wondering, "Am I supposed to still think this guy is an asshole?"

Today I realize that I didn't understand C.J. Or at least didn't understand his situation.

Here was a guy who was super, super busy. He was in the chassis business and you've got to hustle, hustle, hustle, to survive. C.J. was in contact with hundreds of people, with a lot going on.

When he brushed me off I thought that was rude. But today I realize that he wasn't rude; he was just *busy*. Knowing what I know now, I'm a lot more understanding of that. I might be more polite about it, but I have told people the same thing: "I don't have time to visit with you right now."

We took C.J. up on his offer and quickly incorporated the new Rayburn chassis into Jerry's operation. The Rayburn was a good car and we were steadily getting better.

My very first super late model win came in this car, at Bulls Gap. Jerry was the crew chief, and Chris Fox was with us too. Mark Douglas had been the dominant car there in recent months, and I was alongside Mark on the outside pole for the start. I got into the lead and I was running the snot out of our car.

I've always worn earplugs, and naturally you're always listening for cars around you. Every time I was running up by the wall I could have sworn that another car was right there, right on me. It was actually the sound of my car echoing off the wall, but I didn't realize that.

I got to lapping cars, and then I was lapping *good* cars. At that point I figured I must be running pretty good!

The scoreboard is visible from the track at Bulls Gap, and I could see that Vic Hill was third and Mark Douglas was second. I just about caught up with Vic, and I could see Mark just a little bit ahead of Vic.

That was a great thing to see, let me tell you.

I eased up and followed Vic, and we cruised on home. That was an awesome night, and an awesome experience. To get my first late model win at my home track, in front of our home crowd…wow! On our cooldown lap I could hear the people cheering. What a feeling! It's a feeling that gets in your blood, you know?

After the race Chris said, "Why'd you slow down? You could have lapped the whole field!"

I shook my head. "That's not why we were here," I said. "We were here to win the race and that's what we did."

Another great experience came a little later at Tazewell, where we beat Scott Bloomquist at a $10,000-to-win race. It was a daytime event, and whoever got to turn one first was probably going to win. I got there first, and I knew Scott would be right on my rear bumper. The track was narrow, and it was just about impossible to pass. When we got to traffic I slowed my pace, and Scott was all over me. I knew he had no chance of passing me, so I kept my cool and maintained my distance between me and the lapped car. Scott finally blew a tire on the last lap and spun into the infield.

That win is still a fond memory, believe me.

9

Never Give Up

Ups. And downs. That's the inevitable part of racing every young driver has to learn to deal with. I won a lot of races in open wheel modifieds—a couple hundred races, in fact. Some were mighty big races with a big purse. We also won the UMP National championship four times: 1998, 2000, 2001, and 2002.

Those were "ups." Those were good times.

Hey, guess what? When I stepped up to race late models, all those wins and championships didn't mean anything.

What we did in the past didn't matter much. In racing, it's not about what you did last year, last month, or even last week. It's all about what you're doing right now, tonight, in this race car right here.

What a rude awakening! I had got to where I expected to win every time I climbed in the modified. In 1999 we won 49 races in 65 starts, and that messes with your mind. You start thinking you're supposed to win every dadgum race!

Then we got into the late model, making the transition to the pinnacle. In our form of racing—short track stock cars—super late models are the top. In money, in prestige, in everything.

There was still so much I wanted to achieve: I wanted to prove we could run with the best, we could win crown jewel races, and we could make a living as a traveling professional racer.

But man, all of a sudden we weren't the big dog. Not even close! We were almost like a beginner all over again, learning and making mistakes. Every now and then—if things fell exactly right—we could win.

What a humbling experience. I'm a humble guy, but dang…I wasn't ready to be humbled quite *that* much.

But it was good for me. It taught me—or maybe just *reminded* me—about things like dedication, and focus, and patience. Most of all: don't give up.

This period was a great learning experience. If I could sit down with a young racer who is struggling, that's the main thing I'd tell them. When you're down, and it feels like you're going backward and can't seem to get anything going, don't give up. You've got to believe in yourself, even if nobody else believes in you.

I truly believe that if you want something bad enough, and you work hard and stick with it, you can make it.

But if you quit, you're done.

So don't quit.

Yes, a great learning experience. But definitely not easy.

I never felt like giving up, not really. I guess I'm just stubborn, for lack of a better word. I had enough confidence to continue to believe in myself. Shoot, if these other guys could win races, so could we! After all, I was a winner in modified racing, so if we could just learn more and get ourselves better, we could be successful at the next level.

Those first few late model wins, with Jerry Weisgarber's Rayburn chassis, were a big step. When you're down, and struggling, it's impossible to overstate how much a win means. Victory lifts you, and fills you up with something. It fuels you to keep pushing on. When wins are few and far between, winning a race is like good medicine. It makes you feel better all over. Actually, it lifts the entire *team*.

But even when we won now and then, we weren't at the level we wanted to be. We were getting better, but I couldn't help but notice that all the wins we scored were in conditions favorable to me. When the track is exactly as you like it, and your car is set up real nice and runs good, you *should* win.

We needed to get to a place where we didn't have to have favorable conditions to win; capable of winning *any* race, regardless of the conditions. And, honestly, that's the level you must reach to survive as a traveling racer.

That comes with experience. The more I improved, maybe we could get there.

During the 2003 season I connected with Arnold Fuller of Mach 2 Motorsports. Arnold was from Charlotte, and we connected through a mutual friend, Jim Long. Jim and his family run Fayetteville Motor Speedway, and I got to know Jim in my days in the modified. Jim was working to get modified racing stronger in North Carolina and we became friends.

Arnold mentioned to Jim that he was looking for a driver, and Jim suggested he call me. That's the beautiful part of racing; you develop friends who are there at the right moment to put in a good word for you.

I was still driving Jerry's car, and during a break in our schedule I traveled over to Gaffney, South Carolina to run Arnold's car. We teamed up a couple of times during that season, kind of trying each other out. Arnold actually had two cars, with Ricky Weeks driving the other car.

As the 2003 season finished up Arnold and I talked about going racing together on a full-time basis. We agreed to give it a whirl and would start the 2004 season as a team. This was the beginning of my time as a full-time late model racer.

Connecting with Arnold was another good experience. I was eager to travel, and Arnold was good with that. Arnold likes his stuff to be nice; he's a good guy, very clean-cut, and his cars reflected that. He provided us with excellent equipment.

Arnold ran a MasterSbilt chassis, a four-bar car that was very different than the swing-arm chassis I had been running. This took some getting used to. We raced a lot in the Carolinas, against tough competition. Chris Madden was good, along with several other guys. We could win some races; it was challenging but we had a good time racing with those guys.

I was still very much in learning mode, and I didn't know enough to make a lot of major changes to our car. I'd call the MasterSbilt shop and talk to Keith and Tater Masters, describing our setup. They said we were running a pretty basic deal and would offer suggestions and explained how this change or that change should impact the car.

By this time I had built a few modified chassis, so I understood the importance of a good baseline setup. This is critical, because if you wander too far on your setup and get yourself lost, you can go back to that solid baseline and start over. With the MasterSbilt chassis we never went too far from our baseline. I was with the Mach 2 team for two years, and it wasn't until toward the end that we had enough confidence to try major changes to our setup.

Besides, I was more focused on my driving. I always figured that if I can't outrun a guy who is on the same setup as me, I'm not good enough yet. I didn't want to beat them with setup until I could beat them with driving.

Dirt racing is constantly all about learning things, soaking in knowledge until it becomes ingrained in your brain. I learned from many different people along the way, starting with my brother Kurt. There were other important people like Donnie Adams of Lightning Chassis. Donnie is very creative.

We started out running cars with leaf springs and learned to do all kinds of crazy things with that suspension. The trend shifted along the

One of our early late model wins! This is Richmond, Kentucky on June 15, 2002.

Kurt was helping us on this night. Must have been a good combination...we won!

way to four-bar cars, and we ended up running an old asphalt chassis with a swing-arm suspension. We did well with that car and won several races.

When Donnie and I went racing together I began to feel like I was starting to understand it. I mean, understand what the chassis was doing and how you adjust to make the car faster. I've always been mechanically inclined, and I like to improve things. But I would not call myself creative, not in that way. Creative is making things from scratch that nobody has seen before; I'm probably not that guy. However, if you introduce a concept to me I can ponder on it a while and maybe make it better.

In September of 2003 our area—and all of racing, really—suffered a terrible tragedy.

Duayne Hommel was a rising star in racing, from right here in Newport. Duayne and I went way back together, and our career had a similar path. We raced modifieds together a lot, and he was a friendly guy. He and his family are good people.

Duayne and I weren't tight, but we talked fairly often. One night in September 2003 I stopped by Duayne's shop to visit. We sat there and talked, and he explained how excited he was to be a father. His boy, Deagan, was maybe a year old. He was very excited about that little boy!

The next day I got the news that Duayne had been in a terrible car accident not far from his shop and suffered severe injuries. He was life flighted to Knoxville, and things looked grim.

Duayne survived, but it's been a very difficult road for him. His injuries left him in need of almost constant care, and it's been a tough situation for him and his family.

A few years ago Melissa and I built a house not far from our shop, in an area that was developed by Duayne's dad Junior. We still run into Junior and his wife Gayla and Duayne around Newport. It always brings a smile when we stop in a restaurant and they happen to be there, it's always a good visit.

What happened to Duayne was tragic. Awful! He had a lot of promise and potential and it's a shame he didn't have the opportunity to fulfill his racing career.

When I joined the Mach 2 team I had to call C.J. Rayburn to let him know we wouldn't be running his chassis any longer. It was a very interesting conversation.

I began by telling C.J. that I was going to drive for Arnold next year, and

In the Mach 2 Motorsports Rayburn car at Cleveland, Tennessee in 2004. (Rick Schwallie photo)

C.J. Rayburn was a GIANT in our sport, no doubt about it. (Bob Markos photo)

they ran a MasterSbilt car. I told C.J. that I really appreciated everything he did for me, but this guy has plenty of equipment and I'll be able to race nationally instead of just regionally. This was a good opportunity, I explained. I thanked C.J. for giving us a chassis and I told him that I felt kind of bad that we weren't going to run his car any longer.

"Don't worry about it, Jimmy," C.J. said. "You don't have to worry about things like that. Make no mistake, I didn't do it to help you."

I was almost speechless when he said that.

"You didn't?" I finally said.

"Nope. I did it to help *me*. You see, if my car helped you win races, it helps me twice as much. When I help someone win races, that sells race cars."

It was starting to sink in but I still didn't quite know what to make of this guy.

"Well, do you want your car back?"

"No, just keep it," he said. "I'll call you when I need it."

So after a while—I'm talking many months—C.J. called and asked if we still had his car. Yep, it's sitting right here in my shop. He needed it, so I loaded 'er up and drove up to Whiteland. We sat down and ate dinner and had a nice time.

See, many people might not understand C.J., and realize where he was coming from. But what he said was absolutely true. A chassis builder isn't providing you a car just because they're kind and generous; they are doing it because they believe it will promote their business.

There is nothing wrong with that. It's just that when you say it out loud, it might seem a little too direct.

This was a good lesson for me, a part of me slowly opening my eyes to how things work in this world. I appreciated C.J.'s honesty. I was not offended at all, because it made sense to me.

And we *did* help C.J. When we ran well in a Rayburn chassis, that looked good for him and his cars. And believe me, I wanted to help C.J. because he was *the man*. Throughout his life he provided a race car to tons of different people. Lots of guys.

When we were running his car, I probably didn't call C.J. as much as I should have. Whenever I was at his place I could see that he was constantly on the phone, and I don't like to bother someone who is that busy. I would call him and let him know how we ran last weekend, but that's about it.

C.J. knew about things that are way over my head. He was great with numbers and chassis dynamics, but maybe not quite as polished with people. He could be brutally honest at times and some people just can't handle that kind of honesty. But that was C.J.

He was good to just about every racer out there. If I ever have a chassis company, I would like to build an affordable car so that the average guy could do what I've done. I'd like to help them, just like C.J. helped me.

C.J. recently passed away, and when I heard the news I regretted that we didn't talk as much as I'd have liked. I should have picked up the phone every now and then and called him. It would have been a fun conversation, always. Truth is, I'm not good with calling people and just making conversation. But with C.J., you didn't have to worry about that issue… when he answered the phone, the conversation was going to take right off. Guaranteed!

It was while I was driving Arnold Fuller's car that Melissa and I started dating, and after a while she decided to go with us on one of our racing trips.

We headed over to Longdale, North Carolina. Just as we entered the track the leaf spring on our trailer broke, so we were thrashing around, getting the car ready but also figuring out how to get our trailer fixed.

Melissa decided to take a shower. Right about that time I went into our truck looking for something, and I reckon I didn't realize Melissa was in the shower. It felt kinda stuffy in the truck, so I opened the windows and went back outside, not thinking anything about it.

A few minutes later Melissa stepped out of the shower, and she was standing there drying herself off. She thought she heard voices, so she casually turned and looked in that direction.

She was quite surprised to see a crowd of people standing at the open window, staring at her. Did I mention that she was naked as a jaybird?

Melissa hollered and jumped away from the window. After hiding for a couple of minutes the people all went away and she was able to get the windows closed and get herself dressed.

I heard about that one for a long, long time!

In January 2004 we were still running the modified some, and we headed for the three-night Open Wheel Modified Winternationals at East Bay Raceway Park. We won the race in 2003, so we were shooting for a repeat win.

We used Arnold Fuller's truck to pull our trailer to Florida, but the truck broke down in Georgia. It was an automatic shift and wouldn't upshift, and we limped to a truck repair center for service.

The delay caused us to miss the opening night, which put us behind the 8-ball from the start. On the second night we got torn up, so we weren't in the best mood when we woke up on Saturday morning.

The lineup for Saturday night had us deep in the E-main, a daunting situation. I could picture all that carnage and we were going to be right in the middle of it.

I tracked down Al Varnadore, the promoter at East Bay. I lobbied Al for a past winner's provisional so I could skip all that chaos. We were the defending race champion, after all.

Al kinda hesitated.

"Well," he said finally, "you're in the race, Jimmy. Don't worry about that. But I need for you to try to race your way in. Just try."

I was a little grumpy, but okay.

We got through the E-main, and made it into the D. I drove back to our pit, and we decided to keep going. We got through the D, and made it to the C.

"Hell, let's keep going!" It was starting to get exciting, I had to admit.

We lined up for the C-main and got through that one, too. By this time people were all fired up, and you could feel the energy. This was not at all a scenario we would ever choose, but it was working out okay!

The B fired off and we worked our way to the front. We scored a transfer spot and headed back for our pit to get ready for the feature race, which paid $8,000.

We started deep in the field and started moving forward. We got up with the leaders, and Jeff Leka and I were racing hard for second, chasing leader Chad Kinder. It was a good race, and we were going at it pretty hard.

In the late going Jeff and I got together and tore up our right front shock and flattened our tire, and that dashed our hopes of winning. We changed the tire and got back out and finished ninth.

Even with the disappointing ending, it was an exciting night. Tons of people came by our trailer after the races, and it was fun.

Here's an interesting thing I remember. After the race a guy with a pocketful of money was looking to buy a race car. He came by our pit and asked what we wanted for our car. I shot him a fair price—nothing stupid, just a straight price of what the car would bring anywhere else. He kinda shook his head, and went down the way and bought another car. I was amazed. I mean, seriously? You don't want the car that passed nearly every car on the property tonight? But, oh well. People must think differently than I do, I reckon.

That night was a long time ago, but the memory lives on. Every time we go to East Bay, somebody comes by our pit and remembers that night. I remember it, too!

10

Uncertain Times

Teaming up with Mach 2 Motorsports expanded our horizons—by a lot. We raced throughout the Carolinas and traveled to Florence, Kentucky a few times, including our first North South 100.

Man, Florence was hard to figure out, and we couldn't hit our butt with both hands. We also traveled throughout the southeast to several Southern All Star races.

We mostly kept the car at our place in Newport, with Chris Fox and Kenny Holt part of our team. That's the shop we built and still work out of yet today.

As we began to travel with the late model some people knew of us because of our modified racing. In fact, when we went to Eldora for our first World 100 in 2004, I was amazed at how many people wanted our t-shirt. We were busy enough that I finally had to quit selling shirts out of the back of our hauler because I didn't have time to race!

That first World 100 turned out to be a big weekend for us. We qualified good and ran well in our heat race, and had a good starting spot in the main. We were right in the thick of it and on lap 48 I slid Billy Moyer to take the lead.

We were leading the World 100.

That makes me kind of pause when I say it today. Just a couple of years after moving to late models, *we were leading the World 100.* That moment was everything I had dreamed of. The best guys in dirt late model racing were all behind me—for the moment.

As it's happening in real time, you don't have time to think about that stuff. I was just trying to run hard and clean and take care of my race car. We had a good car, but I didn't dare think far enough ahead to dream of winning the race. It's just one lap, one corner, one moment at a time.

On lap 62 my right rear tire went flat, and that was it. We got in to change the tire, but we didn't have near enough laps to get back to the front. Chub Frank won it, and we ended up finishing 15th.

It was a bad break, but that's the way it goes. I raced and raced and raced and was so into it, I didn't have time to think about shoulda-woulda-coulda. When you're leading a big race, you're not sitting there thinking, "I'm gonna win the World 100!" It doesn't work like that. You run every lap and nothing sinks in until it's done.

Later on, when you slow down and look back, things take on more meaning. The wins mean more to you, because you're able to see them for what they really are: success.

Our two seasons with Mach 2 were good ones. We gained a lot of experience and learned a ton.

As time went on there was some friction between Arnold and me, and we began to disagree on some things. I was taking his stuff and racing closer to me and farther from him, and that was an issue. He had to travel to watch his race car.

There was a race at Atomic, and we wanted to go but Arnold didn't. I might have gone anyways, I don't remember. But at any rate we ended up cussing each other a little bit afterwards.

I was younger then, and probably didn't show Arnold the appreciation I should have. I am the most appreciative guy in the pits, but I don't express it like I should. That wasn't just because I was younger; I *still* need to work on that. Looking back, I would definitely have handled things differently.

It would have benefitted me along the way if we'd had a couple more mentors at the right time. There were times when I didn't have people around me to guide and advise me on the right way to deal with people, or handle a situation. That's not an excuse; it's the truth. I made mistakes with how I dealt with people because I flat didn't know any better.

My view of a team owner today is very different than it was at that time, and my view is more accurate today. A team owner is paying all the bills, and almost every racing operation is a liability on the balance sheet. No matter how you figure it, this person is spending money for you to race. Usually they are doing it because they enjoy watching their race car. It's expensive, and you're an expense. At the very least you need to make sure—*damn* sure—they understand how much you appreciate what they are doing for you.

A race car is optional, you know. They could choose to quit whenever they want.

At any rate, at the end of the 2005 season it was time for Arnold and I to go our separate ways. I was out of a ride and had to figure something out right quick if I wanted to race in 2006.

Tazewell, Sept. 4, 2005...our first Lucas Oil win! We were excited to share the moment with (L-R) Kurt Owens, Chad Bryant, Jeremy Sheppard, Kenny Holt, Chris Fox, and Michael "Snarf" Phillips. (Rick Schwallie photo)

Driving for the Harrod Farms team was a great time, all around. Those guys knew how to race, and win, and still have fun! (Rick Schwallie photo)

In the years after Arnold and I split I sometimes wondered if I had properly thanked him for our time together. A couple of years ago the Lucas Oil series had a weekend at Portsmouth where they suggested everybody use a throwback paint scheme on their car. We decided to make our car look like Arnold's No. 20 from our time together, and it was great. Arnold came to Portsmouth and we went racing together, what a fun weekend. I was able to tell Arnold how much I appreciated him giving me a chance in his race car all those years ago.

Unfortunately Arnold passed away just a few months ago. Rest in peace, buddy. It was an honor to go racing with you.

From there I wasn't sure where to go. It was late in the year, and I talked to Ken Schrader and asked if any of his NASCAR friends were thinking of starting a dirt late model team. Ken said he was going to Atlanta that next weekend and would talk to some people. It was a short conversation and I didn't think about it much beyond that.

I was surprised a week or two later when Ken called me back. "Do you want to run my car this weekend?" he asked. They were headed for North Georgia Speedway and then Cleveland, Tennessee.

Ken's guys got me situated in their car and we ran a few races together. We ran pretty good at Cleveland and finished third behind Dale McDowell and Scott Bloomquist. But this was just a one-weekend deal and I was still looking for something long-term for the 2006 season.

Another conversation was with Scott Bloomquist. He had told me once, months before, that he might want me to drive for him someday. So I called Scott and explained that I was looking for a ride.

Scott said that he wasn't set up for running another car at the moment. But he said that if I didn't land a ride by such-and-such time next spring, I could run his back-up car for a few races. That meant a lot to me, because I look up to Scott.

As it turned out, another door was just about to open.

Jeff and Eddie Harrod are good 'ol boys from Kentucky, part of a big farming family. Along with Justin Sims, a Kentucky state trooper, they are one big happy family and they are a lot of fun to be around.

They love to race and they've got enough money to do it right. Harrod Farms is in the heart of Kentucky, on Hwy. 58 just off I-64 near Frankfort.

My phone rang and it was Jeff Harrod. He thought it would be cool for me to drive their car a time or two. Well, I immediately thought it would be cool, too! So away we went. Now we were a part of that big, happy, fun-loving Kentucky family.

Lots of happy smiles after this Bulls Gap win in 2006! That's Jeff Harrod in the blue shirt. (Rick Schwallie photo)

Eldora, June 10, 2006 with the Harrod Farms car. (Rick Schwallie photo)

The Harrod Farms guys had good stuff. They ran a Rocket chassis, and later on we also purchased a Rayburn car.

They were awesome people, probably the most fun I've ever had racing. We'd cut up and laugh and it was great. Of course we were serious about trying to win, but when things didn't go our way we didn't act like the dog just died. We'd just push on and didn't let stuff ruin our day.

We ran over at West Plains, Missouri for the Show-Me 100, and scored a transfer position in our heat race. This was a big deal, making the Show-Me 100! But instead of going to the scales I drove straight back to our pit, and we were disqualified. It was just a mental lapse on my part, and I felt awful. I actually did this twice in their car; they ended up putting a big sign on the dash: SCALES!

We kind of went back and forth with our two cars—the Rocket and the Rayburn—and I liked the Rayburn better. They teased me about that, and when we won in the Rocket they had a good time razzing me. But we gave 100 percent, regardless of which car we were in.

Our engine program wasn't where it needed to be, and we talked about that quite a bit. I explained that at Mach 2 Racing we had experienced good luck with Cornett motors. I'm not a horsepower freak, but the engine we had in the Harrod Farms car wasn't very drivable. It made decent power, but just didn't work with my driving style or something.

After we hem-hawed for a little bit they finally bought a Jay Dickens Chevrolet motor, and we won the first night we put it in. That was a big weight lifted from my shoulders; I had talked them into buying the motor, and I was glad it turned out okay.

We won seven or eight races together that season, not bad at all. We also had lots of fun.

One night we were traveling home when I parked on an exit ramp to get some sleep. Jeff was asleep in the back. A cop came along and knocked on the door and told me that we'd have to move the truck off the exit ramp. I fired the truck up and started to move, and I could hear Jeff flying from the back of the truck. He poked his head into the cab and his eyes were as big as headlights. He thought for sure the truck was rolling down the grade.

On another weekend we were going to run Eldora, and I drove up to their place near Frankfort. We jumped in the truck and took off down the highway, and we were hardly even down the road when all of a sudden Jeff looked around and said, "Where we at?"

"Man, what do you mean, 'Where we at?' We just left!"

"Have we been through Cincinnati?"

"Yes."

"Well, shoot…I'm so danged tired, I don't even remember!"

It was in the Harrod car that I had my first experience of going wide open around Eldora, never lifting the throttle. What a rush! Eldora is unique because turns one and two are slightly different than three and four, and often you can run wide open through one and two but not quite through three and four. So one day during qualifying I flat-footed one and two and when I got on the backstretch I was determined to keep the throttle mashed to the floor through the other end.

We ripped down the backstretch and I was gritting my teeth, bracing myself.

"I'm gonna do it," I kept saying to myself.

I kept the throttle down and turned into the corner, running right up by the wall. Man, that thing sounded great, wide-ass open up high. The car turned nice and got through the corner without getting into the fence and the next thing I knew I was seeing the flag stand on the front straightaway.

That's an important thing, that first wide-open lap at Eldora. From that moment you know it's possible, and you know you can do it. It's never quite the same after you've experienced that feeling.

We had a good time with the Harrod guys, all of us. One of the things I liked about those guys is that it wasn't just about them. They were genuine, good people, and even though our time together eventually ended, they were very gracious and understanding. When the time came for us to part we shook hands and, as the years came and went, we have continued to be good friends.

Man, that's my kind of people.

Part of my experience in the Harrod Farms car was the 2006 World 100. We didn't run all that great; we won our heat race, but ended up 24th in the feature race. But it was at that race when a conversation took place that would have a huge and permanent impact on my racing career.

A guy approached me and introduced himself. His name was Michael, and he smiled and asked if I had a minute to talk. Sure do, I said.

"We're from Tazewell (Tennessee), and my dad is looking to start a new race team," he explained. "He is willing to spend whatever it takes to have a top late model team. He wants to run a national schedule and he'd like to talk to you about driving for us."

Well, he certainly had my attention.

"What's your dad's name?" I asked.

"Mike Reece."

Well, there you go. My next racing adventure was about to begin.

11

Dreams Come True

If you're around racing for any length of time you develop a natural suspicion of people. You become a little guarded, a little cynical, a little skeptical. That's because you discover that, for whatever reason, people often promise more than they can deliver.

People approach racers all the time with a "great deal!" They want you to use their product, they want to sponsor you, whatever. All that is good, of course, but many times the reality doesn't live up to the promises.

So when the opportunity to go racing with Mike Reece cropped up, I wasn't sure. I didn't know Mike personally, and didn't know anything about him. This man was promising to spend whatever it takes to field a top super late model team on the road, and he was offering me the chance to help organize the team and drive the race car.

To be honest, it sounded too good to be true.

Well, it *was* true. Looking back, I can testify that Mike did everything he promised. He was very good to me—still is—and he changed the course of my career and my life.

When I got back from Eldora in the autumn of 2006 I met with Mike and we talked. Mike owned a monument company, and he was a very successful person. He was promising many good things, and my head was spinning. I was overwhelmed, to be honest.

Mike was sort of new to racing. He had helped another guy previously, which gave him some experience, and had also bought a Bloomquist race car. But Mike didn't have a race shop or hauler, or many of the other things you need to go racing. He was eager to get started and wanted me to put everything together and make it go.

I was still a little uncertain. I tried to find out more about Mike; you know, is he a reputable guy? Everybody I reached out to said, yes, Mike is good. He's solid.

Obviously, this looked like a golden opportunity. I thought real hard about what I should do. Should I jump at the chance and go for it? When I posed the situation to my mom, that's exactly what she said I should do.

"Go for it, son!" she said. Good ol' mom. Always a positive gal.

Another thing rattling around in my mind was this: I liked driving the Harrod Farms car—a lot—and the thought of quitting them made me feel guilty. I definitely felt torn.

But I had to set aside my emotions and ask myself a simple question: was Mike Reece presenting an opportunity that would benefit my career? That was a simple answer: Yes, he was.

If we passed up this opportunity, I might regret it for the rest of my life. If it turned out to be nothing, well, so what? I could always get a ride with somebody else. But if it was for real…man, it could be the break I had been hoping for.

We *had* to try. I had to see if this thing was for real. So I told Mike I was his guy. We shook hands and I walked out of Mike's office with a big smile on my face.

We were still smiling, but when I realized how much we had to do in order to put everything together, it felt like being in the middle of a tornado. All of a sudden there were a million details to chase, and the clock was ticking until our first race in early 2007.

The number one thing we needed was a crew. The first guy I approached was Chris Fox. Chris had cut back his racing involvement for a little bit, but he was eager to get back into it. Shannon Green also helped us out, along with Bud Orr. My brother Kurt jumped in and helped, as well.

Another piece of the puzzle was George Gantt of Gantt Appraisals. George was a good, kind friend who had told me for a long time that he'd like to get involved and help with our racing program. I approached George about the new opportunity with Mike, and he jumped on board as one of our sponsors.

I had built a nice race shop behind our old garage at David Prizer's, and had been renting the space to Scott Hicks and Mike Ottinger, a couple of asphalt racers from Newport. They had just vacated the shop, so the timing was perfect. We started rounding things up and building cars and our shop was booming with activity.

It's amazing how much it takes to go racing: tools, fixtures, parts, spares, engines, frames, wheels…whew! And when the delivery truck backs up to your door with all your new stuff, you've got to organize and assemble everything.

It was tons of work, but we liked it. We were working and making jokes and having fun while we put everything together. It was a good experience and I smile now when I think back to that winter.

We had one Bloomquist car to start with, and Mike had just ordered two more cars. I checked with Scott and the cars were over at his place, so Shannon and I drove over to help get everything finished up.

Mike and I were still debating which motors to run. Mike was fond of Clements, and they do a nice job. We raced Fords when I drove for Mach 2, and Mike's existing car had a Ford. My idea was to run another Ford, and we'd have two of them. I've never been a "brand" guy—Ford or Chevy—but it made sense to stay with what we already had.

We made up our mind to go with Jack Cornett, and ordered two motors. Mike told me, "Just have Jack send the bill to me."

I laughed. "Man, he's *got* to send the bill to you…I sure can't pay for something like two motors! Are you kiddin'?"

We also needed a hauler. We decided to buy a rig from 5150, up in Lewisburg, Tennessee. They had a new black conversion truck and trailer nearly complete, with the conversion built on a used truck chassis. We were able to select how we wanted it finished, and I drove up there a couple of times to check on things and show them what we wanted.

Then came the day when we picked up our new rig. Well, there's a problem: I've never driven a tractor-trailer before. The one time I had tried—in Alvin Renue's rig—Alan nearly crapped his pants because I was all over the place.

My buddy Cheyenne Kite rode along with me to Lewisburg so he could follow me home in my pickup truck. Well, I jumped in our new hauler and acted like I knew what I was doing, but…I had no idea. I managed to get 'er in gear and release the brakes, and away we went!

It probably wasn't as bad as it sounds. We didn't hit anybody, and by the time we got to middle Tennessee I had the hang of it. Kinda.

Pretty soon it was time to stop for fuel. I eased into the truck stop, climbing down out of the cab like a big rig trucker. Say, look at this big black hauler! Ain't it nice?

I fueled the tank on one side of the truck, and Cheyenne fueled the other side. When we finished I went inside to pay, and somehow in the confusion—there was always some confusion in those early days—one of us didn't take the fueling hose out of the tank.

We wheeled back out on the Interstate, and I'm rollin' down the road feeling good. A trucker pulled up alongside me and he's waving like crazy, pointing and telling me to pull over. So I flicked on the signal and eased off the road, wondering what in the world was wrong.

That's when I saw the fuel nozzle and hose, still stuck in my filler opening with the hose dragging on the ground.

An early start in Mike Reece's car at Florence, June 2, 2007.
Good things were happening! (Rick Schwallie photo)

Getting our shocks ready for the World 100 in 2007. (Rick Schwallie photo)

Boy, this is great. I'm gonna get fired from my new ride before we've even run a race! Plus, they are going to be awful mad at me back at the truck stop, and as I dialed their number I had visions of major explosions and people burning up from some fool driving off and breaking the pump.

I was worried to death, but the guy at the truck stop just laughed and said no problem. They've already got it repaired, he said. Apparently the hose and nozzles just snap together. "People do this stuff all the time," he said. Well, that didn't make me feel any better.

Everything finally came together for our new team, and lo and behold things went according to plan. We put our new cars together and got our trailer lined out and we were ready to hit the road and go racing.

Hit the road...that was music to my ears. For years I had dreamed of traveling and making a living driving a super late model. Now it was happening.

Mike did everything he promised. He funded the race team and allowed us to call the shots and put everything together. He made it possible for us to continue racing for years to come, through one of the most productive periods of my career.

I've said it so many times through the years that people are probably tired of hearing it: Mike Reece made my dreams come true. It's as simple as that.

When money is tight, that affects how you race. There's no doubt about it. There were many times in my early years where I felt like we weren't racing to our full potential—sometimes even in my own race car—because maybe we didn't have the best motor or fresh tires.

You learn that you can pinch pennies on certain things, but not everywhere. The bottom line is that you've got to spend money in the areas that matter most, such as motors and tires.

I was very much aware that Mike was spending a lot of money, particularly when we were putting the initial program together. There was stuff I had collected through the years—tools and fixtures, for example—that I used to stock the shop and trailer, trying to avoid spending money where we could. But with buying the cars, the engines, and the hauler, Mike still spent a lot of money.

My goal was to make enough money with the car to keep us going. If we could make enough to pay our fuel, our crew, and other expenses, we wouldn't have to keep going back to Mike and asking for more money. I didn't want to have to go back to the well any more than we had to.

Things went well for us, right away. We went to Volusia in February to kick off the 2007 season, and we were competitive at the get-go. The

Winning our first World 100 in 2007! There is nothing like this feeling. (Rick Schwallie photo)

Bloomquist car handled nice and I liked it. Scott offered a lot of good input, and that was a boost as well. My confidence was starting to take off.

Anybody who has raced will tell you that confidence is *huge*. I felt like I could take any car and could win with it. We now had everything needed to travel and win races at a national level.

A helpful factor was getting to race just about every weekend. There was nothing keeping us from getting out there and racing. We were *full-time* racers now.

We raced an open schedule, running some Southern All Star events, World of Outlaws events, and Lucas Oil Late Model Dirt Series events. I didn't care where we went; I just wanted to race!

That's when it really hit home with me: I love driving a race car.

There's a ton of day-to-day stuff surrounding every race team. Work in the shop, dealing with people, working on the business side of things and paying the bills, keeping your crew together, traveling up and down the road, doing media interviews, all kinds of stuff. I was learning how everything worked, but most of all, I loved every minute I was inside the race car.

In the car, it was my own little world. Just me, all alone, competing with these other guys.

I was living my dream, and was just starting to realize it. Most of the time we were too caught up in what we were doing to appreciate what was happening; that's common, especially when you're younger. But there were moments when it came into focus. In the middle of a race, going wheel to-wheel with a really good racer, and realizing...hey, I'm holding my own with this guy! In fact...we can *beat* this guy!

What a great feeling!

As summer heated up in 2007, so did we. We were steadily picking up the pace and on June 15 won a Lucas Oil race at North Georgia Speedway. The following day we traveled to Talladega Short Track, where we won again.

Back-to-back wins in Lucas Oil competition; that's nothing to sneeze at.

On July 6 we won another Lucas Oil race, this time close to home at Tazewell. It was great to win in front of our home people in the stands! And it was especially sweet for Mike Reece to see his team win at his hometown track.

We traveled to LaSalle, Illinois on August 6 with Lucas Oil and won again, and the following weekend traveled to Florence for the North/South 100, one of the most prestigious events in dirt late model racing.

We had never run worth a dang at Florence, never. But we won the North/South that weekend and picked up a winner's check for $50,000.

I remember that weekend well; the weather was hot, as usual, and there were a bunch of hot chicks in victory lane. We had champagne and everything!

Winning that race was important, partly because it was a breakthrough at Florence. Again, it's that "confidence" thing. I was starting to prove to myself that I had a shot at winning at any track, on any day, against any field of cars.

When I say confidence, I don't mean arrogance. There is definitely a difference. I'm not an arrogant person; exactly the opposite. I'm a low-key guy and you will pretty much never hear me brag or talk smack. At the same time, I believe in my ability to win.

It had been a good four-week stretch for us. After winning the North/South, I remember Scott Bloomquist telling us, "Well, now you've gotta win the World 100!" Scott pointed to recent statistics which showed that whoever won the North/South would also win the World.

Win the World 100? Hey…that sounds like a good idea!

Three weeks later we headed for Eldora. I'd like to say we had high hopes, but I'm not sure that was true. Yeah, we expected to run good, but a race of that magnitude, you don't want to let your dreams get out of hand. Still, we felt pretty good; as we unloaded our car we had won 11 races in 33 starts at that point in the season.

We qualified well and set fast time, and that was a good start. There were 203 cars on hand; man, when you out-qualify 202 guys, that ain't bad.

A big storm swept through on Saturday night just as the program was getting started. Part of the pit area was flooded so they postponed everything to the following day.

The next day we ran third in our heat race and lined up 13th in the main event. I got a nice start and picked my way forward, passing Scott Bloomquist for the lead on lap 10.

I was out front in the World 100! But I had seen this movie before, and it hadn't ended well. So I concentrated on making good laps and tried to take care of our car.

Steve Francis slid us to take the lead on lap 18, and Steve drove away from us a little bit. I was starting to sense that I didn't have anything for him. But I coached myself to stay calm and don't make any mistakes.

Sure enough, I started reeling Steve in. On lap 87 I passed him and from that point it was just a matter of finishing the deal. We rolled across the finish line in the lead and…well, that was a mighty cool deal.

Everybody was whooping and hollering, but I didn't get too excited. Deep inside I was elated, for sure, but I fought to not show a lot of emotion.

We scored $40,000 at the World, but we weren't finished. The following weekend we won the $20,000-to-win Racefest World Championship at West Virginia Motor Speedway. We kept winning and closed out our season with the $10,000 Blue-Gray 100 at Cherokee Speedway in Gaffney, South Carolina, a prestigious race in its own right.

The 2007 season had been good for us. Our relationship with Mike Reece had begun in a positive way, and things were just getting started.

A few days after our World 100 win, the race coverage in *National Speed Sport News* began with this paragraph: "*Jimmy Owens has officially arrived as a dirt late model star.*"

It feels a little weird to think about things in a dramatic way like that, but the 2007 season was a milestone for our racing career.

I was proud, of course, but mostly I was proud of Mike and Chris and our crew. We did it together. It was a season where nobody quite knew what to expect, and it couldn't have gone any better.

As someone who has always struggled with this kind of thing, it meant a lot to read stories like the one in *Speed Sport*. Now, don't get me wrong: it's dangerous to read your own press clippings, because it can make you overconfident. I wasn't about to let *that* happen. Still, it boosted my self-esteem a little and gave me permission to believe in myself a little more.

It felt like *validation*. After a season like 2007, I didn't have to apologize to anybody anymore. You know, the "*who does he think he is!*" thing.

Winning felt good, and I liked it. There ain't nothing wrong with that.

I believe it was Ozzie Altman who came up with the "Newport Nightmare" nickname. Thanks, Ozzie! (Rick Schwallie photo)

Racing with Rick Eckert at Hagerstown in 2008. (Rick Schwallie photo)

12

Following The Series

The 2007 season was a game-changer for everyone with the Reece Monument team. We were no longer looked upon as regional racers, and we had traveled farther—and more often—than ever before.

Our plan was the same as we started the 2008 season. Instead of following just one series, we built our schedule around the events that made sense. Obviously, the biggest purse and the shortest tow are always a consideration. Plus, if you're running an open schedule, most of us tend to run more often at the places we like. That's one element that changes when you commit to running full-time with a series.

We had a pretty decent year in 2008, and started off good. In February we ran the Dart Winternationals at Golden Isles Speedway in Georgia, winning three races and the overall points title. We won 14 races in 2008, including several $10,000-to-win shows including the March Madness at Cherokee Speedway, the Scorcher at Bulls Gap, the Ralph Latham Memorial at Florence, the Bluegrass Classic at Bardstown, Kentucky, and another $10,000 race at Bulls Gap.

The biggest payday of the season came at the Hillbilly 100 on Aug. 31 at Tyler County Speedway, our first visit to the track. Man, one look at that place and I knew why they called it "the bullring!" Tim Dohm had built up a big lead and we were running second, and got a caution flag. That put us right on Dohm's bumper, and our car fired off real nice and we got the lead. We hung on for the $40,000 win.

The headline that next week in *Speed Sport News* said, "*Jimmy Owens Is $40,000 Hillbilly.*" That suited me just fine!

But as 2008 went on things were getting kinda tough. The economy began to take a crap, and that affected a lot of things. We started to hear rumors of tracks not paying the purse, racers getting bad checks, things like that. It created uncertainty and that's not a good feeling when you're trying to keep a business going. A race team is like any other business: you get nervous when you think about money not coming in.

Plus, the cost of fuel had jumped way up. Not just racing fuel, but *diesel* fuel. Man, it takes a lot of fuel to get up and down the road, and you've got to have money coming in to cover that. It's nerve wracking when you have all these expenses and you're not sure where the money will come from.

Plus, the idea of getting stiffed at the payoff window is a very big deal for any racer. It isn't just financial; it's an emotional thing. You worked all week in the shop, drove half-a-day to get to the track, raced your butt off, and put everything on the line. You did everything you were supposed to do; you held up your end of the deal. To do all that and then have somebody say, well, sorry I can't pay you guys because I'm short of money…man, that's a very emotional deal.

That's when we thought about our options for 2009, and started thinking about running the Lucas Oil Late Model Dirt Series schedule as a full-timer. Lucas has always been solid, and that's what we were looking for. They had things in place to assure the racers that we'd get paid properly at the end of the night.

It was kind of a natural choice, really. We ran a lot of their races in 2008 and finished eighth in series points, but we didn't get any points money because we hadn't competed in the minimum 80 per cent of the races.

We talked it over with Mike and decided to run the Lucas deal in 2009. We liked the idea of the purse being guaranteed, and a good bit of their travel was close to home. It was logical.

Many of the tracks on the Lucas Oil schedule were familiar to us. Florence, Cherokee, Fayetteville, Bulls Gap, Tazewell, those were almost like hometown tracks. But running the full schedule meant traveling a little farther and running many new tracks.

One of the first new tracks came in May at the Diamond Nationals at Lucas Oil Speedway in Wheatland, Missouri. This facility is probably one of the best we had ever visited, and our first impression was good. We had heard so much about the track, and were eager to run there. We didn't have a good day on that first outing, and ran 12th. But in time we would learn the track a little better and it would become one of our favorites.

A couple of weeks later we ran the Show-Me 100 at West Plains Motor Speedway. This was the final Show-Me at West Plains, and the following year it moved to Lucas Oil Speedway. We set quick time and led the first 19 laps before Brian Birkhofer passed us and went on to win, and we finished 4th.

Our first trip to West Plains had been with the Harrod Farms car a couple of years earlier, when I drove past the scales after transferring from the consy. Still, I learned a lot that weekend.

On May 30 we were back at Florence, where we won the Ralph Latham Memorial for the second straight year. After some rough nights in my earlier years at Florence, the track was turning out to be good to us.

In early June we headed for Eldora, and the Dream. We set fast time, but didn't have the car we needed in our heat race and did not make the transfer. We ended up using a fast qualifier provisional to make the show, and along with Chris and the guys we threw some things at the car to try to get it at least competitive for the feature.

We hit the setup just right, and from the get-go we were fast. Our provisional had us starting 19th, and that's pretty deep against such a stout bunch of cars. But right away we started passing cars on the bottom like crazy.

About 25 laps into the race our oil pressure light blinked. At least that's when I first saw it. I kept going, and a few laps later saw it again. After that it was on my radar, and it was blinking a little more often. I looked down at the gauges; I had oil pressure, so I moved up the track a little bit and the light didn't seem to blink as often.

Tony Stewart and Scott Bloomquist were running 1-2, and I started running them down. We were past the midway point when I caught them, and I could see my car smoking. I wanted to make a move for the lead, but when I pushed my car hard the oil light would blink. Doggone it!

I starting thinking…we came from 19th to third, and I'm good with that. So I took it easy and rode behind them for what seemed like an eternity.

Well, it *seemed* like an eternity; it might have only been half a lap. I was still thinking: you know what, I might not win, but these guys are gonna know I was here, one way or another.

So I decided to go. Mash the gas.

Tony and Scott were dicing for the lead, getting after it. Our car was so dang good I passed them both on the same lap.

I remember it like it was yesterday. I passed Scott through one and two, and got beside Tony on the backstretch. He was moving up the track and it looked like I was gonna get pinched against the wall, so I let off the gas and turned left and drove by him on the inside. I'm not kiddin', our car was that good. I could run anywhere I wanted.

Once I got the lead I backed off as much as I dared, still watching that oil light. In the late laps I came up behind a guy I wanted to lap—I mean, *really* wanted to lap—but I restrained myself and just rode behind him, trying to baby my sick motor.

We hung on to win for another big payday at Eldora.

It was a great night when we won the Topless 100 in 2008, and James Essex interviewed us on the PA. (Rick Schwallie photo)

With promoter Carl Short after winning the Hillbilly 100 at Tyler County in 2008. Carl has done a lot for our sport! (Rick Schwallie photo)

Most of the time I don't hoot and holler after a win, because that's not my style. But when they interviewed me that night my voice was cracking and I felt a whole lot of emotion welling up inside me.

It was just a heckuva night. To come from 19th to win the Dream, that's special. And something else was on my mind: It was finally sinking in to me just how meaningful it is to win big races like this. I had begun to realize how much it meant to Mike Reece and my crew, and all the people who support us. Family, friends, everybody. Standing there that night, I was thinking about all those people, and I just felt a huge happiness that we had helped them have a wonderful night.

I'm not a party animal, but if I was, we would have rocked the house that night. It was a great night and I'm glad it's still so fresh in my mind.

Afterwards we sent the motor back to Jack Cornett, and he tore it down. Apparently our distributor had cracked and Jack called and said he had no idea how that motor lasted as long as it did; he said there is no way it could have made another lap. So I guess Lady Luck was riding with us that night.

I like racing at Eldora, although that's the site of the most serious wreck I've ever experienced.

It was the 4-Crown Nationals in 1999, the year after Jack Hewitt won all four features at the 4-Crown. Hewitt winning four features in one night was just about the coolest feat I'd ever heard of, and we wanted to go up with our modified and watch Hewitt race, and try to win against him.

We were quick time in qualifying and started 8th with the invert. There was a pile-up right in front of us, and everything happened fast (it always happens fast at Eldora). I was running wide open and hit the guy in front of me, and a split-second later somebody hit me so hard that it broke off the pedals in my car.

My back popped, and I immediately knew that wasn't a good thing. My leg was hurting, and when I looked down at my feet I could see daylight through the floor of the car.

I crawled out and walked to the top of the track and sat down. The reason I sat down so quick is that my ankle swelled up real big and I couldn't put any weight on it. The guys in the ambulance checked me out, but luckily we didn't need x-rays or to go to the hospital. I kinda limped around for a couple of days, and we had one badly wrecked race car to fix.

Eldora is a badass race track!

As the 2009 season wore on we were good, but not great. We were consistent, but didn't score as many wins as we wanted (what racer doesn't say that?). We ran second in points much of the season, but Scott Bloomquist built up a pretty good points lead and although we closed out the season strong we weren't able to cut into his lead.

In August we had another good weekend when we won the Topless 100 at Batesville Motor Speedway. Chris and the guys worked their butt off all weekend, and we had a real nice car for the feature. We caught Scott in traffic and took the lead early, and from that point hung on to win it. It was a $40,000 payday and a good night.

I'm a fan of Batesville, but I've never been much of a fan of taking the roof off. It's cool to watch, I'm sure, but as a driver it's *not* cool. These cars are heavy, and I've seen guys flip and the cage works like a shovel, throwing dirt in your face. If the ground is just an inch from my head, I'd just as soon avoid that, you know? It's nerve wracking.

But there are a lot of cool people up at Batesville, and lots of history. The promoter, Mooney Starr, tries to take care of the racers. He promoted some big modified shows up there, and I liked that. He put up big money—$10k, $30k to win—and in the early years it was a struggle to get enough people. But he hung in there and now he's got the place rolling good.

On our first visit to Batesville we got to visit Billy Moyer's shop, which was cool. Larry Shaw, a very successful car builder, is in the area as well. The Topless continues to grow and that's good for everybody.

One week after our win at the Topless we won a Lucas Oil race at Tazewell, and two weeks later won at Portsmouth Raceway Park.

Knoxville Raceway in Iowa was a late-season tradition for the Lucas Oil series by that point, although we actually made our first trip out there in 2008 and finished second to Tim McCreadie at the Late Model Nationals. Knoxville is a special place, different from most other places we had raced.

I remember the first time I saw the place. I looked things over and immediately thought, "Now this is a big-ass race track! Wow!"

But it's a lot more than just a big track; there is so much history and tradition there. My first visit there was a lot like my first trip to Eldora some years earlier; you think about the fact that some of the greatest racers in American history have turned laps there. All the signs and banners hanging around the track, and the sprint car museum just outside turn two, it was awesome. I enjoyed that first trip and it's turned into a track I've looked forward to running every year.

We closed out the 2009 season year pretty well, but Scott's point lead turned out to be too much to overcome. We finished second in series points, and we felt like it wasn't a bad finish considering it was our first time running the full Lucas Oil schedule. Our season included seven wins, including the Dream and the Topless. Not bad.

But I was reminded that we still had a lot to learn. When we looked back at the season there were too many instances where I took it too easy, trying to be conservative. A couple of times we were running bad, so I pulled in. When you're racing an open schedule, that's okay. But it's not okay with points racing. You've got to stay out there and get every point you can. If I got lapped I'd want to pull in, and that costs you points. Your motor starts smoking, you run bad, well, I'll just pull in! You have a flat tire and pull in, well, no need to go back out, you know? I did that a several times before I realized, "You big dummy, you can't pull in!" You've got to get every position, every point you can.

The more I thought about it, I realized we didn't compete like we should have for the championship. Sure, we finished second in points. Fine. But we could have done much better. We could have kept it way closer; maybe we could have won it? You don't know unless you give it your all.

That was a very important lesson learned.

It was still a good first experience, though. One of the keys was that we had good help, with Chris Fox as our crew chief. Kenny Holt, another longtime friend, was back on board and everybody worked real good together.

One of the things I liked about running the Lucas Oil series was that we didn't spend all week debating where we were going to race that weekend. We had an established schedule, and we didn't have to take any time with that sort of planning. That suited me because I don't like fiddling around with stuff like that. It was nice to have the schedule already mapped out for us.

After the Lucas Oil season finished we ran the World Finals at Charlotte, where we won the final night for $10,000.

I liked going over to Charlotte, although I remember a few nights when the track was very rough. I made my first trip there with Mach 2 Motorsports a few years earlier, and ran there several times. We were running a limited late model there once, and a big-ass wreck happened right in front of us. I was trying to miss it but somebody spun right in front of me and I blasted that poor guy in the back. It ruined our car, and probably his, too.

That same night we also ran a super, and they did a pill draw after your heat race, like a redraw. It paid $1,000 per spot passed, and we drew a 16 starting spot and won. That had been my biggest race payoff to date, I suspect. We were in a Rayburn car, and as I recall we passed Donnie Moran for the win.

One of our best nights at the World Finals came in a Bloomquist car. We ran the C main, transferred to the B, then transferred to the A. We started deep and drove up to third, contending for the win. I think it was Scott and Chris Madden and us. Although we finished third we got a lot of "attaboys" and pats on the back for the most cars passed that night.

But that first win in 2009 was cool. It's a big deal, the World Finals. The coolest part is the four-wide salute, when they bring all of the cars from all divisions out for a parade lap. That is really, really awesome. When you're out there in that group of cars, you feel like you're a part of history. The crowd is big and boisterous it looks great from the race car. Very exciting!

13

The Road

Ah, life on the road. Ain't nothing like it. Now, I didn't say it was *good*; I just said there ain't nothing like it. When we made the decision in 2009 to follow the Lucas Oil Late Model Dirt Series full-time, it changed almost everything about my racing life. It was a learning experience, because chasing a series full-time is a different way to race and a different way to live.

When you're racing locally, you settle into a groove. Most of your tows are short, and you're sleeping at home most of the time. But when you begin to travel, it's a different setup. The logistics, the planning, everything is more complicated.

Not to mention the intangibles. You're away from home, your crew is away from home, and everybody gets a little homesick. You get on each other's nerves a little bit and people get to fussin'.

Nothing ever replaces your family, of course. But we discovered that with a traveling series it becomes like your second family, your family away from home. Everybody rides up and down the road, facing the same challenges. Lonesome, homesick, tired, stressed...everybody faces that stuff. Nobody is immune.

Racers, series officials, parts people, sponsors, fans, media people... they're all part of the family.

Watching from a distance, you might see rivalries on the track and think, "Oh, Jimmy and Scott, they hate each other." Well, it ain't like that. Even though you compete with other racers, you take care of each other. If you break down on the side of the road, you don't have to worry that nobody will help you.

What happens on the race track is one thing. You get mad at somebody, or they get mad at you, and that's real. Over time, that kinda heals up and

Rolling eastbound on I-40...here we go again! (Dave Argabright photo)

I do most of the driving in the truck, and that's the way I like it. (Dave Argabright photo)

you move on. But off the track, if somebody is broke down on the side of the road and needs help, you instantly forget what happened on the race track and you help that guy. You do whatever you can to help him get on home, or get to the next track.

That's how it is and I like it that way. Whatever fussin' you've got going on with another driver, or his crew, you leave that stuff at the house and help out when needed.

After a season on the road with Lucas, I realized that I didn't miss the drama you often have at local race tracks. You've always got the Hatfield and McCoy stuff going on, and even when you race regionally you get caught up in other people's crap and that gets tiresome.

I don't know exactly how to explain it, but when you get on the road with a touring series it's different. Even though you're racing with the same people every weekend, you don't have the petty stuff you see at the local level. Maybe it's that "family" thing, I don't know. Or maybe we're so danged busy with everything we don't have time to fuss with each other.

The logistics of traveling are different, obviously. If you're going back to your shop every night after the races, you've got the opportunity to fix your stuff and replenish your trailer. But when you're gone for weeks at a time, man, you've got to plan a whole lot of things to make it work.

If you tear up your stuff, that's a problem. Not only are you away from your shop, but you also don't have all week to fix it. Believe me, that is on your mind when you're in the race car. Maybe I can pass this guy, but it's risky…what if I destroy the car? We won't be home for two weeks, and that is gonna make things complicated. So maybe you settle for a spot here or there.

Plus there are the finances. It costs way more to get to the race track when you're towing six, eight, 10 hours. Running a safe fifth-place pays a whole lot better than wrecking and hitting the wall.

That first year we were still learning about all this. In time, experience teaches you how to race on the road, and how to live on the road. It's not easy and it's definitely not always fun.

But I'm not complaining. Through all my younger years in racing, my dream was to be a professional, traveling racer. By the end of the 2009 season, I could finally say I was a full-time traveler.

We've been on the road for many years, and I reckon we ought to know what it's all about by now. It's a mixed bag…some good, some not-so-good. If you want to be a professional racer that means you're on the road, which means spending great chunks of time sitting in a seat, holding a steering

Earl Pearson Jr. and Eddie Carrier Jr. are great friends and traveling buddies. (Rick Schwallie photo)

I am right in there working with my guys, and I wouldn't have it any other way. (Rick Schwallie photo)

wheel, staring through a windshield at the endless highway. That gets to be a drag, you know?

Oh, don't get me wrong; after I stay put for a couple of weeks I'm pacing the floor, itching to go somewhere. But we definitely get weary of all that highway time.

One way to make things a little more enjoyable is traveling with some of the other racers when you can. Traveling together means following each other on the highway, and we stop together at a restaurant to eat. In addition to Mike Marlar, we've traveled quite a bit with Earl Pearson Jr. and his guys through the years, and also Brad Neat and Eddie Carrier Jr. when they were following the Lucas Oil series. It's good to have people to hang out with.

We started to get to know Earl in the early days of running the Lucas Oil series. Chris Fox was good friends with a couple of guys on Earl's crew, and it kind of took off from there. Earl is kind of a low-key guy, and we hit if off pretty good. Earl loves to hunt and fish and enjoy the better things in life, and he is a good friend.

We've had lots of fun with Eddie Carrier Jr. I get along good with Eddie because I can walk right up and tell him how ugly he is. And right off, he will come back at me with something. Whatever it is, you know it will be funny. No telling what it will be!

The best thing about these guys is that when we're away from the track, we don't talk about racing. Shocks, springs, tires…we leave that stuff at the track. Instead, we talk about any ol' thing…except racing. It's a nice way to get some distance, kinda keep our mind right.

The haulers we have today are a tremendous improvement over what racers used to have to deal with. We have air conditioning and we're able to sleep in a comfortable bed right there at the track. That is a luxury!

When we got our first dually pickup truck—a diesel—the big super truck stops and travel centers were just starting to crop up along the Interstates. Part of our challenge was figuring out which exits had diesel fuel. There were many times that we nearly ran out of fuel, sweating bullets.

It's still possible to run the big trucks out of fuel, and we've done it a couple of times. It's a terrible feeling, knowing you're about to run out of fuel, because it's an extra round of hassle you don't need. You're usually tired and eager to get to the track, or home, and you danged sure don't want to mess around with running out of fuel.

Riding in the truck ain't what people think it is. The trucks look big and fancy, and they are. But they ain't smooth! Not in any way. One of the most important things you learn is this: it ain't cool to stand up and pee when the truck is going down the road. I don't care how accurate you think you are, you ain't gonna hit the toilet when the truck hits a bump and you bounce off all four walls in your little bathroom. You'll be peeing every which way and hitting everything including the walls, the sink, your shoes, and the ceiling. Not cool! So you've got to set aside that big male ego and sit down. That's just a fact of life.

Lots of people get motion sickness when they ride in the back of the truck. It's kind of dark and you're tossed around a lot, which is not a good combination. I have always been one to get motion sickness, especially when I was a little kid. My mama would always pack a change of clothes and a wet washcloth, because somewhere along the line little Jimmy was going to throw up. That's the worse feeling, I'll tell you.

I could do some serious throwin' up at the fair! I was that kid you didn't want to ride next to on the Spider. I thought I grew out of all that, but a couple of years ago Nathan and I went to the county fair. I figured I could ride once, you know? Nope; I got sicker than a dog. And it's funny, after that I couldn't ride in the back of our truck for several months without getting sick. I'd have to sit up front until I was so tired that I could get into the back and fall straight asleep.

Going in circles on the track doesn't bother me, because I'm used to it. But every now and then if there's a wreck and I swerve real hard back and forth to miss it, I can feel my stomach turn flips and for a second it feels like everything is coming up. That's when an open face helmet would be way better!

I do most of the driving in our truck, because that's what I want. I am a much better driver than rider, I reckon. There are times when other guys drive, and that's okay. Sometimes I can't go any more, and I need a break.

I like music when we're going down the road, and when a station begins to fade I'll get Pandora on my phone and stream it to the truck radio. Usually classic rock, maybe '80s or '90s rock. I like a lot of different music. I sing along all the time even though I know I can't carry a tune.

I've never seriously considered getting a motorhome. For one, I'm not one to abandon my crew. I wouldn't feel right. I need to be right there with 'em, going up and down the road. If it's good enough for them it's good enough for me.

The highway exposes you to as much danger as the race track, I think. That is always on my mind, every mile. I feel a powerful responsibility to be careful and protect my crew riding in the back.

Some crew guys we've had through the years are a little heavy-footed when they drive the truck. They're eager to get to our destination, I get it.

But our entire race team is in their hands when they're at the wheel. Three or four people, two expensive race cars, spare motors, wheels, tools, our truck and trailer, everything. That's several lives and 35, 40 tons rolling down the road. I don't care if you think you're a skilled driver, when you get a big rig in trouble at 80 mph, it's probably not going to end well. I've had to scold guys about going too fast, and it's not something to joke about.

One of the enemies is sleep. Or, lack of it.

Everybody in racing can tell stories of travel adventures, and near misses. People falling asleep, or almost falling asleep. It's a big deal and we've all struggled with it at times.

It's weird how your mind works when you're sleepy. Weird and kinda scary.

One night—a long time ago—I was helping Kurt with his car at David's garage, and I was working the graveyard shift at TRW. I hadn't slept in probably a day and a half. It was around midnight when I left the garage to drive back to the house on old Hwy. 411 and when I reached the highway—US 25-70—I must have fallen asleep at the wheel.

I was driving a Volkswagen Beetle, and I woke up and realized I was sitting at the stop sign at the highway, engine running. One foot on the brake, and one foot on the clutch. I kind of looked around and realized what had happened. I have no idea how long I'd been sitting there; one minute or 10 minutes or 30 minutes. No idea.

It's amazing that you can actually fall asleep like that. I guess you can only stand so much, and when your brain fades, out you go.

A few years later I was coming back from racing in Somerset, Kentucky. I was driving for Danny Yanders, or maybe it was the Harrod Farms car. I had borrowed Kurt's Ford Fiesta, and on the way home it was the wee hours and I started getting sleepy. I got scared that I was going to fall asleep and wrap myself around a tree along the highway. I was doing everything to keep my eyes open…radio blaring, windows open, talking to myself, the whole deal.

I got as far as Exit 8 on Hwy. 25E and man, I couldn't go another mile. I pulled off the exit and parked at a Shell station which was closed at the time. I shut the car off and leaned the seat back and was out like a light.

But I started to dream…a vivid dream that I was back on the road, fighting sleep. In my dream I could see the tires inching toward the edge of the road, closer, closer, closer…and sure enough there was a big ol' tree. I was headed straight for it at 70 mph. Holy shit!

I woke up in a panic, yelling my fool head off and wrestling with the steering wheel, slamming my foot on the brake. My hands were all clammy and I looked around, and there I was, parked peacefully at that Shell station, perfectly safe.

After just a second I realized I had been dreaming. It felt very silly, but there wasn't anything I could do but laugh at myself.

That stuff can happen to anybody.

One night Chris Fox was driving us home, and we had borrowed a Dodge diesel truck from Curt Hoffess. We had raced up in Kentucky and were driving home through the night. I was sound asleep, riding three-wide in a single-row truck.

All of a sudden the truck was pitching and swaying and we woke up with terror in our eyes. Chris was sawing at the wheel, trying to get 'er whoa-ed up. In a moment he had it back under control and I looked around and could see that we were entering the rest area at mile 419 on I-40 eastbound, not far from home.

"What happened?" I hollered at Chris.

"I went to sleep," he admitted, kind of a sheepish look on his face.

It took a moment before we realized what had happened. He had dozed off and the truck eased off the right side of the highway, and in a miraculous piece of luck happened to go off exactly at the ramp. I mean, exactly at the ramp.

We must have hit that ramp running 70 mph with the race car hanging on for dear life on that little trailer we were towing.

Whew! That was a close one!

14

Getting Closer

Behind the scenes—I say behind the scenes because I've always been private when it comes to my family—my world changed totally on January 23, 2009.

A few years earlier Melissa had a bout with breast cancer, and went through all the treatment. The cancer had been dealt with and life went on, and in 2008 she began to feel some symptoms similar to when she had cancer. Obviously she was very concerned and went right to the doctor.

The oncologist did a bunch of blood work. He sat her down and said, "This will go away in seven months."

"But the previous chemo was just six months long," she said. "Are you telling me this is worse now?

"No, I'm telling you this will go away in seven months because you're going to have a baby."

Melissa's daughter Shelby was 17 at the time, and Melissa was shocked.

"But you told me before that I could never have another baby!"

"I know what I told you, but you are definitely pregnant," he insisted.

She hurried home to tell me the news.

"You can't be pregnant," I told her. "They told you it wasn't possible!"

But sure enough here comes Nathan.

Before that moment, I was the world's worst at thinking about what it would be like to be a dad. I thought the idea was impossible, and crazy. No way I could be a dad! No way!

But when little Nathan grabbed my finger on that January day, his first day here on earth, I was done. It was over. Everything I thought about fatherhood…all the uncertainty, all the fear, man, that just disappeared. It was the greatest feeling I've ever experienced, way beyond any other thing in my life.

Tazewell, 2009: Our new little traveling buddy!
Ain't he something? (Rick Schwallie photo)

Greeting folks at our souvenir trailer in early 2009
at Brownstown. (Rick Schwallie photo)

Soon enough we had a little traveling buddy. And so much more! Wow…life is so, so good.

We kicked off the 2010 season and things were picking up. The economy was starting to come back, and some of the worry and anxiety of the past couple of years was fading.

We got going pretty good in the spring, and had some good runs. We won at Brownstown, Indiana on March 27, and won the following series race at Bedford, Pennsylvania on April 23. During a break in the Lucas Oil schedule we hauled up to Kentucky to race with the World of Outlaws at Bluegrass Speedway, and won there. The following week—May 15—we won with the Lucas series at Wythe Raceway in Virginia.

Three straight Lucas Oil wins was a record for the series. And, for the first time in our career, it also put us in the points lead, with Scott Bloomquist second. However, the following weekend Scott got back into the points lead.

We went back-to-back with wins at Cleveland and Bulls Gap on June 17 and 18, but Scott was running good, too. Even though we were gaining momentum, it was shaping up to be a real good race to the championship.

On July 17 we won the Diamond Nationals at Lucas Oil Speedway in Wheatland, our first win there. In time Wheatland would be very good to us, but that first one took some work to get done. The track was still kind of new to me, and unlike tracks around home we just didn't have a lot of laps there. But each time we made the trip out there we were a little better.

I guess the track just suited me. That happens, you know. Just like with Scott Bloomquist at Eldora, he's hard to outrun up there. Wheatland, that just suited me, and we've won in every type of car we've raced there. We don't do anything different, really. Just turn the wheel and mash the gas.

A couple of weeks later we towed all the way up to New York, where we won at Fonda Speedway on July 27. New York is a long way from home, for sure! Fonda was a fun, fun race track. The only time you let off was in turn one, where you'd only lift for a second and then you were back on the mat. Man, it was exciting. Tommy Greco, a native of that area who was a longtime crew chief for Tim McCreadie, was telling us about the tire choice.

Tommy is a great guy, lots of fun. He's like all those New York people, he's got a funny way of talkin'. But when he talks about picking tires at Fonda, you ought to listen.

"Put the Hoosier 28 on," he said, "and you'll be fine."

"Yeah, but the track is dirty, and—"

"I'm telling you, put the 28 on."

We did what he said, and when we started the race the track was real dirty and I definitely had second thoughts about that tire. But then the track cleaned up and, man, we walked the dog and put it on those guys. It was fun!

We should have won both New York races—the other was two days later at Utica-Rome Speedway—but our fuel regulator caused a fire at Utica-Rome. We loaded up and headed to Hagerstown, Maryland and scrambled to change a bunch of stuff that was burned up.

On August 14 we won the North/South 100 for the second time. This was a big deal, for a lot of reasons. Obviously, winning $50,000 is always special. But I've always been concerned about people thinking a big win was a fluke. When you back up a big win—or a good year—you prove yourself, in my opinion. Winning once is one thing, but winning again—and again and again—is tough. Easier said than done. Consistency means a lot.

That has always motivated me. One thing you never have to worry about with me is resting on our laurels. Sure, I'm grateful when we have a good year, and I'm happy, but I don't want to fall short the next year. I'm fired up to do it again and prove that the good year wasn't a fluke.

We closed out our year with another win at the World Finals at Charlotte. There was something about that event I liked, and it was beginning to grow on me.

The 2010 season was good for us, but once again we fell a little short in the Lucas Oil points race. Scott Bloomquist ended up beating us again, and although we were disappointed I wouldn't call it a frustrating experience. We had a good year, and did our best. I felt like Scott beat us fair and square, and we didn't give him anything at all. He was very strong and we had a few key moments where things didn't go our way and that proved to be the difference.

At that point we were feeling good about things. We had some momentum and were definitely going in the right direction. We were getting better, stronger, and more consistent. I felt like we had all the pieces in place to win the Lucas Oil title, and if we kept working hard we could get it done.

There was no doubt in my mind that the Lucas series was where we needed to be. We were making more friends, and began to travel quite a bit with Earl Pearson Jr. and Brad Neat. Earl finished right behind us in points that year, but we never had any kind of problem with each other. We could race each other hard with no problem and still be good friends away from the race track.

It's that family thing I was talking about earlier. We hung out together, and it was like family. I had never experienced that before in racing. I guess I am something of a loner, and always preferred to do our own thing. Which, I'm still like that to a degree. I like being on my own. But it's also nice to have people to sit with at the restaurant and enjoy their friendship.

Racing has been good to us in that way. We have made *lots* of friendships around the country through the years. Just the other day I was telling Nathan that we could break down in almost any state and there were people I could call and ask for help. That's a great thing, man. *Great.* It means a lot.

When the 2010 season wrapped up we were offered a chance to race a midget at the Chili Bowl in Tulsa, Oklahoma. The Chili Bowl is a unique deal, a dirt race held indoors in January on a little dirt track at the Tulsa Expo Center.

A deal had been arranged through one of the series sponsors, Rockstar, to offer the Lucas Oil series champion a Chili Bowl ride. Scott Bloomquist had ran the Chili Bowl before, but apparently wasn't able to run the 2011 event. With us finishing second in series points, the ride was offered to us.

Heck, yeah! We figured the Chili Bowl would be lots of fun, and we figured right.

The adventure started on the trip to Tulsa. We decided to take our toter home so we'd have a place to stay while we raced. It was early January, and we rolled west across I-40. Mike Ottinger and his wife rode along with us; they are into RC racing, and a big RC race takes place in Tulsa that weekend as well.

As we got into Arkansas we hit a big ice storm. All the big trucks were in one long single-file line, and pretty soon it started snowing. I mean, snowing. The visibility was very bad, whiteout conditions at times.

The truck in front of us hit the brakes and started a chain reaction. I backed off, and our toter home slid sideways. Man, our toter home felt awful big and long at that moment. I looked in my mirrors and cars and trucks were going every which way behind us.

Lo and behold, we got straightened out and somehow kept rolling. Now there is no traffic behind us, because they've all wrecked! We rolled on for several more miles, kinda tip-toeing along. We ran into another pile-up ahead of us, but I was able to get stopped before we hit anybody.

It was snowing like hell, and we were sitting there stopped with our flashers on, the last vehicle in line. I turned and looked at Kurt and just as I said, "I don't like this…"

WHAM! Two young girls in a little car hit us a ton. We ran back to check on them, and when the one girl got out of the car her feet hit the ice and she did a complete flip. She actually slid under their wrecked car and we helped her get to her feet.

They were okay, but the one girl kept saying, "My dad is gonna kill me!"

Her poor car, they hit us so hard it busted their motor mounts. We managed to get the car started and drove it a few feet further into the median to get it out of oncoming traffic. The girls piled into our truck and we drove them to the next exit where her dad could pick them up.

Our truck wasn't hurt, so we kept rolling. A few minutes later a guy in a BMW drove past us and his car kicked sideways and slid into our lane. I changed lanes right quick and missed him by no more than an inch or two.

I looked at Kurt and said, "Okay, that's enough for today." We had planned on getting all the way to Tulsa, but we'd seen enough. It was just getting dark and we made it to an exit ramp and parked at a truck plaza.

When the weather cleared we pushed on to Tulsa. The delay caused us to miss the first round of practice, which was probably for the better. It was one less opportunity for us to tear up any equipment.

The midget was a different experience. The little 4-cylinder engine, the short wheelbase, that tight little track…it was a handful. And it didn't take me long to put it on the roof.

We raced with Kenny Brown Racing, and after the first round of hot laps on our qualifying night they told me we didn't look too bad. I asked if they could slow the steering down some, and that helped.

The guy said, "You did pretty good, but you need to try to get to the bottom of the track."

I said, "Dude, you don't understand. I was aiming for the bottom of the track...but it was already plumb past when I finally got there!"

Kurt pointed out that we were pulling the front wheels off the ground coming off the corner, and I explained that the car wanted to rear up like that every time I stepped on the throttle.

In our second practice session I was on the gas when the car got up on the right rear and I panicked and hit the brake. *Ooops!* Man, I took a major flyer, one of those flips you see on the highlight reels.

They repaired the car and we lined up in the C-main, and I transferred into the B. We passed quite a few cars in the B, and finished just out of the transfer. I was starting to get the hang of it a little…we got on a clear track and turned some pretty good laps, the fastest of the race. But we came up a little short and didn't make the show on our qualifying night.

They have more than 200 cars at the Chili Bowl—sometimes over

300—and on Saturday we were in the F main. That's right, the F main. The track was heavy with a big cushion, and as we were in the lineup chute I was watching the previous race on the big screen. Man, this racing was wild…and these guys know what they're doing! When I saw so many other cars getting on their head I felt a little bit better that we weren't completely out to lunch.

I'd already flipped our car once, and I felt bad about them having to repair it. That was enough for me to kinda cool it, and I just rode in the middle and stayed off the cushion. We finished 6th in the F main and that wasn't enough to transfer, so our Chili Bowl experience was over.

It was probably not a good idea to go out there without getting some practice laps under our belt. It was just too different, and that's the wrong place to start from scratch. If I ever run it again, I would definitely want to get a bunch of laps to practice and get the hang of it.

The team had brought five cars to Tulsa, and the other guys had lots of experience in these cars. It was a nice bunch of guys, but I think they looked at me as a bit of an oddball…they were all cocky young dudes, and I was this older guy who drove some kinda stock car.

One funny moment came when the Lucas Oil TV crew came to our pit with their camera. The TV crew walked right past the other guys and came to see me, and that made me laugh. It was funny.

I felt bad that we didn't run better, but when it came time for the Saturday night feature the other guys on the team were standing there watching it with me—they hadn't made the show, either. No kidding, that's a tough race to make the lineup for the final event.

Despite our struggles, it was a fun experience. And definitely very different than anything I've ever tried. I was tickled that we'd passed a bunch of cars in the B main on our qualifying night, so that felt good.

But it was cold! It got cold enough to freeze the water pipes in our truck, and we had a heckuva time getting them thawed out. But finally all was well.

What a weekend!

The bonus of our Chili Bowl experience was meeting Chris Davis for the first time.

I was standing next to our car when up walked a tall, lanky guy with a real direct style. We had already raced and crashed in a big way, and he looked our car over and kinda shook his head.

"Well," he said, kinda slow, "no offense, but you probably need to stick to late model racing."

That was my introduction to Chris Davis of Midwest Sheet Metal in

Springfield, Missouri. This guy was direct! I knew that from the get-go... and I knew I liked this guy.

We hit it off from that moment. He asked if we'd be interested in working with his company on a sponsorship deal for our late model, and we said, sure, absolutely. His sticker has been on our car ever since.

Through the years Chris and I became close friends, visiting many times and talking on the phone a bunch. Whenever we're in Wheatland we're sure to connect with Chris, and we'll often see him at other tracks such as Batesville. Chris is a strong supporter of dirt late model racing, a genuine fan. He loves this sport, through and through.

Chris is someone I can share things with, and I value his input. He is a smart guy and a good businessman, with a lot of business—and people—experience.

Chris is a very kind person, very considerate. He took us fishing, and it was great. I hadn't been out fishing for many years, and I enjoyed the heck out of our outing. Chris kept asking me, "You sure you're having a good time? We can go back if you're bored."

I kept telling him, "Aw, man, this is great!" Just sitting out on the lake, I'd forgotten how good that feels. Chris was worried about me being bored, but I could have sat out there all day and night. I love fishing but somehow I've lost that connection. I was reminded how much I enjoy it.

Midwest Sheet Metal has grown a ton since our first meeting. Chris and I are both very busy, and sometimes it's hard to stay in touch as much as we'd like. But Chris knows that if he ever needs anything, I'm here. And I know the same about my buddy Chris.

15

We Did It!

When the 2011 season got underway we were ready to contend for the Lucas Oil championship. Now don't get me wrong, we were contenders in 2009 and 2010, yes. But we still didn't have our ducks in a row like they needed to be. We weren't quite there.

After two seasons of falling short we stepped it up. There wasn't anything specific we did differently; it was just a matter of improving the small things and getting all of us on the team pulling in the right direction, together.

Mike Reece was still providing us everything we needed. I was on the same page with our primary crew—Chris Fox and Kenny Holt. We also had several part-time helpers, including my brother Kurt, and between everybody it was a good group. Jack Cornett was building us some good strong Ford motors and they were running good.

The year got off on a positive start when we won at East Bay Raceway Park on February 12. Now, I can't exactly tell you why, but I've never run worth a crap in a super at East Bay. I'd won there in a crate car and an open wheel modified, but we couldn't do worth a dang in a super. But finally in 2011 we got it done. It was a daytime show on Saturday afternoon, but the track was actually pretty racy. We passed Austin Hubbard early in the race and hung on to win $10,000.

As the season got going it looked like it might be a repeat of the past two; Scott Bloomquist got into the points lead and we were second. On an off weekend for the series we won a $10,000 race at Bulls Gap with the Ultimate Super Late Model Series, which gave us a little bit of momentum.

On May 28 we won the $30,000 Show-Me 100 at Lucas Oil Speedway. It was our first Show-Me win, and it was a big night. We were building a nice following of fans and friends there in Wheatland and everybody had a great time celebrating with us after the race.

The following weekend we won at Cleveland, Tennessee on Thursday,

It was a little dirty for our win at Cleveland
on June 2, 2011! (Rick Schwallie photo)

ran third at Tazewell on Friday, and on Saturday ran second to Don O'Neal at the Ralph Latham Memorial at Florence. It was another consistent weekend and it allowed us to take the points lead from Scott.

We were hitting our stride. But Scott came back strong and won three straight in early July—Portsmouth, Muskingum County, and Magnolia Motor Speedway—to regain the points lead. We stuck with it and won again at Fonda, New York on July 27 and when we loaded up that night we had regained the lead by just five points.

At the moment we were so caught up in the racing we didn't have time to think about the points. But that didn't stop others from thinking about it, and all of a sudden that's what *everybody* wanted to talk about. I remember the media asking me about it a lot. It got to be a little nerve-wracking, and as the season went on I kinda had enough of the topic.

On August 13 we won the $50,000 North/South 100 at Florence, our third overall North/South win and second straight. A week later we won at Bulls Gap, where lots of local people were cheering us on.

Our confidence was already good, but big wins pumped us up even more. We headed for Eldora and the World 100 feeling pretty good. The nice thing about the World 100 weekend is that, since it has no impact on the Lucas Oil points, you can forget all that and just think about the race.

It was a good weekend. We scored our second World 100 win, and that was a great moment. You know, I believe the second win meant even more than the first. When I won in 2007, I'm not sure I fully appreciated the history of the event. Even though it paid real well and there was a lot of hoopla, it almost felt like just another race. With that first win I believe I didn't fully understand the impact, the importance, of the World 100.

But the win in 2011 felt a lot different. It felt more important. More *satisfying*, you might say. It's probably like this for a lot of younger drivers; as time goes on you start to sense the history of a great event and understand what it means.

People could probably see that I was more excited in 2011. We had backed up our first win, and I understood the prestige of the race.

Here's something kinda interesting. When I was standing on the victory stage, looking out at all the photographers with the camera flashes blinding me and hearing that big grandstand cheering, I suddenly thought about how many other drivers wanted to be standing where I was at that moment. It was the first time I had ever thought about that perspective…I remember that very clearly.

Scott Bloomquist went on a tear again in September, winning four straight races, including Virginia Motor Speedway on September 18 to

Making some new friends at Bluegrass Speedway in 2011. (Rick Schwallie photo)

Celebrating our first Lucas Oil series title at Atomic in 2011. Wow! (Rick Schwallie photo)

retake the point lead. But we kept digging, and weren't about to give up. We won a preliminary race at Knoxville Raceway on September 29, our first ever win on the big half-mile.

But man, the points were tight! With just three races left on the schedule—Dixie Speedway, Rome Speedway, and the Dirt Track World Championship at Atomic Speedway in Chillicothe, Ohio—Scott was leading us by just 15 points. Everybody kept telling us that it was the closest points race in series history.

To be honest, by that time I was completely tired of the discussion. I just wanted everybody to shut up and go racing, period. I don't even like looking at that stuff until the end of the year. Where you end up, that's it. If you win, great; if not, we'll try again next year.

I tried to explain to people that I've never actually set out to win a championship specifically. That's the truth; sure, we knew it would be cool to win the Lucas Oil title, but we specifically didn't set that as a goal. Our idea was to just go race and if things fall our way, fine.

Scott won at Dixie, and we ran fourth. That pushed Scott's points lead out to 65 points. As we headed for Rome the next day I was honest about the situation. If Scott ran good at Rome, he'd be hard to catch. You couldn't help but look at the points at that stage.

That's when we had one of those moments where things played in our favor. Scott was leading the feature at Rome, and we were right behind him. As we went along I spotted a small trail of smoke behind his car, and then it got bigger. I knew he would run the thing until it quit. And sure enough, it did.

Scott's motor finally melted down and he pulled in, giving us the lead. We hung on to win and the tide had turned. I felt bad for Scott, but that's racing. He would say the same thing, I'm sure.

We now had a 50-point lead going into the Dirt Track World Championship on October 15.

The pit area at Atomic was packed to the gills with race cars for the 2011 Dirt Track World Championship. After many years at Pennsboro, West Virginia, promoter Carl Short had moved the event around some. It had been at Chillicothe for several years and after an absence of a couple of years it was back there for 2011.

I wasn't keen on it, but the points race continued to be the burning topic in the pit area. It seemed like everybody who came by our pit wanted to talk about it. I reckon that's natural, because it was one of the closest races in series history. Plus, because we had been running better the past few years, people were now starting to talk about a rivalry between Scott and me.

It was a great moment, sharing the championship spotlight with Mike Reece. (Rick Schwallie photo)

Having my family there to celebrate meant a lot! My sister Tammy, Kurt, cousin Paige Davis, Sherri and Chris Fox. (Rick Schwallie photo)

And now here we were, with the championship down to the two of us.

I had to grit my teeth and listen to all the questions. I finally snapped a little bit when a reporter asked me, "What are you going to do today to win the title?"

"Listen," I said, "it ain't up to me. I've got the lead. You need to go ask him what HE'S gonna do. All I need is a good finish."

I don't think the reporter liked my answer, because I was a little bit hateful when I said it.

The track that weekend didn't turn out like anybody had hoped. It was narrow, one-lane, and not at all racy. It took rubber during the last consy race. They were calling us out for the feature, with no track prep at all. We were amazed. Why didn't they work on the track and at least try to get it to where we could race?

But out we went. Don O'Neal got into the lead right off, and I was right behind him. Our car was way better than Don's, and a couple of times he left the door open for us. I could have doored him and got past, but I wasn't going to run over him. That ain't the right way to win.

I'll admit, the championship was on my mind. I needed to run second, and I couldn't afford to cut a tire down. That would have been a disaster, you know. We couldn't be aggressive, and there ain't no doubt: that sucks. Points racing, and not being able to take that extra chance, sometimes that's no fun. It takes a little bit of excitement away for everybody: drivers, fans, everybody.

We followed Don to the finish, and ran second.

So we won the Lucas Oil Late Model Dirt Series championship.

We did it.

My guys were real happy, and so was Mike Reece. We had lots of fans who were celebrating like crazy and that was fun.

It was a great accomplishment for our team. We worked hard, we stuck with it, and we completed the deal. We represented Mike Reece and our sponsors the best we could, and it paid off.

Plus, we outran a bunch of good racers. Scott Bloomquist, he ain't no slouch. All the other Lucas regulars that year—Don O'Neal, Steve Francis, Earl Pearson Jr., and a bunch more—are very good racers. You've got to be on your game to beat 'em. That's what makes a championship mean something, because it never comes easy.

Most of all I was happy for our guys. Man, this racing deal is a hard life. You work in the shop all week, busting your butt, then you sit for hours in the truck riding to the track. When you get there you work long hours outside in the hot, the cold, and the dust. Win or lose, you load the car and make that long ride home and do it all again next week. For the guys working on the car, there ain't any kind of glory at all. So when I see how happy my crew guys are when we do something special, that means everything to me. I'm not kidding.

Of course, it works both ways. When they've worked real hard and given me a good race car and I make a mistake or do something stupid that costs us a win—or destroys our stuff—it feels awful. I'm the one who gets to have the fun in the race car, but there's some pressure with that fun, too. You have to face the questions when you don't run well.

We had a nice time celebrating the championship, but in our business you don't have much time to stop and smell the roses. We had to get right back at it and get ready for next season. Just like winning a big race, you want to back it up and prove it wasn't a fluke.

That's what was on our mind, almost from the time we climbed out of the car there at Chillicothe. I wanted to show people that we weren't a fluke.

Somebody told me the other day, "Jimmy, even though the 2007 season was real important, I'd say that 2011 was your breakout year. You had a great year and won the Lucas Oil title, and that season really put you on the map."

I told them that's not how I thought about it, not at all. I don't care about being on the map. It was a great year in 2011, sure, but I didn't feel like soaring at the time. I still don't. I'm probably like a lot of racers: I'm remembering the races we didn't win, the mistakes I made, the ones that slipped away.

That's the stuff that stays with you for a while.

Emotionally, racing is a tough deal. Many things knock you down. Stuff with the race car, naturally, but other stuff, too. People talking, people fussing with you, talking trash, it wears on you. In order to deal with that you kind of put up a wall, and you don't let yourself take things too seriously.

It's just racing, after all. It ain't life or death.

16

Good Things

I mentioned earlier that the measure of a great racer is the ability to "back it up" after a big win or championship. So, after savoring the good vibes of winning the Lucas Oil Late Model Dirt Series title in 2011, right away our mindset shifted to winning it again in 2012.

That's the way every good racer thinks. What's the most important race of your career? The next one. Which race do you want to win more than anything else? The next one. What you did last week, last month, last year, people forget that pretty quick. And you better forget it, too, or you'll lose your hunger.

There's also another thing in play. A championship-caliber racing team has a lot of pieces: The driver, crew, team owner, engine builder, chassis, shock provider, sponsors, people helping with logistics…there are a lot of components and you have to get them all working in sync, working together. When that happens, you build momentum.

Momentum is a big deal, and I'm not just talking about on the race track.

Once you gain momentum as a team, you don't dare ease up. Everybody has to be committed and positive and pulling together, and if you stop and smell the roses for too long—maybe a minute or two—you lose your momentum. If you're content to lay back and "savor" stuff, you ain't gonna be savoring it for long.

That was definitely on my mind as we got our stuff ready for the 2012 season.

The season started out good, but a little frustrating. In the first 16 races we finished 2nd 12 times! You would think a guy would be excited to be running that consistent, but after a while you start thinking it ought to be your turn to win a dadgum race!

We finally broke through in May at Batesville, one of the most unique

Matt McRae had my name in the pool, and he won this Mustang when we won the Bad Boy 98 at Batesville in 2012! It was cool! (Rick Schwallie photo)

We won a new Camaro that night, and Nathan was eager to jump in and start blowing the horn. What a memory! (Rick Schwallie photo)

wins of my career. The promoter at Batesville, Mooney Starr, is always looking to hype things up by being different. Which is good, of course. This time Mooney arranged for the winner of the Bad Boy 98 to receive $10,000 and a brand new Chevy Camaro from Mark Martin Chevrolet in Batesville.

But the really cool wrinkle was that they selected a number of fans in attendance to represent each of the drivers in the race. If your driver won, you got a brand new Mustang from Mark Martin Ford. Now, I don't know about you, but if I knew I was gonna win a brand new Mustang if my driver won the race, I would be cheering for that dude at the top of my lungs!

Billy Moyer started on the pole, and we were alongside him on the front row. Chris Fox and I decided to set our car up for the longer runs, figuring we'd see a good stretch without a caution. That's always a little risky, because if the race has a bunch of cautions you're at a disadvantage on the restarts.

We fell back a little bit on the start, but got it going and passed Moyer for the lead on lap 12. Luckily, there were only a few caution flags, and that played to our setup. Moyer pressured us some when we got to traffic, and Scott Bloomquist came up to make it a three-car race for the lead. We got to traffic in the final laps and Moyer was right there, but we hung in there for the win.

Before I even shut my car off I was already thinking about what I was going to do with that new Camaro. My son Nathan was three years old, and I figured I'd just hang on to the car and let him have it when he turned 16.

The fan who had my name in the pool, Matt McRae, was a 19-year-old kid from Quitman, Arkansas. Man, he was wired when they presented him with that new Mustang. "I am now the biggest Jimmy Owens fan," he said on the PA. It was great!

I got more excited for him than I was for myself. Seriously, it was so cool to see this boy win a new car. That made it lots more fun.

After we got all loaded up that night and headed back to the motel, I started having second thoughts about that Camaro. Was I really going to hold onto that thing for 13 years? Then I remembered them saying something about the winner having an option to take a cash payout instead of the Camaro. So I called Mooney, and his wife answered the phone.

"How about you guys keep the car and I'll just take the money," I said. We kind of talked it through, and I finally decided to go ahead and take the car with me back to Newport.

We parked the Camaro in the garage and just kind of looked at it for a while. We were so busy racing I didn't have time to fool with it right then, anyways. After a couple of months, one evening I said to Melissa, "Let's take this thing out for a drive!"

The first thing I discovered was that you couldn't see anything out the back of this car. It drove real nice, and it was fun, but the visibility in the rear wasn't worth a crap. Immediately I was thinking, "There ain't no way I could turn a 16-year-old kid loose in this thing…he'd hit everything in Cocke County!"

So I got in touch with Mooney and also talked to Lance Landers, Mark Martin's partner in the dealerships in Batesville. They made me a deal to trade the car in for some cash, and we were happy with that.

The best part of the whole deal—in addition to Matt McRae winning the Mustang—was my memory of victory lane that night. Me and Nathan hopped into the Camaro, and Nathan started blowing the horn. Everybody was laughing and happy, and it was one of the most fun times I ever had. Rick Schwallie snapped a great picture, and it's still one of my favorite racing memories of all time.

We mentioned Billy Moyer a little earlier, and we need to say a little bit about what a great talent he is and how important he's been for late model racing. Billy and Scott Bloomquist are two of the all-time greats in our sport, and for our generation they were the two guys everybody wanted to pursue.

There have been a few times through the years that I've heard my name mentioned in the same sentence as Scott and Billy, and that is probably the best thing a late model racer could ever hear. That kind of compliment will never get old, I assure you.

Billy is a quiet person, and kinda keeps to himself. But I enjoy talking with him at the track, he's a good guy. He's a lot like me, I think, in that it takes a while to develop enough of a relationship for him to open up with someone. I'm not comfortable just walking up to somebody and start talking about stuff; if you walk up to me and start talking, that's easier for me.

I'm not sure when I first raced against Billy. Probably the first couple of years we were in a late model, I reckon. Moyer is fun to race with because he's so respectful, and through the years we've raced with each other a lot.

I've got to tell you about the time I thought I killed Moyer at Charlotte. That was an awful day!

It was just a few years ago and we were running in a heat race at the World Finals. We were racing hard and Billy pushed up the track just as I cut down, and we hit wheel-to-wheel. It was totally a racing incident, nobody did anything wrong. We just hit.

Billy spun out and backed into the wall, really hard. I knew it was a hard, hard impact and I was immediately upset. We were circling the track under caution and every time we went past the wreck we could see the ambulance there as they were getting Billy out of the car.

Man, I was all tore up. I was so messed up mentally that when the race restarted I lost my focus and dropped to third…I just couldn't stop thinking about Billy, worrying how bad he might be hurt.

Billy had hit his head, but didn't go to the hospital. As soon as we finished the heat race I jumped out of my car and ran to Billy's pit. I was scared and upset. I could tell that Billy had a concussion, because he wasn't talking quite right. But he did recover, thankfully.

Man…I was probably as torn up about that accident as anything I've ever experienced in a race car. I thought I'd hurt Billy bad…it was a terrible feeling, and it took me a long time before I got over that.

We had a good season in 2012, very good. One week after the Batesville win we won the Show-Me 100 at Wheatland, then won again at Wheatland on July 14. We scored Lucas Oil wins in Indiana at Lawrenceburg (Aug. 25) and Brownstown (Sept. 22). The Brownstown race was the Jackson 100, a race with a lot of history and prestige. The win pushed our points lead to almost 400.

That's the best way to win a title; by a bunch of points. As we closed out the season nobody was coming around and asking about a tight points race. It's a great feeling, actually, because you're not distracted. You can focus on racing hard and trying to win races.

You'll often hear fans and officials say that a runaway takes the fun out of the deal. Boring, they say. They love the drama of going into a final event when the title is still up in the air, where anything can happen. Lots of drama, lots of uncertainty, lots of intrigue.

I get all that. But I can definitely say, for a racer that deal is emotionally draining. It's exciting, but it's also very stressful.

That's why it was so awesome to have a big points lead going down the stretch in 2012. We were relaxed, and to be honest we probably raced better.

We won again at Dixie Speedway in Georgia on Oct. 6, boosting our points lead to 475 and pretty much wrapping up the title. Two weeks later we headed to Portsmouth Raceway Park in Ohio to close out the Lucas Oil season.

Carl Short had moved the Dirt Track World Championship to Portsmouth, paying $50,000 to the winner. The Dirt Track is one of the biggest races in our sport, with a ton of history. Carl started the race at Pennsboro, West Virginia in 1981, and it immediately became a huge

With track co-promoter Steve Kosiski at I-80 Speedway in 2012. Steve and his brother Joe have done a great job at I-80. (Rick Schwallie photo)

Talking with TV's Erin Bates and cameraman Doug Franke just before the Knoxville Late Model Nationals in 2012. (Rick Schwallie photo)

success. It was a pioneering race when dirt late model racing was in its infancy, and the list of those early race winners is like a Hall of Fame: Jim Dunn, Charlie Swartz, Freddy Smith, Jack Boggs, Billy Moyer, Larry Moore, Donnie Moran. Those guys—and the Dirt Track World Championship—helped put dirt late model racing on the map.

But the Dirt Track was kinda looking for a home in 2012. Through the years it left Pennsboro and moved to several different tracks, including Bardstown, Kentucky and Chillicothe, Ohio in recent years.

Having the Dirt Track World Championship as a season finale was a great thing for the Lucas Oil series. The competitors loved racing for $50 grand, and the fans seemed to enjoy watching a big event to close things out.

We qualified well, and we were relaxed going into the main event. The only pressure we felt was to win the race; the points deal was like icing on the cake.

Don O'Neal took the lead at the start, but our car was strong right off the bat. We passed Don on lap two and took the lead. Every time we'd get deep into traffic I wondered if I'd start to hear somebody coming up to challenge, but several times we had a caution when we got into traffic and that gave us a clear race track again.

We held on to win, leading Bloomquist and O'Neal to the checkered. It was a great weekend all around, and I was in awe at the idea of adding my name to the list of Dirt Track World Championship winners.

Those are the kind of moments that help me understand that a lot of good things have happened in my life, and in my racing career.

We closed out our season by winning back-to-back against the World of Outlaws at the World Finals in Charlotte. Our win total for the year was 12, and that's a pretty decent year by anybody's standards.

Everything was in place for 2013 to try and keep our good momentum going. We got a real good start on the season, winning in February at East Bay and at Lonestar Speedway in Texas and at Hagerstown, Maryland in April. We scored our third straight win at the Show-Me 100 in May.

We headed out to Nebraska in July, where it's always hot enough to melt your eyeballs. The Silver Dollar Nationals at I-80 Speedway paid $27,000, and we scored a big win there. The following weekend we won again at Roaring Knob (man, what kind of name is that for a race track? Ain't that something?) in Pennsylvania, and on Labor Day weekend we won at Attica Raceway Park in Ohio and closed the weekend with a win at the Hillbilly 100 at I-77 Raceway Park in Ripley, West Virginia.

Like the Dirt Track World Championship, the Hillbilly 100 is another iconic event for our sport. We took the lead from Dennis Erb Jr. on lap 62 and drove on to the win, scoring $25,000.

We finished the season with a fifth-place run at Portsmouth for the Dirt Track, and clinched our third consecutive Lucas Oil series title. It had been another good year, with some big wins and another title.

But things were not as peaceful as they seemed. There were some things brewing that would cause us to step back and make some big decisions.

Changes—big, big changes—were right around the corner.

17

No Hard Feelings

When I got into Mike Reece's car in 2007 it was my first opportunity to race extensively with Scott Bloomquist. Scott is one of the most important people in the history of our sport and one of the most dominating winners. Nobody has impacted modern dirt late model racing more than Scott.

I was in awe of Scott in the beginning. How could you not be? I was a regional guy who had won a few races, and all of a sudden there I was, having friendly, detailed conversations with Scott.

I discovered right away that Scott works harder at going fast than anybody I know. He eats, lives, and breathes this deal. There is not a bolt on the race car that Scott overlooks. He's immersed himself so deep into these cars that it's almost like an obsession.

The results speak for themselves. You will never hear me say anything that will diminish what Scott has accomplished. He is completely focused on his race car, and his team, and nothing gets in the way of that. He's almost like a robot, or a computer.

Running a Bloomquist chassis was a very successful experience for me, and for Mike Reece's team. We won three consecutive Lucas Oil titles, a pile of races, and a bunch of money with those cars. It was good, good, good.

Now, let me say this: I am a confident racer and I believe we would have won those races and those titles even if we had gone with a different chassis back in 2007. It might have taken us longer, I admit; but I believe in myself and my team and I will always believe we would have got the job done in a Rayburn or a Rocket or a whatever.

From the beginning, I could sense that Scott was hesitant to let me in his circle. Scott is a close-to-the-vest type of guy, and when it comes to the race car he has a very small circle of people he trusts. In fact, initially there

Talking shop with Scott Bloomquist in 2013. (Rick Schwallie photo)

Racing with Scott Bloomquist at Wheatland. We've had some great, great duels. (Rick Schwallie photo)

was some question whether Scott would be willing to sell cars to Mike if I was the driver.

Not because he didn't like me; I don't believe it was personal. It was because Scott is very careful to keep his knowledge and potential advantage away from anyone he feels could become a consistent challenger to his success.

Scott is first and foremost a racer, and his chassis business is secondary. Think about it: Would it make sense to sell cars to someone who might consistently beat you on the race track?

I remember a conversation prior to the 2007 season. Scott was hesitant to sell more cars to Mike at that point, and Mike asked me what we should do if Scott declined our offer to buy a new chassis. I remember telling Mike that if Scott didn't want to sell us a car I'd just as well stay with the Rayburn chassis.

But Scott finally agreed to sell us a Bloomquist chassis, and we had a pretty good relationship. Scott and I talked a lot—a LOT—about the chassis and how to tweak them and race them. Scott was very helpful to us in a lot of ways, and in return I feel like we helped him in a lot of ways. It was a two-way street and it worked.

At least it worked for *our team*. You'd have to ask Scott if he felt like it worked for him as well.

Scott won the Lucas Oil series title in 2009 and 2010, and we were second both years. When we won our first Lucas Oil title in 2011, Scott finished second.

Somewhere along the way the dynamic started to change between Scott and our team. It wasn't like anything sudden; more of a gradual thing where I could feel a gap growing between us, and a definite coolness to our conversations.

Through 2011 to 2013 we outran Scott more than he outran us, and I could sense that he was getting defensive. But no matter what the situation, I told him the truth about our setups. Now, I didn't *volunteer* any information; just like Scott doesn't volunteer information. But when he asked me about different things I told him the truth.

Then I started to question the things he told me. Is he lying to me, trying to slow me down? That's when I realized: he probably thinks I'm lying to *him*, trying to keep our advantage.

It was not a healthy situation. We had a business relationship, but it was becoming strained.

There were others running Scott's chassis, and I felt like he was more open with them than he was with us. It was like we were getting shuffled outside the circle, and that bothered me. Listen, it wasn't about hurt

Last-minute coaching from Nathan before qualifying at West Virginia Motor Speedway in 2013. (Rick Schwallie photo)

I love this picture! Sharing the moment—and the confetti—with Nathan after winning at I-80 in 2013. (Rick Schwallie photo)

feelings, and it wasn't an emotional deal. I've never been a "group" guy so I don't mind not being in a social circle. And I don't necessarily feel like we "need" information and feedback from other racers. But if we're on a team and everyone else is getting information, we should get it as well.

So I went over to Scott's place to have a private conversation, face to face, to talk it out. It wasn't a heated conversation, no yelling or screaming or anything like that. We just talked and tried to get things out in the open.

"Listen," I told him, "I've never lied to you about anything. I don't expect you to tell me everything, especially the things you've learned on your own. You've earned that knowledge and I don't feel right asking you to share it with me.

"But I do feel bad when you share that data with everybody else, but you don't share it with me."

Scott assured me that wasn't the case, that we were okay. So I went home and figured we were back on track.

But we weren't, I don't believe. There was still a division there, a strain. It wasn't anything I could specifically put my finger on, but I could feel it.

In early 2014 we came out of the gate not running very well at all. We struggled at Brunswick, and struggled at East Bay. We just couldn't hit our ass with both hands, to be honest. Meanwhile, Scott was running good, and Chris Madden was also running good in a Bloomquist chassis.

We—all of us in the Bloomquist cars—were running double-stacked right fronts. But man, I couldn't get going with that setup. So when we got to Volusia, I walked over to Scott's pit to see if he could help me get it figured out.

A year earlier at Brunswick, we were running good and Scott came to our pit. He was asking questions about our setup, and we got down at the back of the car and I let him see everything. No problem. In my mind, that's how the deal is supposed to work.

At Volusia I asked Scott if he had this or that on the car, and some particulars. He said, yes, that's what he was running. And I asked if I could have a look.

No, he said. He'd rather I not look under his car.

Whoa. Really?

It was time to make a change.

From that point we took steps to move to a different chassis. I said it at the time and I'll say it again today: I didn't take it personally and I wasn't mad at Scott. This was strictly business; we paid for his cars and we were a customer. The supplier wasn't able to help us with the data we needed, so it made sense to look for a different supplier.

Working with Darrell Lanigan and his Club 29 chassis was a good experience in 2014. (Rick Schwallie photo)

Tight racing with Chase Junghans, Ryan Gustin, and Eddie Carrier Jr. at Lakeside Speedway. (Rick Schwallie photo)

We felt like the business relationship needed to change, and I suspect Scott did, too.

One of the things that made it more complicated was that Scott and I are totally different personalities. He loves the limelight, and loves to be controversial. I'm the opposite. Sometimes he says things in public—about his competitors, about different situations—that I would never say. Scott and I operate with a completely different set of ideas in everything we do.

We had just two things in common: a love for dirt late models and a desire to win. Other than that, we were different in pretty much every way possible.

As I go through life I've learned that it isn't good to let things get personal, or let things get under your skin. There were times through the years when things were heated between Scott and me at the track, but that's just racing. You race long enough, it's likely you'll have a brush with somebody and people get mad. You have to let it pass and move on and forget it.

One time we outran Scott at Batesville and he was pissed. He told his crew to go and look at our tires, because he couldn't believe we beat him on the same tires. His crew came to our pit and looked and reported back to Scott: same tires we're on, man. He said, bullshit, there ain't no way.

I wasn't upset by that. I figured it was just Scott being super-confident. He is so totally confident in his ability, he doesn't want to believe anybody could ever outdrive him. And that's okay, that's just who he is. He's just an extremely confident person.

Fact is, he *is* a helluva driver. People talk about his knowledge of the race car, but don't overlook the fact that the man can wheel a race car. When he gets his stuff together he's one of the toughest racers you'll ever face.

Me and Scott are natural rivals if you think about it. Listen, I want to win. And so does Scott. We can't both win…so that is a conflict. I look at Scott as just about the best ever, and I want to beat the best. When we're on the race track together I'm going to try my hardest to beat that guy. And I think, if he'd admit it, Scott has enough respect for me that he wants to beat me just as much as I want to beat him.

I've heard people say that me and Scott race each other harder than other people. Maybe that's true, I don't know. I feel like I'm trying as hard as I can every time out. But it is definitely possible…maybe Scott and me bring out a little extra in each other. And there ain't anything wrong with that. It's a healthy thing and it probably makes us better racers overall.

People get jealous of Scott but he's worked his ass off. I love racing, but compared to him my deal is almost like a hobby. It's almost foolish how

The Chicken Head! Our buddy Keith McGuire from Alabama always makes it fun with his chicken costume.

Talking with MAVTV's Dave Argabright and cameraman Mark Wildman after our win at the Topless 100 in 2014. (Rick Schwallie photo)

much Scott is ate up with this deal. If he's not running good, it eats him up so bad he can't stand it. He's all torn up.

Scott loves playing mind games with the rest of us with the things he says. He likes that stuff because, for a lot of guys, it gets under their skin. They let Scott get in their head. I learned pretty quickly that you've got to tune that stuff out. ALL of it. And, really, as much as Scott loves playing mind games, sometimes he messes himself up as much as he does everybody else. But that's just my opinion.

When I was running his cars and we were both winning a lot, I joked with him that we needed to take advantage of the situation. We should have been talking shit about each other and stirring up our rivalry for the fans and the media, because I think we could have done it and neither of us been offended. But we never took that idea and ran with it.

It's been several years now since we decided to go in a different direction with our chassis. The business relationship between Scott and me ended at that point, but we are definitely not enemies. In fact, we probably talk more now than we did before. Still not a lot; but we are certainly friendly. We're probably not going to go over to Scott's house for dinner anytime soon, and I doubt he'll come by my place to hang out. But we have a good relationship.

If Scott needs something, he knows I would help him, and vice versa. A while back I needed a black nose piece, and Scott had one. So he loaned it to me. A short while after that I got a call from one of Scott's crew asking if we had a front valance we could spare. We did and were glad to loan it to them.

That's how it ought to be. Help each other out, then race your ass off against each other. With no hard feelings.

Darrell Lanigan was on a roll with his chassis business in early 2014. Darrell had raced a Rocket chassis for several years and had developed some ideas of his own. So he basically applied his ideas to a Rocket chassis and the car became a Club 29 chassis.

Darrell was based in Union, Kentucky, just up the road from Florence Speedway. I was not close with Darrell, although he seemed like a nice guy. He was a strong racer and had a ton of success, but as a person he is very quiet. I didn't know him very well, and even after working with Darrell for a couple of seasons I'm still not sure I know him very well. He is very reserved and very private.

Several guys on my crew had talked with Darrell and were friendly. Somewhere along the way—and these conversations dated back well before my visit with Scott at Volusia—there came a discussion about us possibly racing one of Darrell's chassis.

So Darrell brought a car down to Volusia in 2014, and we ran it one night. We were pretty good—we set quick time in qualifying—but we got roughed up in our heat race and elected to park it for the night. Darrell was still short of cars at that moment and it wouldn't be cool to tear up his stuff when we were just giving it a try.

Mike Reece and I talked it over and decided to buy Darrell's Club 29 car. So, I guess you could say, that was when we officially moved over to the other side after running Scott's cars for the past seven seasons.

A lot was going through my mind at that moment, I'll admit. I was ready to change, for several reasons. Mainly I had an intuition that we were trending in the wrong direction. Yes, I realize we won three Lucas Oil titles in a row. But 2013 wasn't quite as good as 2012, and 2014 started off like a real dud. So something told me—beyond the situation with sharing information—it was time to make a change. We weren't where we needed to be.

Sometimes you can hurt yourself by staying in the same chassis for too long. There is a real benefit to shaking it up and getting a fresh look at things.

Actually, we flirted with another chassis in 2012, but not on a full-time basis. We were waiting for a new car from Scott, and he was so busy they were delayed in getting it finished. Scott and I were butting heads a little bit on the new car, and we were having some trouble getting the pieces and parts we needed.

Mike Marlar had purchased a Barry Wright car and ran it a few races, and we decided to buy the car from Mike and run it a few times. Honestly, we were just trying to spice things up and kinda poke Scott a little bit to get our car finished. We were running second in the Barry Wright car at Charlotte when a bar broke and we dropped out, and it turned out we only ran the car that one time.

But Mike Reece and I made the decision to buy the Club 29 car and make it our primary car. Darrell helped get us a bunch of deals on parts and other stuff so it was a good setup all around.

Despite my worries, making the transition to the new chassis didn't turn out to be a problem at all. Just the opposite, actually. We had a great season in 2014, contended for another Lucas Oil title, and we were a couple of flat tires away from having the most successful season of our career. So I think the numbers speak for themselves on that deal.

One thing I will admit, a lot of people were asking us why we made the change from the Bloomquist chassis. I'm private by nature, so I didn't share a whole lot of the background at the time. I just kept telling everybody that we felt like it was time for a change and that was it.

Here's a weird thing that I recall from that period. When we rolled out the Club 29 car I immediately had people walking right up and looking under the back of our car. Hey, that never happened when we were in the Bloomquist chassis. I don't know if it's because people have so much respect for Scott that they don't feel comfortable or what, but I literally had to chase people away from the Club 29 car. It's like they felt it was suddenly okay to check out our setup. It was annoying as hell, I'll tell you.

After a little bit of a slow start we heated up in May with the new car. We won at LaSalle, Illinois, and Tazewell before heading up to Florence where we won the Ralph Latham Memorial at the end of the month. That gave us three wins in four starts with the Lucas Oil series, and we closed to just 10 points behind Don O'Neal in the standings.

It turned out to be tight on the points all the way to the end. Don got going good and won a couple in June, but we came back strong in July to win four races and take the points lead. We won the USA Nationals at Cedar Lake on Aug. 2, scoring $50 grand. That was an Outlaws race, and didn't help us on the Lucas points deal. But we won again with the Lucas series at the Topless 100 at Batesville on Aug. 16, scoring another $40,000.

When we left Batesville we had a lead of 145 points over O'Neal. But Don wasn't giving up, and we had a hard-fought race at the Hillbilly 100 at I-77 Raceway Park a couple of weeks later where Don won and we were second.

We had a real scramble at the World 100 the following week. We ended up winning a consy and started at the back, racing our way up to third behind Bloomquist and Dale McDowell.

At Brownstown at the Jackson 100 a week later we finished 12th while Don was second, and he regained the points lead. From there it was on to Knoxville, Iowa.

Remember those old radio ads when they talked about "death-defying race drivers and thrilling action!" That's what we had at Knoxville. And it wasn't much fun at all.

Knoxville is a bad fast race track. You're really hauling it there, and I love it. But at the Thursday night opener of the Knoxville Late Model Nationals I had just about the worst wreck I've ever experienced.

We were running our heat race, coming off turn four onto the front straightaway. We were wide open—like everybody else—when I felt something touch our car and it cut left. Then it felt like somebody hit me a ton, but as they were up against my car I could hear—they were still both feet into the throttle.

The safety crew loads what's left of our car after our crash at Knoxville in 2014. (Rick Schwallie photo)

Talking it over with our good friend Chris Davis of Midwest Sheet Metal. (Rick Schwallie photo)

I felt our car shoot up into the air, and immediately was thinking: "You know, Jimmy, this ain't gonna end very good at all."

I clenched my body and pulled my arms in as the car started rolling over, and every time we smashed down on the track I was cussing. We flipped a long way—it felt like the whole straightaway—and when the car finally stopped rolling I was mad enough to eat a handful of ten-penny nails.

I got out of the car pretty quick—adrenaline kinda takes over sometimes and you don't even realize what's happening—and I looked up to see my good friend, Mike Marlar, running up to me. Mikey had a scared look on his face and I think he was genuinely concerned about me being hurt bad. But my anger—well, maybe it was rage—must have been obvious because Mikey didn't say, "You okay, Jimmy?" or anything like that.

He just looked at me and kinda held up his hands cautiously and said, "Jimmy, don't do anything stupid."

Our crew member Mullet—Jeff Strope—was right there, too, and he was mad enough to rumble with somebody. I grabbed my helmet and started walking back to the infield, and I didn't need to look over the car to assess the damage. That thing was a complete wreck.

I made just a couple of steps when Ben Shelton, the pit reporter, asked a question and pointed the microphone at me. I have no idea what the question was, but I let loose with a few choice words for the car who turned me over.

"He's a f---ing idiot!" I yelled. That was definitely not a nice thing to say on the PA but in fairness to me I had just used up one of my nine lives and wiped out a perfectly good race car. So I wasn't in a good mood.

"Who, Jimmy?" Ben replied. "Who's an idiot?"

"Feger!"

Jason Feger was the car that tagged me in the corner and then kept his foot in the gas. I don't know what Jason was thinking when that happened; years later I still can't figure it out. I believe he intended to wreck me, but I don't think he meant for the crash to be anywhere near that violent. Sometimes you do things and instantly realize, "Oops, that's not how I thought it would go." I've done that myself a few times, in fact.

I got back to our hauler and tried to regroup, but it took a while to get myself settled down. Man, I was hot. Sometimes you're mad enough that a simple "damn it" just doesn't cut it.

We rolled out a backup car and forged on, and on Saturday night ran 7th in the championship feature. As far as me being dinged up, it probably looked worse than it really was. I was sore the next day, but that's about it. Feger and I talked later, but not specifically about the wreck. It is what it is, I reckon.

Having some fun with Nathan at Magnolia Motor Speedway in 2014. (Rick Schwallie photo)

Darrell "Hammer" Pack, Kier "Big Snack" Hoover, and Kenny Holt in a detailed discussion with Jack Cornett at Eldora in 2014. (Rick Schwallie photo)

I will admit that a lot of people have razzed me over the years about my remarks on the PA that night. I am not a fan of swearing on the PA, and that's out of character for me. But it's over and done with and I can't take any of it back. It happened and there ain't anything I can do about it now but smile. It seemed like the right thing to say at the time, if you know what I mean.

When we left Knoxville we were staring at a 145-point deficit to O'Neal in the Lucas Oil chase with just three races to go. We kept digging and ran decent at the next two races—Dixie and Rome, in Georgia—but couldn't make up ground fast enough.

Losing our primary car at Knoxville hurt us, because looking back we trended downward a little bit in performance with our backup car for the next few weeks. (However, Ronnie Stuckey took our wrecked Knoxville car and clipped the frame, and at the end of the season we won at Charlotte with that car.)

When we got to Portsmouth for the Dirt Track World Championship on October 19, we were 75 points behind O'Neal. There were lots of interviews at Portsmouth about the points deal, and we tried to stay in a good humor and work with everybody. I felt like we could still win the title but I knew it was going to be tough.

Don and I each won our heat race, and locked in for Saturday night. I would start third, and Don was to line up sixth. Rain moved in and pushed the feature to Sunday afternoon.

We ran good in the early stages, and got to the lead on lap 40. But a couple of laps later Scott got past us, and we battled for several laps before I got back in front on lap 54. Scott hung in there and finally got around us again on lap 60, and from that point we just weren't able to get enough of a run to make anything happen. In the late laps Eddie Carrier Jr. passed us for second, and we ended up third. O'Neal was fourth, and that was good enough for Don to clinch the Lucas Oil title by 65 points.

And that was the story. We fell just short of our fourth straight Lucas Oil title. We were definitely disappointed but you've just got to face facts. We just were not quite able to get it done.

I was happy for Don, however. You never enjoy losing a race or a championship, but give credit where it's due. In my opinion Don drove one of the best seasons of his career in 2014. He was smart and patient and he learned how to race in a different way than in the past.

Don has always been a tough, aggressive racer, a guy who got 120 percent out of his car every night. If the car wasn't perfect it didn't matter; Don was going to drive it as hard as it could be driven. But when he joined

Don O'Neal did a heckuva job and won the Lucas Oil title in 2014 after a tight battle with us all year. (Rick Schwallie photo)

Not much excitement here! Hanging out with Jason Papich, Earl Pearson Jr., and Billy Moyer at I-80 in 2014. (Rick Schwallie photo)

Clint Bowyer Racing at the start of the 2014 season Don focused on being smarter and more patient. It really paid off and the results speak for themselves.

I realized that Don had adjusted his style a little bit earlier in the year at Magnolia Motor Speedway. I passed Don for the lead there, and in the past I felt like Don sometimes could get down on himself and lose his focus when that happened. But man, at Magnolia he came charging back by us and I thought, "Whoa, what's happened here!"

So I was glad for Don, and for Clint Bowyer, and everybody on their crew.

We had a good year, too, by any measure. We won 15 races, including a couple of crown jewels. So we couldn't complain too awful much.

I was a gracious runner-up in the 2014 championship, and as the afternoon sun was setting there at Portsmouth I was saying nice things in interviews about having a good season and looking forward to coming back next year.

I was smiling and composed and on the surface everything looked peachy. But underneath all that calm, my world was in great turmoil. Aside from changing chassis brands, everything related to our team was changing. In my heart I knew that the coming season was likely to be very different than the past eight seasons.

I'll bet you don't like change. Well, I don't either. But it was coming.

18

A Major Change

The whole thing started innocently enough. Around the middle of the 2014 season I talked with a guy from Oklahoma who wanted to go racing. His name was Bryan Roland, and I called him to put in a good word for a friend of mine. We talked for a few minutes on the phone, and Bryan said they already had their mind set on a driver.

I hung up the phone and didn't think anything more about it.

About an hour later my phone rang, and it was Bryan.

"What about you?" he said.

"What do you mean?" I replied.

"What about you?" he repeated. "Would you be interested in driving my car?"

"I've got a good ride," I said.

I had been racing with Mike Reece for eight great, successful seasons. At that moment I hadn't given any thought to making a change.

Bryan said he would take care of me way beyond what anybody else could do. He was in the oil business and had the resources to make good things happen.

Prior to that conversation, over the past couple of seasons I had turned down two different significant offers from other teams. When I say significant, I mean *significant*. Big base salary, plus 40 percent of whatever the car made.

But I turned down both offers. Why? It's a little complicated, but not really. Number one, I didn't feel like the timing was right. My mama was sick at that time, and I was very concerned about her. One of the offers would require me to move to Charlotte; if I would move from Newport and take Nathan with me, my mama would be very hurt.

And part of my reasoning in turning those offers down was my loyalty to Mike Reece.

You've got to understand, Mike made all my dreams come true. I was an up-and-coming regional guy and Mike allowed me to go out on the road and make my way as a professional, traveling racer. None of that would have happened without Mike.

But by late 2014 there was no denying that things were changing. Mike had gone through some changes in his life, and a couple of times down the line he told me that he was tempted to sell out and quit.

"What would it take for me to hire you?" Bryan Roland was asking me.

"I don't know," I said, and my head was spinning a little bit. This was not a conversation I was expecting to have. Finally I just said, "Look, I appreciate your calling, but I'm not interested."

I figured that was the end of it. But it was just the beginning.

A short while later Bryan called again.

"I'm serious," he kept saying. "I want to hire you to drive for me."

Bryan was very successful in the oil business, and he had recently purchased the Widow Wax line of car cleaners. He was looking for an established, well-known driver to help promote his new brand.

"I'll tell you what," I replied. "I'll tell you the numbers I turned down over the past year or so. If you're serious, it would have to be better than those two offers."

I shared the numbers with Bryan, and he didn't flinch. "That's fine," he said. "I can do even better than that."

Things were getting serious. For the sake of my family, and my future, I had to listen to Bryan's offer.

"Here's the deal," I finally said. "If I'm going to drive your car, we've got to make this right for Mike Reece. Here's his number; you call Mike and if you guys can work a deal where you buy him out, I'll drive for you. Otherwise, I'm staying put."

I called Mike immediately and gave him a heads-up on my conversations with Bryan. I didn't tell him what Bryan was offering me personally; I just explained that Bryan was interested in buying Mike's team.

"I'm not interested in selling," Mike said. "I'm having a good time racing."

We hung up the phone, and I was uncomfortable. This was conflict in a classic sense; what's best for Mike…but what's best for Jimmy?

I called Mike back. I shared all of the details that Bryan was proposing. My salary, the crew's salary, and—also very important—the fact that Bryan was able to provide health insurance for everyone on the team.

"Let me think about it," Mike said.

Even prior to the call, a couple of things came up that brought some tension with Mike and me.

Mike Reece made my dreams come true,
that's for sure. (Rick Schwallie photo)

Sometimes it's hard to ignore the stress and pressure
of this deal. (Rick Schwallie photo)

The biggest problem was the damned Internet. People who don't have anything better to do than try and make others miserable sit at their keyboard all day, making stuff up. Stirring the shit and making life difficult for the rest of us who are actually out there racing.

You know what ain't easy? Staying together as a racing team for eight seasons.

This deal wears everybody out eventually. Friendships and marriages and business relationships, racing can take a toll on all of them. It's a life filled with conflict, even when you're winning. *Especially* when you're winning. Success means money, and money means conflict. That's the best way I know to say it.

Like everybody, Mike and I had to work through various issues as time went on. We were always able to get to an agreement, and that's how we stuck together. It's not that me and Mike are difficult people; quite the opposite, really. It's just that you have to work your way through different scenarios and difficulties.

For example, a sponsor wants the name of their company in big letters on the t-shirts you make. That brings the classic tug-of-war about promotion…I want to promote the names of my sponsors, but people seem to want to see "Newport Nightmare" bigger than anything on the shirt.

One of the main things that kept me and Mike together, I reckon, is the fact that we are friends. Genuine friends. I cared a whole lot about Mike, and always wanted things to be right between us. He was good to me and I did my best to always be good to Mike.

That's why the idea of joining Bryan Roland was so hard. Sure, the numbers he was proposing were very good for me and my family. But the idea of leaving Mike was painful.

In just a day or so Mike called me back.

The numbers Bryan was throwing around…Mike was amazed at the numbers. I was, too. And I stressed to Mike: I'm not asking you to match these numbers. I understand. But I just wanted Mike to know what's been offered.

Finally Mike said, "You know, let me come up with a price. Let this guy put his money where his mouth is."

Bottom line, Mike shot him a price to buy him out, and Bryan agreed.

I was all set to drive for Bryan Roland in 2015.

When I look back today, this is a difficult episode to talk about. Although it was a sound business decision, it hurt Mike to sell the team. He enjoyed our years together just as much as I did. It hurt me, too, and not just a little bit. I was all tore up for several months as we worked through all this.

We all know people who thrive on conflict, and have all kinds of chaos and drama going on all around them. Well, I ain't that guy. I don't like change and I don't like conflict.

When my time in Mike's car ended it was sad and emotional. I wish things would have happened smoother, but I reckon things like that just aren't smooth. It's almost like a divorce; even when people are nice to each other, it's still a divorce. It's painful.

My relationship with Mike went way beyond business, way beyond racing. I had a powerful dream to be a professional racer, and Mike made that dream come true. Obviously, I felt strong affection and loyalty toward him. I could never in a million years repay Mike for what he did for me.

Nothing could ever match what we did with Mike. Those were good years and they mean everything to me.

Mike went on to sponsor Scott Bloomquist for a few years, and they did pretty well together. People might have wondered if I was mad at Mike sponsoring Scott, but just the opposite: I was glad he was still involved in the sport.

The transition to Bryan Roland's team was the second major—and very emotional—change I had experienced in just a few months.

Since the very beginning of my racing, cousin Chris Fox had been right by my side. Through thick and thin, we did it all together. But in July of 2014 Chris and I parted ways and he left our team.

Like I said earlier, this deal wears everybody out eventually. And that's basically what happened with Chris and me; the emotions and stress of working together finally took a toll and Chris left to go do something else.

When Bryan took control of the team and we were putting everything together for 2015, I told Chris there was a place for him here. I laid out what he would be paid, and what he'd be doing. He was welcome back if he was interested. Chris thought it over, but he ended up going to work at Mahle, a manufacturing plant nearby. Hey, I get it; a real job is way more secure than working for a racing team, and a lot more stable for a guy and his family. As it turned out, this was a very good setup for Chris and his family.

Chris and I are still close, and he comes by the shop every few days. Chris follows the University of Tennessee sports and he's real active with that stuff, and with his family.

Every so often we manage to lure Chris away for a weekend and he'll come racing with us. It's just like old times, with Chris jumping in and helping us. He is still very smart and savvy with race cars, and he pitches right in to grind tires or whatever else we need. It's always fun and it is great having him around.

We have a lot of great memories together. Chris and I have a good relationship, but sometimes we are a little too much like brothers, because we get to fussin' and fightin'. Chris is the most contrary person I've ever met. If I say "white," he immediately says, "black." That's just how he's wired. And man, he is stubborn. When he gets something on his mind, there ain't no changing it.

Maybe someday we'll get a chance to work with Chris again on our team. I definitely miss him being with us on the road. But Chris has a real good job, and it's a good setup. I would never want him to give that up to go racing and I wouldn't feel right asking him to.

Chris is my kin and I care what happens to him. Always will. And, through thick and thin, I hope he always knows that. We did many great things together and nothing will ever take away from those times.

Part of my worry for Chris—and any of my guys—is what would happen to them if I got hurt and couldn't race. Think about Knoxville, Iowa, in September 2014. In an instant everything could have changed, everything could have been over. It happened in a heartbeat and it could have turned a lot of lives upside down.

I worry about that a lot, and not just for myself. I think about the other people who would be affected by something like that. These guys depend on their job with the team to pay their bills, and take care of their family. If I had a career-ending crash those guys would work for a couple more weeks and then they'd be out on the street. I hate it that we can't give them a more secure situation but that's the nature of racing.

The personal dynamics of working with Chris and Kenny and my longtime friends is challenging at times. We were friends and family before we started racing, and they helped me since the beginning. When Mike came along and we formed a full-time team they came to work, and they started treating me differently. I wasn't just Jimmy anymore, I was the guy who could fire them.

Man, I didn't like that. I still don't like that.

No matter how much you want it to be, racing ain't all fun and games. A lot of money is being spent and that makes things more serious, more complicated. I always felt a responsibility to the guy who owned the team and wrote the checks—Mike Reece, and Bryan Roland, and later Leon Ramirez—to run the team the right way.

I didn't necessarily want that responsibility, but that's how it fell. I would have much preferred to be a carefree guy who showed up at the track with his helmet, hanging out with my friends all week and having a good time.

Chris Fox and I have shared many great moments together. I wouldn't trade anything for those times! (Rick Schwallie photo)

Dave Braswell of Braswell Carburetion tends to our carburetor at the Wild West Shootout in 2015 as Cory Drips and Bill Schlieper look on. (Rick Schwallie photo)

But it doesn't work that way. Somebody has to be the leader.

Decisions have to be made on how you spend your money. The owner is involved in all the big decisions; which chassis you run, which engine builder you use, that kind of stuff. But most team owners—like Leon Ramirez, for example, who is in the oil business—have a full-time business to run and they don't have time to oversee every little decision on the race team. Somebody at the team level has to make those decisions.

For better or worse, that somebody turned out to be me.

In our early years, Chris took care of a lot of the administrative chores for us. He wrote the checks, he took care of the paperwork, he handled most of that stuff. When Chris left and took a full-time job that stuff fell to me, and I handle it the best I can. I don't like doing paperwork, and I'm not very good at it. But it's got to be done.

One of the biggest challenges is that many of the guys who work on a race crew today are old-school with just about everything. They are focused on the race car and a lot of times they're not thinking about the bigger picture. Sometimes it's hard to get them to understand that we aren't racing a street stock at Bulls Gap anymore. This is a professional level and you have to step up to that. Wear the crew shirt, and conduct yourself professionally.

There are times when we've had to talk with our guys about stuff like this. I understand where they are coming from, because it took me a few years to see the bigger picture myself.

When it comes to working with people, I'm definitely not a dictator. My style isn't to yell and rant and rave. The biggest thing is being able to talk things out. If there is a problem, come talk to me. Because I'm damn sure going to talk to you if I've got a reason to.

This makes it kinda sticky when your crew is filled with family members, or lifelong friends. You hope that you can work through whatever issues and not let it hurt your friendship. But at some point you realize that you must have the authority to direct what's going on and take charge.

When I was a little younger, I reckon I worried about this too much. I worried that if I was "the boss" it would cause people to look at me differently. That bothered me, a lot. But not so much anymore, because I've grown into it a little bit.

Our 2015 season with Bryan Roland was decent, but not spectacular. We finished third in Lucas points, with one series win at Macon in April. We also won the Wild West Shootout finale in Arizona in January ($10,000), and the National 100 at Phenix City, Alabama ($25,000) in October. We continued to run the Club 29 car through the 2015 season.

Racing hard with Jonathan Davenport at Lucas Oil Speedway in 2015. (Heath Lawson photo)

The 2015 season belonged to Jonathan and Kevin Rumley. They had a good race car and it was a heckuva season for them. (Heath Lawson photo)

But 2015 belonged to Jonathan Davenport and his car owners, LeRoy and Kevin Rumley. They won just about everything you could win that year, including many of the Crown Jewel races and the Lucas Oil championship.

People have asked my opinion of how they pulled off such a great season. The truth is, sometimes people just get on a roll. They had a good race car and they looked like a hero. It's amazing how that works!

They had the so-called "Rumley Device" on their car, a suspension setup that was a little bit secretive and controversial. I believe it changed racing somewhat, because it opened things up and got people thinking about new ways to do our thing. They were using aero to the max, and it opened the door to a lot of new ideas.

Is that a bad thing? It's probably a mixed bag. The truth is, the challenge of keeping up with them got me thinking creatively and it made racing fun again. Even though Jonathan was dominant on the track, it was fun to try and chase him down. It opened my mind to some new things and kinda got me fired up again, if you know what I mean.

I have a ton of respect for Kevin Rumley. He is a great thinker for sure. On the flip side, sometimes I felt like Jonathan didn't get enough respect in 2015 for the job he did behind the wheel. There were several races where Jonathan won the race with his driving ability. I can say this because I was chasing him and saw it with my own eyes.

Following the great dominance of Jonathan and Kevin, the officials in our sport made some rule changes meant to rein in some of the stuff they had developed. I wish they had left things alone. I don't know why they want to make rules that take away our creativity. At the same time, I do understand the need to keep costs down. With all the new technology at our disposal it's hard to balance things.

I do know this much: it's real easy to spend a whole lot of money to go fast. Now we're beginning to hear from regional and local guys that they can't afford to come and race with us, and that's not a good thing. We didn't have that before. Data acquisition, computers on the cars…we didn't have that, either.

But on the whole, I enjoyed that season. We had a good time and came up with a couple of cool deals of our own that put us back into contention to win races again. We weren't quite on track with Jonathan and Kevin but we were okay.

One thing's for sure, that 2015 season established Jonathan as a genuine star in our sport. He was capable, night in and night out, of racing with anybody in dirt late model racing.

He had to grow a little and adjust to his new status and I think he did a great job with that. Jonathan's world changed from that point on, like it always does for someone who reaches the top level.

Jonathan came to me with some questions about the logistics of some things, such as putting together a t-shirt trailer. I explained that the number one thing is finding someone you can absolutely trust to run the trailer. I've been super fortunate to have Michael Hayes and his family taking care of my souvenir items and trailer for many years, and they've done a great job.

My advice to Jonathan was that he needed to get that t-shirt operation in place immediately, because you've got to jump on the bandwagon right away. The popularity of being on top—and people wanting to wear your t-shirt—might not be there forever. In fact, it WON'T be there forever. That's a fact of life for every racer who ever lived, no matter how big they are.

I've always considered Jonathan a friend and it was awesome that he asked my advice. That meant a lot to me.

19

People

You have probably figured out by now that my racing career—my whole life, I reckon—has required me to change and adapt to different things. There have been many times in recent years when I realized that I'm no longer a young street stock racer still on the time-clock at TRW.

I don't like change. Most of all, I don't much like having to change *me*. You probably feel that way, too.

But that's the way life works. If you want to accomplish new things, and reach new goals, you've got to learn new things.

That ain't easy. For me, it's been hard to push myself out of the corner and engage more with people. Plus, I wish I was more patient, and didn't let stuff bother me so much. Little stuff and big stuff.

Sometimes I watch how other guys interact with people and I say, "Man! He makes that look so easy."

I like people. I'm fairly social, and easygoing, and I rarely have a serious conflict with anyone. But in the life of a traveling professional racer, you're gonna interact with TONS of people, in many different ways.

That has always been a struggle for me. I'm good with people up to a certain point, and then it starts to get uncomfortable. But…too bad! That's part of the job and I've had to learn how to get through it, to navigate different situations.

The vast, vast majority of racing people are great. They're nice. They make it a pleasure to stand at the back of the trailer after the races and visit.

You get to where you begin to recognize people. We've got a Wheatland crowd, a Knoxville crowd, a Hagerstown crowd, everywhere we go. I like that.

Sometimes people are really funny. I've had people shake my hand and call me John Blankenship. Here while back I had a lady tell me that she was my biggest fan, and then she called me Freddy Smith. I thought, "Dang, do I look that old?"

People stand with me to get their picture taken and you can feel their hand shaking. They're nervous! I try to put them at ease, especially little kids. One time a kid came by my pit crying because when he met Scott Bloomquist a few minutes earlier he was so nervous that he couldn't speak (the kid, not Scott). I hate that for a kid, so I try to make them feel comfortable.

I've tried to impress this upon Nathan. I was that kid who was very shy, and I urge Nathan to speak up and not be shy. If you see a girl you like... tell her. Don't be shy. Who knows, right?

The other night a little kid came into our hauler and gave me a big hug. For a kid to love you like that and not even know you, that's awesome! I'm being part of a memory for a kid and that feels great.

At first all of this was awkward for me. I reckon it goes back to that very, very first night when I felt weird walking around the pit area in my uniform. I didn't have the confidence that it was right for me to be doing this, and it took a while to grow into.

It was intimidating for a while, especially when fans are older than me. I was taught to respect my elders, and when someone older approaches me I'm flattered. That took some getting used to.

Naturally, there have been people who were a little bit of a problem. Some years ago I met some people at the track, just a casual acquaintance. They asked me one night, "Hey, is it okay if we stand on your trailer and watch the race?" I said, well, that would be okay.

Next thing you know, they've invited a dozen of their friends up there with them. And then...they invited themselves into our hauler! These were people I hardly knew, and they just pushed through the door and were enjoying the heck out of sitting in our hauler. I had to chase them out, and the whole thing was amazing to me. Who would do that? But it happens.

The hauler—the living area—is an area most teams consider off-limits to all but a select few people. Think about it: basically, that's our home. It ain't comfortable having lots of strangers traipsing through your home, coming and going.

I reckon every racer can tell some stories of people who were obnoxious. I've had some of that, too.

One night we were working late at Wheatland after we had torn up our car. Me and the guys were working away, long after the races had finished. A drunk came up and grabbed me by the shoulder and pulled me away from the car, and I mean *dragged* me.

"Hey, can I get my picture taken??!!"

Our mood was probably not very good after crashing and having to work late, and I was plumb rude with this guy. But he never even heard me! He took the hammer out of my hand and stood next to me and grinned while his buddy took our picture. "Thanks man!" I thought my guys were gonna come unglued.

Luckily, that stuff is pretty rare. By far and away, most racing people are great to be around.

I will say this: We need to think about security at some of our tracks. It's too crowded sometimes and a driver could be put in a bad situation very easily; people get rowdy and things could get out of hand. Some tracks are flat dangerous, because they allow way too many people in the pit area or the work area. In the heat of the moment you're rolling through a crowd of people in the infield and some hothead could do something to really hurt someone. The world is different now and we have to think about that. Sure, it's a worst-case scenario but it could happen. Eldora seems to have the right idea, their pits are much tighter. Not everyone is allowed to be in the pits.

The upside to all of this is that many people want to buy your t-shirt and wear your hat. They enjoy supporting you, and them having someone special to cheer for makes it all the more fun.

When you buy a racer's t-shirt or other merchandise, you are literally helping that person continue to race. Every racer will tell you how important that is.

This was all a challenge for me at first. The merchandise part is like a separate business, and most of us have no idea how to make a shirt and set up a selling process. No idea at all.

If you're going to operate at our level you've got to sell merchandise. Most likely you'll need to find somebody to help you and oversee that process. It has to be somebody you trust, obviously. A lot of times you'll see a family member handling this for a racer, which makes sense.

In our earlier years we made a few shirts and later had a little trailer that Arnold Fuller purchased. Melissa took care of that part of things, and we'd take it with us to many of our races. We found out right quick that it's a hassle to try and sell stuff from our trailer in the pit area, because it takes away time you need to spend on your race car.

It was probably 2004 when Michael Hayes approached me about handling our merchandise. He had been helping Duayne Hommel, but Duayne had been injured and could no longer race. I didn't know Michael all that well, but I figured it would be okay to try each other out. It has worked out real well, and we're still going strong together.

People seem to love our nickname, and the whole "Nightmare" theme. (Rick Schwallie photo)

We put this guy on the hood and nose of our car back in 2012, and people loved it. When we changed up our paint scheme a couple of years later and he was gone, we had people asking about him for several years. Amazing! (Rick Schwallie photo)

Michael and his family have done a good job. They've worked their tail off.

We eventually bought a truck and a bigger trailer, which helped us a lot. That's a lot more comfortable than selling from a little table when it's 95 degrees outside.

Marketing our merchandise has been a learning experience. We've found that people enjoy variety; if you have only one or two shirt designs you aren't going to sell much. If you can afford to invest in making many different shirt styles you'll sell a lot more. And we've also learned that it's very important to offer kid sizes. We even have dog sweaters! Variety.

We've discovered that people love our nickname, the "Newport Nightmare." I think it was Ozzie Altman who came up with that…we were at Brunswick early on and I was driving Scott Russell's car when we ran off and killed 'em one night. Ozzie was announcing and I believe he tagged me with the nickname. It's worked out well because people like that theme, they like something different.

Welcome to my Nightmare! We actually considered putting that title on this book.

I've always been amazed that so many people like the Nightmare theme. Monsters, skull-and-crossbones, that whole deal. If I put an angel on my car, or a cute puppy dog, nobody would like it. They like the darker stuff, it seems.

Figuring out what people want in the area of merchandise has been a learning experience, and humbling at times. There were items I was sure would be a huge hit, and convinced Michael to make up a bunch of shirts or whatever. Well…*wrong!* That stuff hung in our trailer for months until we finally just got rid of it.

Sometimes when I come up with what I figure is a sure-fire great merchandise idea Michael listens and has that look in his eyes…like, "Okay, here we go again." But he does listen! He likes to kid me a little bit when my ideas don't exactly take off.

It's awesome when people buy and wear my shirt. For people to cheer for us, that never gets old.

Hopefully my skills in interacting with fans have improved through the years. I've tried, anyway.

Many years ago at Charlotte—it might have been a race they called the Colossal—I drew the 18th starting spot and ended up winning the race. They paid a $1,000 bonus for every car we passed, so it was a great payoff. $18,000 just in lap money!

Afterwards back at our pit I was happy as a lark, laughing and cutting

Michael Hayes and his family have done a great job with our souvenir marketing through the years. (Rick Schwallie photo)

This was our souvenir trailer in 2015. We've met a lot of great fans through this trailer! (Rick Schwallie photo)

up with people. Lots of people were buying our shirts when a lady came by and asked if we had a blue shirt. I kinda laughed real quick and said, "I think you're shit outta luck, ma'am."

She was really put off by that, and turned and walked away. I felt bad, because I didn't mean anything by it. I didn't mean to hurt anyone's feelings. But it was a good lesson. I learned right then that you have to be polite, always. Also, not everyone gets your humor, your mood. You have to be aware of that.

I'm better at all of this today, I believe. Not perfect, but better.

Still, there are moments when dealing with people becomes too much. Even when I enjoy it, and people are great, it becomes overwhelming.

It takes a lot of energy to interact with a bunch of people. After a while, you begin to feel like you're all worn out, exhausted. This is hard to explain…maybe I'm the only one who gets this way, I don't know.

Many times when we're racing at the same track for two or three days I'll visit our merchandise trailer on Saturday afternoon before racing gets started. I'll sign autographs and we'll sell shirts and it often runs into an hour or two. It's fun and I like it.

But by the time the session is over, I'm emotionally and physically spent. Flat-out exhausted. So I'll get back to our hauler and try to carve out some alone time to regroup before we start racing.

Don't get me wrong, I'm not complaining about this. It ain't a bad thing, and I wouldn't want to stop doing it. But I have to give myself some time to rest and recover. Sometimes I'm more tired after sitting and signing autographs for two hours than I am after working hard on the car all afternoon. Ain't that something?

A little quiet time is a good remedy on those afternoons. I'll turn off the TV and sit quietly, letting my mind slow back down. I try to not look at my phone, even. I just sit there and breathe.

After a little bit I feel recharged. I get into race mode and pretty soon it's time for the driver's meeting and we're good to go.

Interacting with people is way more than just fans after the races. You also deal with sponsors, manufacturers, race officials, the media, and other racers.

The sponsorship deal has been a big learning curve as well. I suspect every racer in the pit area would tell you the same. When somebody approaches you with a sponsorship deal it starts an interesting conversation.

What's the space on your quarter-panel worth? What's putting a sticker on your car worth? Is it worth whatever you can get, or is there a formula you need to know about? Are you asking too much? Or too little?

I don't know those things. Who does?

You do figure out that you have to decline the offer of putting somebody's big sticker on your car for $200. It's awkward sometimes, but racing today has grown to where you have to ask a lot more money for deals like that. When we were racing the street stock, getting a $200 sponsorship would have us smiling for a week. But at this level things are more complicated, more expensive.

You also learn that if somebody proposes a $75,000 sponsorship deal that would require you to completely rewrap your car and your hauler, you've got to think through the cost of all that. That stuff is expensive and you have to take that into consideration. It has to make sense.

Each of us has worked our deals for personal equipment. I used Bell helmets for a long time; I have a square head and it's hard to get a good fit. I'm Frankenstein. For many years Bell was the only helmet that fit me. Recently I've worked with Aaron Zentgraf of Simpson Race Products and found their helmets fit me pretty well also.

I've worn Design 500 uniforms for several years. I get no preferential treatment or deals there; I buy 'em the same as everybody else.

As for parts and pieces on the race car, that involves many different deals and arrangements. I've been lucky, I've never been forced into using a lesser product for financial reasons. The driver has to have confidence in his race car, and those components are important.

For example, I've had Goodridge plumb our cars for many years. I've had offers from other providers who would supply us the parts for free, but I don't feel the quality is as good as Goodridge. My choice is to have the best and most dependable products on the race car, even if we have to pay for them.

Safety has come a long, long way since I started racing. I still see guys not wearing gloves, and I recognize where they're coming from. In the beginning I didn't like wearing gloves either. I felt like gloves took away from the feeling I was getting through the steering wheel. It was a layer I didn't like, and it took a while to get used to wearing gloves. They're not as comfortable…but maybe by wearing gloves your fingers won't get burned off, right?

We have improved in this area tremendously, and some of that goes back to having good plumbing lines and fixtures. But a guy should wear gloves because it's still possible to have a big fire. Never forget that!

20

A Great Privilege

My deal with Bryan Roland ended in the same way it started: quick and surprising. Our 2015 season was filled with ups and downs. A lot of it was me trying to adjust to so many changes in my racing program.

I missed Chris Fox, for one. We had several guys helping us on the crew, but most definitely we were trying to get used to each other. We were competitive but not as fast as we needed to be.

Throughout the year I had this unsettling feeling that I never could quite shake. This was no knock on Bryan; we just hadn't had time to figure each other out.

I realize now that nothing felt permanent. We could never quite get settled down and get on solid footing.

Bryan was in the oil business, and just as he and I went racing together in 2015 the oil industry experienced a lot of difficulty. The price of crude oil dropped dramatically and it affected a lot of people in that business.

Every racer has a sixth sense about stuff like this, and the natural instinct is to start looking around for a place to land. So throughout 2015 I had conversations with my friend Leon Ramirez from Oklahoma, who had told me for many years that he'd love to put together a car for me to drive.

I also started talking seriously with Barry Wright. I wasn't kidding when I said one of my lifetime goals was to go racing with Barry. As the 2015 season went on our talks got more serious and we began to figure out what a pairing would look like.

It was around the time of the PRI show in Indianapolis that Bryan and I connected and decided to go our separate ways. Bryan came and got his stuff, and that's when R&W Motorsports came together. I was glad

Working with Barry and Lance Wright was a once-in-a-lifetime privilege, I reckon. (Heath Lawson photo)

Nathan and I fooling around at Batesville. (Rick Schwallie photo)

that Bryan and I had the chance to race together and I am grateful for the opportunity.

So this was the plan for the 2016 season: we would team up with Barry Wright and his son Lance to run a Barry Wright chassis. We'd race out of Barry's shop in South Carolina, and Barry would be our crew chief.

Team ownership was a partnership between Leon Ramirez and Tommy Weeder. Tommy and his company, Edge Services, had sponsored us previously. Tommy already had a truck and trailer, Leon had one Clements motor, and Tommy had another Clements motor, as I recall. Custom came on board and built us two more motors.

Barry and I had talked and he had two new chassis in progress for us.

One of my first conversations was at Charlotte with Darrell Lanigan. I explained the change and told Darrell we wouldn't be running his car in 2016. It wasn't performance based at all; this was just an opportunity for me to go racing with Barry Wright, something I'd always wanted to do.

Darrell was cool about the situation, no hard feelings. He's been around this deal for a long time and he has been through many of these same changes in his career.

Racing is a small world and that's why it's so important not to burn bridges. There ain't that many bridges to begin with, so don't be burning any down! Treat people with respect, be honest, and you never know… even though your partnership ended today you might be racing with that guy again down the road.

You never know.

So now, after years of talking about it, I was finally driving for Leon Ramirez. To this day, I'm still driving for Leon. Over the past several seasons he's been there for us, giving us everything we need to race—and win. I appreciate him very much, because he's always been there for us and he's always been honest and sincere.

He and Tommy together were good guys. This was a good bunch to be associated with.

I was excited about 2016. I already had a connection with Barry, because he was building our Loose Gruff modified chassis. As a builder Barry is excellent, because in the beginning he sets out exactly what you're going to get, and that's what you get. No gray area. I like that, because it avoids those little misunderstandings that can crop up.

In fact, those Loose Gruff cars were our original connection with Leon.

Winning the Show-Me 100 was a highlight in 2016. L-R Glen Benson, Chuck Hickman, Lance Wright, Nathan, Barry Wright, Jeff Strope, Michael Hayes and his son Kyler. (Heath Lawson photo)

Nathan catches a ride after we've won the World Finals at Charlotte. (Dave Argabright photo)

His son Dereck ran our car, and Mullet—our friend and crew member Jeff Strope—got to know them pretty well.

I had known Barry Wright for a long time, dating back to the Mach 2 Motorsports days. Barry is respected and admired throughout the sport and there is good reason for that.

In fact, back in that era Barry once offered me a ride. I was just starting to get into the late model scene, and I elected to stay with Mach 2. I believe Chris Madden ended up in Barry's car at that moment.

Barry and I have always hit it off real well, and our time racing together will always be one of the highlights of my career. We elected to go with Custom Engines for our motor program. Custom is based in Knoxville, Tennessee, and they build good motors.

We would maintain and race the car out of Barry's shop in South Carolina. This was very different for me; since the beginning of my career our car was always close by and we were in the race shop pretty much every day.

It was an adjustment, but I kind of enjoyed the change. It was almost like being on vacation during the week, and then on the weekend I'd could just show up and race. I had never had that before, trust me! It was awkward at first but I got used to it.

There is a downside to that setup, I believe. When you're not hands-on with the race car throughout the week, it's impossible to stay as close to all the details. And you need to be close, because if not you're missing something.

Was that a key factor in some of our struggles that season? I don't know. It's not that I know more than the other guys; I mean, Barry Wright is as knowledgeable as anybody in our sport, period. So that wasn't a problem.

But I think it hurt us because I didn't know my car like I need to. I'm a hands-on driver, and being there every day and knowing every single detail on the car as it is built and maintained, that's important to me.

Believe me, just showing up and driving the race car is awesome! But if I'm honest about the situation, it probably is not the ideal recipe for winning. *My* ideal recipe, I mean.

Barry and Lance were doing a great job with the car, that's not the point. And the situation gave us time at home without a race car, and that's good. But it was different, and I don't think I adjusted to it very well.

Barry's shop was about two hours from my home, and I'd drive over about once a week and come home that night.

The chemistry between us was probably the smoothest I'd ever experienced. Barry and I are very similar in personality; I'm not a hard-nosed guy and neither is Barry. Barry and Lance were on top of things

This picture says a lot. You can see the stress and strain weighing on Lance and Barry Wright at Magnolia Motor Speedway on June 18, 2016. (Heath Lawson photo)

Things had changed by August 11 when we debuted our new Rocket chassis at Florence. We're racing here with Steve Francis (15), Jonathan Davenport (6), and Jason Feger (25). (Heath Lawson photo)

and I was confident in their work. We communicated well, and it was no problem talking about what we needed to do to get better. Everybody respected each other.

But, I must say, the results weren't there. Not anywhere near what any of us had hoped.

Some of our issues, I will always believe, began with us putting everything together in a rush. We didn't pull the trigger on things until mid-December, and that left less than eight weeks to get everything together to go racing. And I mean *everything*; building a couple of cars, assembling spares, hiring help, lining up motors, everything.

Right out of the gate we were already way behind.

Our engine package was a big factor, too. We decided to run a Chevy engine built by Custom, and that was a package I wasn't used to. We also had some bad luck with fluky parts failures and stuff like that, odd stuff that doesn't usually happen.

If you race long enough you'll likely experience something like this. Things go wrong with no explanation, no rhyme or reason.

We were just not in the ballpark of running good and I was having a hard time explaining it to the guys. All the pieces and parts and people were good, but the package wasn't right.

I had raced Ford motors since I started racing, and now I found myself in a different chassis with a Chevy motor from a different engine builder. And we were struggling. That figures, right? It was hard for me to give our guys the input they needed to improve things. We didn't know if our car isn't handling because the motor isn't running good, or vice versa. Or maybe we were just not handling.

Larry Clark at Custom Engines never hesitated to try to make things better. In fact, all the guys at Custom worked hard to help us find the right combination. I definitely can't fault them.

From the get-go we were running in the middle of the pack, and we never got better. We did win the Show-Me 100 at Wheatland in late May, but other than that there weren't many bright spots.

Right away the situation started gnawing at me. 2016 was a challenging season in terms of results, and...well, just challenging.

The worse part was people stirring things up, asking me why we weren't running good. Man, that was miserable. It really was.

I probably should have sensed that things were about to come to a head as we got into July and August, but I held on to the idea of pushing our way through this bad stretch. I was confident we would get things sorted out eventually.

We raced at Macon, Illinois on July 26 and there was a break in our schedule, giving us a weekend off. On the way home I was informed by Tommy to bring all of our stuff back to my shop. I was riding in the hauler with Barry in front, and I explained the call from Tommy.

"Am I fired?" Barry asked.

"No way," I told him. "I don't think anything is changing, Barry. We'll push on and get through this deal."

Melissa and Nathan and I had planned a camping trip, and I was eager to get away and forget about how bad we were running.

At our campsite we were out of phone service, and that was a great three days. Wonderful! No phone calls, no texts, nothing…just quality time with my family. We had a great time and then we packed up our campsite and headed for home.

As we got back into cell service my phone immediately started chirping. I had a bunch of Voicemail messages from Tommy, so as soon as we had enough signal I called him as we rolled down the highway.

Tommy explained that they had purchased a new car from Rocket and I was to go up to West Virginia right away and pick it up. I was then to go to Barry's shop and load up our two cars and bring them to my shop in Newport. I would take over the maintenance and operation of the team, racing out of my shop.

Effective immediately.

What could I say but okay? I wasn't in a position to say no; I didn't own the team. When the guys who own the team buy a new car, you tend to feel like you need to run that car, you know?

Tommy wasn't a jerk about it. He told me to run whichever car I wanted—the Barry Wright chassis or the Rocket. But they urged me to try the Rocket. And either way, they wanted us to race out of my shop, with me overseeing everything.

When we got home I climbed into our hauler and headed for West Virginia. That's when I made the phone call I was absolutely dreading.

I just laid everything out for Barry, explaining the situation. I felt especially bad that, just a few days earlier, I had assured him that things were okay. I swore to Barry that I did not know about the Rocket purchase beforehand. Barry said he believed me, but there is always that doubt, you know? That situation has bothered me ever since, because I would never, ever be dishonest with Barry.

The whole thing was just tough, all around. No fun.

We got home and put the Custom motor in the Rocket and headed for Florence for the North/South 100, where we didn't run any better than we had been running—15th.

It would take quite a while to get things ironed out and get the team going in the right direction, but we eventually did.

We missed the show at the World 100, and that was no fun. We were pretty racy at Knoxville in September, and were passing for second-place when we lost an engine.

We tried Clements engines for a while, but they didn't fit me much better than the Custom. All the people at Clements were great, and they tried hard to help us. You won't find anybody who will say anything bad about Glenn Clements or anyone with the company—but their motor just didn't fit me.

Looking back, I wish we could run the 2016 season over again from the start, and put things together properly. We would have done things much better, I'm sure of that. I don't feel like we gave Custom motors a good shake because we were in a car I wasn't familiar with. And we could have given Barry's cars a better look if we'd been using a motor I was more familiar with.

At the same time, I don't regret that season. I got to go racing with Barry Wright and that was a great privilege.

It sucks to run bad, always. But it especially hurt in that situation because I wanted to run well for those guys. It made everybody look bad and I don't like that.

That episode has gnawed on me ever since. It probably always will.

21

Never Again

If you are a racer and you have some old tires—more than a year old—out in your shop, I have some advice for you: get rid of those tires as quickly as you can.

Haul ‘em to the dump. Shred ‘em. Bury ‘em. Make a tire swing for kids.

Better yet, if there is another racer you hate, give the tires to that guy. Because there is a good chance that you can make his life totally, completely miserable with those tires.

Whatever you do, don’t put those tires on your race car.

Old tires have made a heckuva mess for me over the past few years. The first episode of misery happened because I just didn’t know; the second episode happened because I was naïve.

Now I know. And I won’t use old tires in any way, shape, or form. Never again.

Twice in four seasons—once in 2013 and again in 2016—I was punished for running tires that were deemed to be treated with chemicals that are not allowed in competition. The problem is, I didn’t use any chemicals on my tires.

To be caught cheating is one thing; to be labeled a cheater when you weren’t cheating is just about the worse feeling in the world.

How do you prove you didn’t do something? It’s impossible.

The first round cost me $20,000, and the second round cost me a whole lot of pride and stress and aggravation. But through it all I have learned a lot, and what I have learned does not give me much confidence that this issue is going to go away.

In 2013 my tires were deemed to be illegal after I won a big NDRL race that paid $20,000. I lost the $20,000 and it was a bitter pill to swallow. I chalked it up to experience—it stunk, but it was an experience—and moved on.

Then in June 2016 I was among a group of five guys who were disqualified by UMP and Eldora Speedway after running the Dirt Late

Model Dream. All of us protested our innocence and we even filed a lawsuit to challenge the ruling. But we ultimately took our punishment and tried to move on.

I did not cheat my tires in 2013, and I did not cheat my tires in 2016. No matter how much you might want to believe I did, you're wrong. I know what was going on and I know we didn't treat our tires. It's that simple. All I can do is tell you the truth. That's all I know to do.

But man, it sucks. To know that people look at you as a cheater is a very bad feeling. It's not something I would wish on anyone.

I've raced for a long time, and I've had my share of ups and downs. But this deal with the tires was just about the hardest thing I've ever faced. Other than the death of my parents, nothing has troubled me like this.

I'm a lighthearted guy and I'm usually smiling. But there weren't any smiles during these two episodes.

Tire chemicals have been around for a long time. They first appeared in oval racing maybe 40 years ago, and they've never gone away.

Racing tires are manufactured based on certain specifications. The tires have varying degrees of softness, and by changing the ingredients and manufacturing process each model of tire can have different characteristics.

Tire manufacturers use a very specific manufacturing process to combine a series of ingredients, forming them into a tire that fits an exact set of dimensions. The tire company builds hundreds of tires at a time, and when the tire comes off the mold it is stamped to indicate the model number of the tire, the lot number, and the date.

If you change any step in the process—the ingredients, the chemicals, the manufacturing sequence, anything—it can potentially change the characteristics of the tires that are produced. Even though they are the same model, tires from different lot numbers can be slightly different—if the ingredients or process has changed.

By the early 1980s racers had figured out—particularly on pavement—that a softer tire makes you go faster because it provides more traction. But it also wears out quicker, which means racers have to buy more tires. Sanctioning bodies and tracks stepped in to try and save the racers from themselves, and they mandated tires with a harder compound.

That's when chemicals entered the picture. If you applied a certain chemical to a hard tire, the tire was softened and you now held a serious advantage over your competitors. These chemicals were quickly banned, and you were disqualified if they found that you were using them. A new phrase was now a part of the sport: "prepping your tires."

Some types of racing—go karts, for example—decided that it was too difficult to police the chemicals so they didn't restrict their use. Just about everybody in go kart racing today is treating their tires, and it's all out in the open. No secret at all.

In recent years the chemicals continued to evolve, and they found their way to dirt racing. That's when people started to realize there was more to it than just softening the tire. Sometimes the chemicals could allow an old tire to have new life, and be competitive. Sometimes the chemical helped your tires fire off quicker. There were lots of different theories and ideas about how prepping could benefit the tires.

Some years ago—10 or 12 years, maybe—a buddy of mine was selling a tire prep chemical, which was still somewhat new to dirt racing. Although officials were beginning to realize tire treatments were being used, they hadn't yet made up their mind on what to do about it. At that point the use of chemicals was perfectly legal.

So we tried some of the prep and took our treated tires to Brunswick, Georgia and just killed 'em. This was the first time we'd ever used tire prep in late model racing, and what a learning experience. Those tires were bad fast. The chemicals had enhanced certain oils in the tires and they performed a lot better. The treated Hoosier LM 20 tires were faster than the softest tire Hoosier made at the time. At that point the officials weren't sure how to deal with tire chemicals and their use was still allowed.

I was running the Lucas Oil Late Model Dirt Series at the time, but I was kinda new to the series as a full-time competitor. I was still trying to figure out how I fit in there, and to be honest I was having a hard time because our relationship—particularly between myself and series director Ritchie Lewis—was strained. We butted heads a lot.

I can be a stubborn person, and so can Ritchie. We had what you might call a difference of opinion; he had an idea of how the series ought to be ran and I had a different idea. It wasn't open warfare, but it was stressed.

Slowly, gradually, we began to respect each other. We began to see eye-to-eye. And much of it was Ritchie helping me understand the big picture, and why it's important to look at things from a wider angle. I was a typical racer, thinking only of myself and my team, and he helped me see that there is more to it than that.

But when it came to the tire chemicals, I was defiant. There was no rule against it, and my buddy was selling it. This was a friend who had helped me in the past, and I felt like by helping him—I even put his product decal on my car—I was doing the right thing.

What makes this topic a little more complicated is the fact that there are some legitimate benefits to prepping your tires. If you're a racer on a budget, the chemicals can help you take older tires—which probably cost you much less than a new tire—and be competitive. Yes, the treatment costs money, but the argument can be made that in some situations it is cost effective.

Downside? That's where it's kinda murky. The chemicals themselves are dangerous, and have supposedly—I say supposedly because, shoot, I don't know about stuff like this—been linked to health problems. Which is obviously not good. If that's true, you don't want this stuff in your shop, around your crew, around your family. But at the same time, what about all those people in go kart racing who are using it openly? Are they being exposed to harmful chemicals?

Like I said, it's murky.

All of this depends on who you ask. Some people say the chemicals are bad, others say they're okay.

At any rate, I gradually began to feel that using tire chemicals was not good for the sport.

After the Brunswick races Ritchie and I were still butting heads on the issue—not the stuff itself, but the sticker. We stopped using the treatment after Brunswick, but I kept the sticker on my car because I wanted to help my friend. That sticker irritated Ritchie and we went back and forth.

"We're trying to police this stuff and you're running the product sticker on your car!" he said.

"So now you're trying to dictate who my sponsors can be, and who my friends can be?" I told him.

We went round and round. It wasn't fun.

Finally one day Ritchie came to me and he was very diplomatic. I will tell you, his approach was a big help. He didn't come down and threaten me and hit me over the head. He was respectful and he explained all the reasons that tire chemicals are a bad idea.

Looking back, I realize that I wasn't seeing the big picture. I was trying to help my friend, and it caused me to not consider all the angles of this thing.

I thought about Ritchie's suggestion. I thought about the big picture, and I decided that it would be better not only if we didn't use the stuff, but it would be better for the sport if *nobody* was using the stuff. So we went one step further. We began to help the Lucas Oil series develop a way to test for the prepping chemicals. We gave them treated tires, we gave them samples, and we helped them in any way we could.

My interest was in creating a way to properly check tires and eradicate the use of the treatment products. If you're going to make it illegal, you have to find a way to effectively test for it. If your testing isn't consistent, if

Chris Fox working hard at siping one of our tires. (Rick Schwallie photo)

Hoosier brings a big load of tires to each of our races. (Heath Lawson photo)

it isn't scientific, it's useless. You won't catch the guys using it and clean tires will mistakenly be found illegal. That's a lose-lose all around.

At that point I never used the chemicals again. I figured the issue was closed, and that the sport had figured out how to deal with treated tires.

In April 2013 we ran a couple of races with NDRL, a brand new series. We ran second to Josh Richards at Paducah, Kentucky, and the following day we won $20,000 with the series at I-55 Speedway in Pevely, Missouri.

We knew going in that the NDRL officials would be checking tires, and that's one of the reasons we wanted to run with them. I wasn't interested in racing against treated tires; that's like bringing a knife to a gunfight. If the other guys are running treated tires, you are at a serious disadvantage if your tires are clean. So when we heard the officials would be checking tires we figured everything would be good.

A week or two after the Pevely race we were at West Virginia Motor Speedway. Mark Richards, one of the owners at Rocket Chassis, mentioned that he heard that one of the tires from Pevely had come back illegal. Mark asked me what I thought about that news.

I wasn't surprised, because I figured somebody got busted for treating their tires. I didn't pay the conversation any mind and went on down the road.

A couple of days later I sent a text to the race officials to ask about getting my $20,000, and they said the payoff was still pending, waiting for the results of the tire tests. They assured me that all was good and the money would be going out within a few days.

Lo and behold, a day or two later I got a phone call from an NDRL official. They said one of our tires came back bad.

"You're kidding, right?" I said.

"No, one of your tires is bad."

There was not much else to talk about, basically. I wasn't going to get my $20,000 and that was that.

I immediately asked Chris Fox about the tires we ran at Pevely. Chris said the tires—Hoosier LM 40s—were the ones we had planned on running at Eldora for the Late Model Dream in 2012, but we missed the race. So we saved the tires (which were date-coded in 2011) for the World 100 that September, but we missed that race, too. So we tossed the tires in the back of our shop and the next chance we had to use them was the NDRL events at Paducah and Pevely.

When we finally used them in April 2013, those tires were about two years old.

Then we remembered something: right around 2011 we experienced a slight change in how our tires were performing and people throughout the sport were wondering if there had been a change in the manufacturing process.

"Hey, maybe that's why the tires checked out wrong," Chris said.

So we sent some tire samples to another lab for testing. Sure enough, everything checked out okay; *except* for the tire with the older date code. Which made me think there was surely something different about the tires date-coded for 2011. The only thing the lab would report is that the older tire did not match the specified chemical makeup that the tire company had provided.

My education was beginning.

It's extremely difficult to detect if a tire has been prepped. You might think that you could just examine the rubber for a trace of the chemicals contained in the treatment, but it isn't that simple. There are all kinds of chemical interactions going on, plus the manufacturers of the tire prep could add an agent that masks the presence of the other chemicals.

It's way more complicated than I can figure out. I'm not a chemist and I don't know what the inside of a laboratory looks like.

In seeking to help with the testing process, tire manufacturers began to provide a baseline chemical makeup—like a map—to the testing laboratories. If the tire sample doesn't exactly—literally, *exactly*—match that baseline the lab assumes the tire has been treated with a foreign chemical. When Hoosier Tire updates their date codes, they provide the laboratories with the updated information. But there is a problem: if the tire is older, and there has been any change in the manufacturing process along the way—even the slightest change—the older tire will not match the baseline. The process only works if the tire manufacturers and laboratories keep track of the date codes and any manufacturing changes. Early on, there seemed to be some question about this part of the process.

It's like this: Hoosier Tire provides a baseline chemical profile for their LM 40 tires as they are made today. You bolt an LM 40 tire from 2013 on your car—a tire that was laying in the back of your shop, or maybe you're a budget racer and you're running somebody's old tires—and they check your tires. If anything has changed in the manufacturing process since your tire was built in 2013—the type of oil used, the recipe, the finishing process—it will probably not match the baseline chemical profile of the current LM 40.

You're thinking an LM 40 is an LM 40, and what difference does it make how old it is? But the age of the tire could mean everything if you get tested.

So I reached out to my friends at Hoosier Tire and asked them if they have changed anything in their manufacturing process over the past couple of years. Now all of a sudden things are getting more complicated. And awkward. Hoosier is like any company; they're not very excited about the idea of opening up their robe and letting everyone see exactly how they do things. So whether or not they changed anything, I can understand why they would be reluctant to talk about it publicly.

Part of what made this difficult was that I've had a great relationship with Hoosier Tire for many, many years, and the people there are my good friends. Genuine friends. People I don't want to hurt in any way.

I can't really cuss Hoosier. I wanted to cuss the guys at NDRL, but really, they're in a bad situation, too. Everybody in this deal is going to look bad.

But I did reach out to some other people, including Ritchie Lewis. I explained the situation, and Ritchie asked if I still had the tire. Yes, I do. I explained that he would just have to trust me, that I have not touched the tire in any way. It hadn't even been washed.

I gave Ritchie the date codes. We tried to find another tire with that same date code, but nobody had one. Well, they *told* us they didn't have one. We'll leave it at that. But we finally found another tire with the same date code and Ritchie sent a sample to the lab.

The tire matched the profile of my tire. The person at the lab told us what kind of prep had been applied, and the manufacturer of the prep. Very confident.

Problem was, the tire we found was a brand new tire with the stickers still on it. So somebody put tire prep on the tire without taking the stickers off? That ain't very likely.

The next development was that Ritchie and officials from a couple of other series sat down for a meeting to discuss the tire situation. The Lucas Oil series uses a different lab than the other series, and they consulted a rubber expert who is more educated on this topic than anybody else. Over the past few years, as they developed their testing procedure, the Lucas Oil guys saw just about every different scenario with tire prep.

Throughout all of this discussion, and listening to everybody on all sides, I began to realize something: the testing process is not foolproof. We have not yet found a way to deal with all the different scenarios, especially if it involved older tires.

All of the series have one thing in common: they don't want to find anyone cheating. This is as big a headache for them as it is for any racer.

And it's a giant headache for the tire manufacturers. They don't want to mess with this, not in the least.

You can't race today without spending a lot of time and effort on your tire program. (Heath Lawson photo)

Tire cheating: the topic has been a massive headache and has left a bad mark on our sport. (Heath Lawson photo)

I'm a baker, and I'm selling cakes. You like the cake, so you want to know my list of ingredients and my recipe. Obviously I'm not going to give you that information. I'm not going to give you all my secrets. That's the position the tire companies are in: they are asked to provide proprietary information to laboratories, information that could very easily be shared with another tire company. Not cool.

When all this was said and done, nothing changed. I called NDRL and asked how we could get finished with all this stuff, and move on. But it was made very clear to me that I wasn't gonna get my $20,000. I was out of luck. Simple as that.

But the stories in the racing newspapers continued on: Jimmy Owens's appeal is denied. End of story.

"He's a cheater, and he lost," they might as well have said in the headlines.

The only good thing to come out of that episode is that my friends, sponsors, and associates stood by me. They believed me when I told them I didn't prep that tire. Although it didn't change the outcome in any way, it meant a lot that people believed in me.

So we fast-forward to 2016, and the tire issue was well behind me. Although it cost me $20,000 and a TON of headaches, I had moved on. I was no longer talking to anybody about how tires are tested, and I minded my own business and focused on racing.

In June 2016 we loaded up and headed to Eldora for the Late Model Dream, which was sanctioned by UMP. We looked at what tires we wanted to bring, and we had some Hoosier LM 40 tires at the shop which were basically a year old. Honestly, I never thought about there being any further issue with older tires, because I was confident that the process had improved since 2013 and everything was cleared up.

We ran pretty decent on Thursday night, and finished third in one of the qualifying races. That was just good enough to have them take samples from our tires, but I never thought anything more about it.

On Saturday night we didn't run worth a monkey's butt. We loaded up and headed back to Tennessee and had no idea what was in store for us.

A couple of days later the UMP officials sent an e-mail to Michael Hayes, who runs our souvenir trailer. The e-mail said I had been disqualified after my tires failed a laboratory test. As you might imagine, Michael called me immediately.

"Hey, what's the deal with you getting disqualified from Eldora?" he said.

"Disqualified?" I said. "What for?"

"For tires."

"That's impossible."

"No it ain't...the e-mail says you're disqualified."

So I found the e-mail real quick and was immediately in shock. Sure enough, it said that five of us had failed the tire tests. Myself, Scott Bloomquist, Gregg Satterlee, Brandon Sheppard, and Ricky Thornton Jr. had all been disqualified.

Right away, I was in disbelief. First of all, some of the other guys who were involved—particularly Randall Edwards and Robbie Allen, crew chiefs for Sheppard and Satterlee, respectively—are not guys I would ever suspect of cheating their tires. I've known Randall and Robbie for a long time and the idea of them prepping their tires...there is no way I would believe it. When you race for a while you develop an instinct on who is likely to cheat, and those two guys in particular were not people you would ever suspect.

If this would have just been among me and Scott Bloomquist, we would have pointed our fingers at each other and gone on about our business. But because it included some guys I believe would never cheat their tires, I felt like something was definitely wrong.

It was the same exact disappointment—and the same exact emotion—of three years earlier. I was being accused of something I didn't do. I felt rotten and I knew the other guys felt rotten, too.

And it hurt to hear and read some of the reaction. "Owens has been busted before for cheating his tires! He's surely guilty this time, too!"

See how this deal works?

As a group, we consulted a lawyer and a lawsuit was filed. Looking back, I don't think this was the correct approach. If I had it to do over again that is not the path I'd take.

We appealed our disqualification and it went before some officials and was upheld. We went through a second appeal process and our disqualification was still upheld.

This situation was somewhat different than my experience in 2013. This time we were up against World Racing Group (WRG), a corporate entity that owns the World of Outlaws and UMP. It's an intimidating feeling as an individual—even a group of individuals—to go up against a company. At least that was my perception. I felt like there was no way we had the resources of a corporate entity.

It was apparent pretty quickly that we were facing a difficult scenario. The problem with a situation like this is that you are trying to prove that either an official made a mistake, or there is something wrong with the process. Now, do you suppose racing officials are excited about admitting a mistake? They're human, and they ain't very enthusiastic about admitting they are wrong.

Plus, they are looking to protect the integrity of the system. Hey, if one part of the system is flawed, that means there might be other things wrong too. Get it? So right away the officials will circle the wagons and dig in and man, it's on. It's total war at that point, because there is a lot at stake.

And there was a distinct feeling—at least on my account—that this was a good time to make an example out of people and try to scare the racers into stopping the use of tire prep.

Which is all well and good, except for one thing: My team did not treat our tires. Plain and simple. We did not.

There was another underlying political element to all this. Four of the five teams—all but Ricky Thornton Jr.—were regulars with the Lucas Oil series. The Lucas series is a rival to the World of Outlaws, which is owned by WRG. WRG insisted that politics had nothing to do with this, but in terms of public perception it was definitely being talked about.

Guys on the Internet message boards went crazy. They said this was proof that Lucas Oil hadn't been checking tires, and that their guys had been cheating all along.

That is complete bullshit. The Lucas Oil guys have been out in front of all this tire stuff, and worked their butt off to develop a testing program that could be trusted. They had gone the extra mile all along and to say otherwise was just stupid. People who said otherwise don't know the facts.

In fact, that was one of the arguments we made in our appeal. In my opinion the process Lucas Oil has in place to police tires is more stringent and more consistent than other programs, and I felt like it was reasonable to run the tire samples through the Lucas Oil process and consider the results. But WRG wouldn't agree to that, and that was disappointing. However, I do understand the dynamics at play here. That would be like WRG admitting that a rival system was more effective, which is a pretty tough thing for any series to admit. That probably caused people to dig in their heels even more.

Our disqualification prohibited us from competing in any UMP event for three months, which meant we couldn't race at the World 100 at Eldora in September. That's a tough penalty, because the World is an important race for everybody in our sport.

In September 2016 a judge dismissed our lawsuit, and that pretty much ended the process. As the new year came and went, four of the five teams involved—myself, Scott Bloomquist, Gregg Satterlee, and Ricky Thornton Jr.—paid the fine and moved on (Brandon Sheppard had dropped out of the lawsuit earlier that summer). We were allowed to return to Eldora in June for the Dirt Late Model Dream.

So that's it, right? The tire cheaters were busted and they paid their fine and all is good, right?

Not from where I'm standing.

My belief, and the reason I wanted to push the issue through whatever channel I could, is that the process is flawed. There are still inconsistencies in how tires are checked.

In my heart, I know I'm right.

I've had guys show me lab reports that says their tires were clean, and they admitted to me that those tires had been prepped.

At the same time, I know of cases where guys purchased their tires at the track on race day—making it pretty much impossible to prep them—and lab tests later said those tires didn't match the proper benchmark.

I don't know why the tire companies do not step forward and become more involved in the process. Maybe they don't have confidence that policing tire prep could ever be done properly, I don't know. All I know is that Hoosier has a wonderful, modern manufacturing facility filled with people who know an incredible amount about tires. If *anybody* was smart enough to crack this nut and figure out how to police tires, it would surely be smart people like that.

Maybe the guys at Hoosier—or any manufacturer—don't really believe us, the racers. Maybe they suspect that we really *are* prepping our tires, no matter how much we deny it. And what if they stuck their neck out for me or somebody else, and it came out that we were lying? That would put them in a terrible position.

This episode has changed the way I look at things, and maybe it's even changed me as a person. I've always been a happy-go-lucky guy, but some of that has gone away. Racing is not fun when it's like this. I'm bitter about this process, and cynical. This was flat-out wrong.

What was at stake in this situation was the system. There are a lot of people who believe, no matter what, that the system must be upheld at all costs. That's fine, except when the system is wrong. And when you get caught up in one of the system's flaws, you're ground up like hamburger and tossed out back to the dogs. Because, see, if the system says you've done something wrong, they *must* be right. If the system is right, that means you are wrong. End of story.

Someday I hope I can sit down privately with the people involved and talk through some of this. Whenever there is conflict like this it becomes so emotional that the truth is often lost. People are trying to protect their turf and I understand that. But I still feel like we can work together and create more confidence in how we police the use of tire prep.

It has not been easy, but I've tried to put all this behind me. Telling my story here has kinda helped, because at the very least I got my side of the story out there.

I will continue to race with UMP and the World of Outlaws now and then. I just want to come and compete and be treated fairly. At the same time, I've tried to be fair here. I've tried hard to see their side as well as my own. I disagreed with the process and I disagreed with the outcome, but there ain't anything to do now but get over it and move on.

For what it's worth, the Lucas Oil series has not had a big ruckus with their process. I believe they have developed a system that is correct and can be counted on.

As for me, I will never use an old tire again. We will buy our tires at the race track and I will personally check the date stamp on every one of 'em. And I would recommend that other racers do the same.

There will be people who read this and laugh. They might say, "Well, Owens the cheater is whining about getting busted!"

Maybe you're one of those people.

You're entitled to your opinion. Based on what you've seen and heard you've formed an opinion of me and maybe it's not favorable. That's fine.

But try to imagine this scenario. Imagine that $100 comes up missing from your workplace, and somehow the people there—your boss, your co-workers, your customers—come to the conclusion that you took the money. But you didn't; no matter how much they say it's true, you know you're innocent. You didn't take the money. They don't believe you, and pretty soon everybody in town hears that you got fired for stealing money.

So you spend all your time trying to tell people the truth, trying to prove you didn't do something. But they just kinda smirk and nod, and it's obvious they don't believe you.

That's a sick feeling, and all the rest of your life when you look people in the eye you're wondering: do they think I'm a thief?

Substitute the word "cheater" for thief, and you'll understand how I feel about tire prep and the events of the past few years.

You don't need to be a Jimmy Owens fan to understand what a helpless feeling that is.

There is one final thing I believe needs to be talked about, and it's something that would probably be a very controversial topic.

When we began the appeals process in 2016, the people reviewing the case were all connected to WRG. That certainly does not make the racer feel like they're getting an impartial hearing. The second appeal went before people outside of WRG, but as is usually the case all of the people on the panel have a background as a racing official. Again, the racer feels like this is not exactly an impartial group, because it's extremely likely that those folks will view things from the perspective of a fellow official.

I believe it's time to diversify the appeals process, and not just for WRG. For every series in racing.

I'm not advocating for a driver's union, or anything like that. I know that would give the racing industry serious heartburn and I understand. That would be like throwing gasoline onto a fire; instant explosion.

But why can't we have an appeals panel that represents many different sides of the sport? Surely we could find a half-dozen people of integrity to serve on such a panel. The group should be diverse: a racing official, a media person, a sponsor, a driver, a team owner, a manufacturer.

I make mistakes all the time in the race car, and in the shop. I'll bet you make mistakes at your job, too. We're human. Nobody is immune, not even racing officials. So there ought to be an impartial process to determine if something might have gone wrong, and try to correct it.

Sometimes our sport pits people against each other. The dynamic of racers-versus-officials has been part of our sport for more than a hundred years. What people might not realize is that, in the end, we want the same thing: we want the baseline of the sport to be built upon a foundation of integrity and doing the right thing.

That's what it's all about.

22

Love, Rediscovered

I will always remember the winter of 2016-2017, because that's when I fell in love with racing again. It's not easy to explain, but by that point I was feeling pretty low about my place in the sport. Our team had changed dramatically—several times—and it was stressful. I was worn out, burned out, used up...whatever way you want to describe it, we were about done.

It got to where I didn't even want to get in the truck and go. Nathan was getting a little older, and spending time with him was the highlight of my life (still is). If Nathan would have looked at me and said, "Daddy, I don't want you to go racing anymore," that would have probably been enough for me to quit altogether.

Honestly, I was pretty much sick of everything.

At the end of the 2016 season Tommy Weeder stepped away from the team ownership side, and we sold all of our Custom and Clements motors and stuff.

Leon Ramirez was fighting some health challenges, and it felt like everything associated with the racing deal was a struggle. Thus far things hadn't gone nearly as good as we hoped and we were all griping.

Leon called me in late 2016 and explained that Tommy wouldn't be a partner, and wouldn't be sponsoring us in 2017. Leon and his family had become my dear friends, and I knew Leon would always be honest with me.

"You got any plans?" Leon asked me.

"Nope," I replied.

"My family would go broke before they'd put you out of a race car," Leon said. "So I'll go ahead and do it for them. You should probably start looking around for something for next year."

I told him that I understood. Especially after how bad we had been running in 2016.

At that point I had had just about enough of racing. I had nothing lined up for the 2017 season, and it seemed that maybe racing had had enough of me.

When Barry Wright and I teamed up, I had told him, "Barry, this is my last hurrah. If this deal doesn't work, I'm done."

"Me, too," he said.

(We are both still racing, so...we lied!)

But I meant it when I said it. I was pretty burned out, and I'd been up and down these roads for many years. I'd had enough. And when you're not running good, it grinds on you night and day. It really is a drag.

Plus, times were changing. When I started racing, nobody knew how you ran last week. But with the Internet, social media, smartphones, message boards...now people immediately know what's going on. Instead of just saying hello after the races, people want to know exactly why we're not winning 20 races this year. Or why we are running that particular motor, or shock package, or...whatever. Real quick they want to tell you what you're doing wrong, and how you should go about things.

Good, bad, or indifferent, things have changed. That's the world we live in now and we have no choice but to deal with it the best we can.

So I closed out 2016 with no plans for the next season. All our stuff was still sitting in my shop, and the truck was parked outside. I had no idea if we'd be racing or not and that suited me just fine.

I enjoyed spending the winter months with my family. Since I probably wouldn't be racing I had made some plans in the spring to do some disaster recovery work. Seriously. At least for a month or two, to get a little money coming in.

Nathan had a field trip for school, and I came along. In the middle of the field trip my phone rang, and it was Leon.

"What are you doing?" he said.

"I'm on a school field trip with Nathan."

"No, I mean with racing. You got a ride yet?"

"Nope."

"Well, what do we need? Let's go racing."

I had to make a decision: did I want to keep racing?

It didn't take but a minute to know the answer. Yes. I wanted to race. We weren't done yet.

I know this probably sounds ridiculous, but from that moment I suddenly loved racing again. A big sense of excitement came over me and I was fired up at the idea of getting in the race car.

Here's another thing: For several months the question of continuing to race had nagged at me, dogged me. Once I made the decision to continue, it was like a weight was off my shoulders.

It's funny, a break of just a few weeks was enough to help me realize how much I love the sport, and how much I would miss it.

Maybe I realized that I liked racing a whole lot more than I thought I did.

I'm going to guess that every professional racer has moments when they're sick of the whole deal. They're weary and frustrated and physically and mentally worn out. I've said it over and over—this deal is a grind and it's very demanding. I'm not immune to all that. I get tired of the travel, tired of my crew guys, tired of dealing with people, tired of disappointment, just. . . *tired*.

But that's how you define a professional: somebody dedicated to their deal and willing and able to endure the hardships and challenges. Of course it's not easy.

The off-season of 2016-2017 wasn't any longer than any other. But for a few weeks, I was mentally and physically unplugged from racing. I mean, *completely* unplugged. I had accepted the fact that I was done, at least with full-time racing. I didn't worry about anything except spending time at home and enjoying my family.

That little break was just what the doctor ordered. I came out of it refreshed and recharged. And maybe, just a little bit, more aware of how important racing is in my life.

I reckon we take things like that for granted. At least I did. And when I was away for a little while, I came to understand something: racing isn't just what I do. It's who I am.

We didn't run all that well in 2017. We had our ups and downs, but that's okay. I enjoyed what we were doing.

I knew things were different—and better—when I found myself getting restless after just a couple of days at the shop. Man, we need to be going somewhere!

R&W Motorsports was now known was Ramirez Motorsports, and we had nearly all of our parts and pieces in place from the year before. Our Rocket cars were ready, and with the slight change in ownership our engine program was redefined.

A year earlier Tommy Weeder had bought out Bryan Roland. Now Tommy was selling some stuff, and it gave us a chance to buy back some of our old motors. We ended up with several Cornett engines, motors that I had raced a lot.

Sharing last-minute thoughts with Scott Bloomquist moments before the Show-Me 100 in 2019. (Heath Lawson photo)

Winning close to home is always special because your family and friends are in the house. Sharing victory lane at Smoky Mountain Speedway with Nathan, Melissa, and daughter Shelby. (Heath Lawson photo)

Jack Cornett and I had enjoyed a very good relationship for quite some time. Ever since I got into a late model I had mostly ran his motors. I've got to admit, it was a sad day a year earlier when I had to tell Jack that the team was going with a different motor builder.

But now we had our Cornett motors back, and I was fired up. (I couldn't help thinking…I wish we'd had these motors in Barry's car.)

Leon asked if there was anything else we needed, and I told him we should try one of those new Durham RY-45 motors. We had one of them with Mike Reece and Bryan Roland, and I liked the way they ran. I wanted to try it again. This was essentially a Ford engine, but using a Chevy radiator, bell housing, and other stuff.

With our motor program lined out we started running better. Our 2017 results weren't spectacular by any means: six overall wins, 5th in Lucas Oil points, and four series wins. But definitely an improvement from the year before.

Everything felt like we were back in a good place. Leon was excited about racing, and we were too. This would be the nucleus of the next several years for us.

Jeff Strope—aka Mullet—was still with us, and we had a couple of different guys rotate on our crew. One big addition—notice how I phrased that?—was the arrival of Kier Hoover, aka Big Snack.

My brother Kurt also started traveling with us and helping our program. That was great, for a lot of reasons. One, Kurt knows a ton about the car and is generally very helpful. Two, it gave us a chance to spend a lot more time together.

We were kind of finding our way during this period, and I suspect most other teams were in the same boat. The officials tightened up the suspension rules after Jonathan Davenport had such a strong season in 2015, and we were working within a smaller window.

That set us looking for other places on the car to improve. When I say "improve," I mean that literally. It ain't just about finding some trick item to make you faster, but it's also about getting the car to operate more smoothly, more efficiently. Everybody was paying close attention to small details, small gains.

One of the changes we made was on our shock program, from Ohlins to Integra.

The decision to move from Ohlins was not easy. I have built a great relationship with the Ohlins rep, Jason Young. Jason and I have a lot of rapport and we work well together.

But Ohlins was developing some new technology at the time and they weren't where they needed to be. This was something Jason and I talked openly about, no problem. They were working hard but sometimes it takes a while to develop and implement some of this technology.

For a while I had been dead set against changing. But we finally reached a point where it made sense to change, so we did.

We were getting a lot of good performance information from Mark Richards and everyone at Rocket, but we were having trouble adopting those changes on the Ohlins shocks. Most of the top Rocket teams were on Integra shocks, and their setup info was based on those shocks. We were not on the same page, you know what I mean? Finally we decided it just made sense to get on Integra and see if it helped us.

The first night on Integra—July 8, 2017—we won at Smoky Mountain. That was encouraging…but Smoky Mountain is one of our favorite and best tracks, so it was hard to gauge how much impact the shocks made. But there was no doubt that we were able to use the information better on the new shocks. We were back in the ballpark and that was a real boost.

Throughout the rest of the 2017 season we were trending in a better direction, and we won six races that season and finished 5th in Lucas Oil series points. That was better, but we were nowhere near where we wanted to be. We had a lot of work to do.

23

Negative Talk

When I began racing super late models in 2004 it wasn't long before I was winning a few races. Then I teamed up with Mike Reece in 2007 and we won some big races, almost right off. By 2011 we won our first Lucas Oil Late Model Dirt Series title and ultimately scored three consecutive series titles.

That was great, and it's always good to be on top. You don't have to be at the *very* top; but if you're among the top few guys around the country that's a pretty good feeling.

But from 2016 to 2019, we weren't on top. Our number of wins was down quite a bit during that period and we were not among the top two or three in Lucas Oil points.

You know what comes next: people started to talk.

"Jimmy has lost it."

"He's done."

"Wonder why he's fell off so bad?"

"I guess Jimmy ain't got it anymore."

That talk never fazed me, and I'm being real honest here. It didn't.

I didn't question myself or my ability during that time, not once. Think about it: *I never said I was great.* Why would you question yourself if you never thought you were great to begin with?

Early on, after we won our first super late model race, we got better every season. Our results proved it. 2008 was better than 2007; 2009 was better than 2008. It kept going, for several years.

And then one year we didn't trend upward.

I knew the upward trend would stop someday. It *HAS* to stop, because nobody in history has trended upward forever. But our good trend lasted for many years.

When we were trending upward, I didn't hear too much criticism from people. Oh, there were a few times; "Boy, you should never have got out of the Bloomquist cars." Stuff like that. But overall, people just said nice things about us.

When we began to struggle in 2016 and beyond, we began to hear it from people.

"What's wrong, Jimmy?"

"How come you ain't running as good?"

"Why aren't you winning?"

Let's face it…people can be blunt.

That's a lot of negativity, and you don't have much choice but to listen to it. The whole deal made it not as enjoyable to stand at the back of the trailer after the races and shake hands with people. I like being back there, because I like talking to people and being around them.

But when you have rude people (usually drunk) who come up and lip off that you shouldn't have done this or that, it turns me off. Real bad.

I've been fortunate to win, but I would have kept racing even if I wouldn't have won any races. Let me say that again: *I would have kept on racing even if I didn't win any races.* Because winning is not the only thing it's about.

Let me clarify something: opinions don't bother me, but it's how you express them that can get me going. If somebody politely says I'm not their favorite and they don't want me to win, that's fine. No problem! But if a loud drunk yells it out at the back of my trailer after the races, that is not fine. That is very irritating and I don't like it.

I love racing but I don't enjoy hearing that crap. It makes me want to not talk to people if they can't be respectful and courteous.

But does that kind of negative talk and criticism make me question my ability as a driver? Or my ability to keep a team going?

No. It does not.

Man, it isn't easy to avoid all the negative stuff nowadays. With Twitter and Facebook people are talking all the time, and much of it is just bullshit.

Michael Hayes, who takes care of all of our merchandise sales and marketing, handles our Facebook page. (I have a personal Facebook page, but it is not official and is just close friends and family.)

Michael sometimes has his hands full with the social media stuff. It's amazing to me that people have the time—and bad manners—to write nasty stuff on other people's social media.

You know, this stuff ain't hard: if you don't like me, don't follow my social media. Ain't that just common sense?

But sure enough, people write that I'm no good and can't race worth a damn. These are people who have never met me (well, I hope that's the case!) and are throwing rocks from a nice, safe distance. It blows my mind that people have that much hate and anger inside of them.

Michael usually deletes those comments, but I've told him he doesn't need to. People have an opinion and I don't mind that. However, I draw the line at profanity, because kids often follow my pages. We don't need them reading a lot of cussing.

I tune most of that stuff out because at the end of the day I'm doing what I've always wanted to do. The comments and opinions of other people can't change that.

I look at Facebook a fair amount, but I've never got the hang of Twitter. The racing forums caught on a few years ago and everybody was looking at them in the beginning, myself included. When I saw the stuff people were saying about me, I was surprised. I couldn't figure out what I could have done to get them so worked up against me.

That's when I realized a couple of things. One, people can be very brave hiding behind their keyboard. Two, those negative comments didn't impact my feelings, one way or another. I wasn't hurt, and I wasn't mad. I wasn't...*anything*. Their opinions didn't register with me, I guess. After a while I quit looking at the forums.

On-line comments I can tune out completely; face-to-face comments are a little more difficult. But I'm still working on that.

There were times when I've enjoyed some sweet revenge when people were putting me down. You're not going to hear me talking trash in an interview after the races, and I'll never intentionally stir up a lot of fussing or drama. But behind the scenes there have been times when I really enjoyed shutting somebody up.

For example, back when we were touring in the modified, people would post on the racing forums that I wasn't good enough to win at their track. You know how it goes: "He ain't beat anybody, so he ain't that good!"

Then when we went to their track and won...boy, that's a good feeling. A *good* feeling. It's nice to know you kinda shut people up a little bit. That's fun!

Early in my late model days I was driving the Harrod Farms car and also still running my modified. We were at Glasgow and I was running both classes. I didn't have a chance to hot lap my modified and went straight into qualifying, where I flat-footed my lap and was really fast.

After qualifying I walked over to the concession stand and a guy stopped me. I wouldn't describe him as angry, but he was definitely direct.

"I've watched you run many races," he said, "but I'm just gonna tell you...if you took that MSD box out of that modified, you wouldn't win another race."

I'm usually a happy guy, not too worried about stuff. (Heath Lawson photo)

After years of trying, we finally won Knoxville in 2018. I reckon the look on my face says it all! (Heath Lawson photo)

He was accusing me of using a cheater ignition box. Traction control and all that, you know.

Without skipping a beat I smiled real nice and said, "Well, then, why in the world would I take that box out?"

He stomped off and I'm sure he told his buddies, "He all but TOLD me he was cheating!"

The whole exchange made me laugh.

I said earlier that it's a terrible thing to be labeled a cheater when you know you didn't cheat, and that's true. However, sometimes there isn't anything you can do about that kind of talk other than trying to turn it into something positive, something motivating, maybe even something funny.

When they are accusing you of cheating, you know you're in their head. In a warped kind of way, that feels good.

I described the period from 2016 to 2019 as a "down" time, and in terms of results it *was* a down time. And, as I described our changes with team ownership and all that, there were lots of challenges.

But of course it wasn't all bad news. Not by a long shot.

In fact, by the 2018 season we were trending back in the right direction again. In May we won the First in Flight 100 at Fayetteville, North Carolina, scoring $25k. This was a special win because Jim Long, who was the promoter over there, has been a longtime friend. Jim had a touring modified series in the Carolinas back in the day, and we ran with him every now and then. Jim helped me get the Mach 2 Motorsports ride all those years ago, so I'll always be grateful to him for that.

Another highlight was winning the Knoxville Late Model Nationals in September 2018. Finally!

The first time I ran Knoxville a few years ago we were leading the race and had everybody covered. I wanted to win that race so bad…it's a special place with a ton of history and it means a lot to all of us. The cushion was big and treacherous, and I kept telling myself, "Roll against it easy!"

But I hit a mud clod and knocked the nose off, and that was it. I was so disgusted with myself. From that point Knoxville was a bunch of "almost" nights for us. Ups, downs, and near-misses.

When we finally broke through and won, it was awesome. We put all that "shoulda, woulda, coulda" crap to rest.

I like Knoxville because if you've got a fast car, there ain't anyplace more fun to race. I will admit, I get worried about the speed. Not so much when I'm in the car; if the car is handling good you're comfortable. But when I'm sitting in the infield and the guys come racing past, you really

Winning the Show-Me 100 in 2018. L-R: Gordy Nelson, Michael Hayes, Jake Fancher, Kier "Big Snack" Hoover, Kyler Hayes, Nathan, Becky and Leon Ramirez, Kelly "Trucker" Raynor, Jeff "Mullet" Strope, and Darrell "Hammer" Pack. (Heath Lawson photo)

It was great to kick off the 2019 season with Reece Monument back on our quarter-panel. We're racing with Brandon Sheppard at East Bay. (Heath Lawson photo)

see the speed. I start worrying about my friends. Maybe I'm getting older, I don't know. But it's a bad-fast place, for sure.

Then in 2019 we won Knoxville again, making it back-to-back. It's hard to explain how that works: you struggle with bad luck at a place over and over again, but when you finally break through it's like the second one comes easier. But once we got clicking there, we got better.

Here's a cool story from that first Knoxville win.

We arrived at the track a little earlier than usual, on Wednesday. Normally I'd just hang out in our truck on Wednesday night, but I decided to get out and walk around.

Somehow I went across the street and ended up at the Dingus bar, a legendary Knoxville institution. I'm not a drinker or a partier; I reckon that's why everyone was so surprised when I came walking through the front door.

People came over to say hello, and sitting at a table in the back was Jonathan Davenport. We spotted each other about the same time, and JD waved and hollered at me. He was having a good time.

"Jimmy! Come on back here!"

I walked back and said hello.

"Sit down," he said, motioning at a chair. "I want to sit with you, because you're going to win on Saturday night."

"I like your confidence," I said, sliding into the chair.

"No, you are going to win," he insisted. "I had a dream."

"You had a dream that I was gonna win on Saturday night?"

"I sure did. It's a guarantee, Jimmy. You're gonna win."

Well, sure enough. We won on Saturday night and I was very, very happy.

I love it when JD has a dream like that. I hope he has another one very soon.

Another nice thing happened just before the season started in 2019.

By that point Leon had settled in as the team owner and things were going smoothly. We had talked about whether we wanted to chase sponsors, trying to decide if we wanted other people's names on the car.

In January we were getting ready for Georgia-Florida Speedweeks and the rear quarter-panel on our car was bare. I was standing in the shop looking our car over when all of a sudden I had an idea.

I don't know where the idea came from; it just popped up.

I grabbed my phone and took a picture of our bare quarter-panel. Then I texted the picture to Mike Reece.

"It would sure look nice to see Reece Monument on this quarter-panel," I said.

Since Mike sold the team in 2014 he had stayed involved in racing through Scott Bloomquist. Eventually he was no longer with Scott, and we had kept in touch a little bit. My relationship with Leon Ramirez had worked out great, and I figured it would be wonderful if we could somehow also get Mike back involved.

A few minutes later my phone dinged.

"It sure would look nice," Mike texted back.

So we got Mike Reece back on board with us, and that felt great.

A little bit ago I mentioned that winning races is not the only thing life is about. Stuff like reconnecting with Mike is exactly what I was talking about.

Driving Mike's car was a great privilege. As time went on things changed, and eventually Leon became our team owner and it is a privilege to drive for him, too. And when you can keep those relationships and continue to enjoy friendships with people as you go along, well…that's awesome.

Oh, it's still great to win. Let me be very clear! I love to win. And as we rolled into the 2020 season, that upward trend we've been talking about really came into play.

2020. The Year of the 20. I liked the sound of that.

24

The Year of the 20

I'd like to tell you that our successful 2020 season was the result of careful and precise planning, and that all the pieces were perfectly in place from the get-go. But that ain't how it happened. Not anywhere close.

For sure, our performance had been getting better throughout the past couple of seasons, especially the latter part of 2019. We went into the short off-season feeling pretty good about how we'd run in 2020.

Kier Hoover, aka Big Snack, had been part of our team from 2014 to the end of the 2019 season. Jeff Strope, aka Mullet, was also a longtime crew member, focusing on our tires.

When the 2019 season wrapped up Snack was ready to go home. After several years on the road, he was burned out and needed a break. You can't fault a guy for this, because racing is a grind and eventually it wears *everybody* down.

Mullet was still on board, but we definitely needed some additional help for 2020. I reached out to my brother Kurt, and he agreed to continue to help in the shop and hit the road with us.

Kurt, I should explain, was a package deal. He has two little dogs—Turbo and Oscar—and if he was going out on the road with us the dogs had to come along. I wasn't excited about our hauler becoming a rolling kennel, but I finally agreed. This team is going to the dogs! For real.

We also hired Cody Mallory for the 2020 season. Cody had worked for Scott Bloomquist for quite some time, and they had some good success together. As the winter went along I was starting to get nervous because we still hadn't filled out our crew, and when Cody contacted me it made sense that he come on board. We needed one more guy and Cody filled that spot.

We entered the 2020 season with a couple of other major changes to our program.

After our win at East Bay in May at the Lucas Oil "Reopening Tour" it felt like things were going in the right direction. (Heath Lawson photo)

Winning at I-80 in September with Cody Mallory, Jeff "Mullet" Strope, Chris Davis, Leon Ramirez, Nathan, Kurt Owens, and Jake Fancher. We really had it rolling at that point! (Heath Lawson photo)

The first change actually came a few months earlier, in August 2019. That's when we debuted a new Vic Hill Chevy engine at Florence.

We had been running pretty well with Andy Durham's RY-45 motors, and we'd worked with Durham for a long time. We probably could have stayed with Durham, but Leon Ramirez and Mike Reece and me got to talking and decided we were ready to try something different.

When you have success with an engine builder, they are always trying to improve their program. Usually that means making more and more horsepower. It's a slow, gradual thing, and sometimes you realize you're not where you need to be with your program. You're making more power than you ever have, but you ain't running good at all!

It seems crazy but that's how it works. It ain't just about making horsepower; it's about finding a motor with a power band that fits your style of driving. It comes down to how the engine "feels" to you.

I can find an engine that fits me perfectly and win a bunch of races, but if the next guy bolts that exact engine in his car he might not hit his butt with both hands. That's because how you drive the car—and how and when the power comes in—makes a huge difference.

There is definitely no "one size fits all" when it comes to racing engines.

Our decision to try a different engine package kind of evolved over time. We kicked the idea around, and after a while it started to make some sense. The idea was to try something different and see how it felt compared to our existing program.

I have known Vic Hill for a very long time. Vic is from just up the road near Bulls Gap, so our paths crossed many, many times through the years. A lot of guys have won races with Vic's stuff and I always figured that sooner or later we'd get together and I'd give his motors a try. This seemed like a good time to make it happen.

Mike Reece was also on board with the idea, so that was another voice in favor.

I would not make a decision like this on my own. Anything that might cost the team a significant amount of money, I won't make that decision on my own. But Leon was good with giving Vic a try so we reached out and put the deal together.

When we showed up with his motor at Florence it was pretty hard to keep it a secret. There aren't many secrets in racing anyway, but when people spotted Vic messing under the hood of our car they figured out right quick what was happening.

I'm not big on sharing stuff like that; if we run good, I don't particularly want everybody knowing what we're doing. But like I say, it's hard to keep a lid on that kind of information.

I liked Vic's motor right off. It made good power, and it felt nice. I liked the way it took off, and I liked how it ran. It felt a lot like my old Cornett, which was a good feeling.

We ran pretty decent from that point in the 2019 season, so when we started preparing for 2020 we were very comfortable continuing with Vic Hill power.

Another major change for 2020 was our shock program, as we were back with Ohlins.

We had gone pretty good on Integra, but eventually I felt like we were identical to everybody else. As I've said before, a lot of Rocket teams run Integra which means there is lots of good information being shared. At the same time, if you're working with the same info as everybody else it's much harder to gain an advantage.

When we moved from Ohlins to Integra a couple of years earlier Jason Young of Ohlins continued to stay in touch with us. Ohlins was doing some significant development, and Jason kept me up to date with their progress.

"Jimmy, I'll tell you when it's the right time for us to get back together," he kept saying. Finally, in late 2019, Jason called me.

"We're ready," Jason assured me.

So at the PRI show I tracked down the Integra guys and told them we were moving back to Ohlins. I'm a strong believer in delivering that kind of news face-to-face; There might have been some hurt feelings but we parted on good terms. At least I hope so.

We put the Ohlins shocks on our car and we were good right off the bat. That change was one of the keys to us doing so well in 2020.

Me and Jason have a good rapport. We communicate real well and he is down-to-earth. We work well together.

We won three races at Volusia in February before the virus kind of shut things down in the spring. I wasn't sure we'd be racing at all in 2020, so I started helping a friend of mine by driving a dump truck around home.

During that few weeks, it was nice to have a job. No, seriously. I liked it. I liked the structure—you start at a certain time, and you quit at a certain time. That was kinda nice. I just kept my head down, got my stuff done, and went home at the end of the day. It was also nice to not have anything to worry about when I got off work. It wasn't hard; show up on time, pay attention, don't give anybody any problem. Simple.

As a truck driver, I wasn't nearly as good as the other guys. It took me longer to turn around, dump, all that. The other guys would get one more load in each day because they were faster—more efficient—than I was.

When I started I told them right off that the moment racing resumed, I had to quit driving the truck. But even with that, they were eager to have me. They explained that it was a real challenge to find guys willing to take the job.

That amazed me. It was a pretty good job, and definitely not all that hard. The pay was pretty decent and it was hard to believe that nobody else wanted the job.

The Lucas Oil series announced a "reopening tour" in May, and we were eager to get back to racing. Like everybody else, I'm sure.

We hit our stride pretty quick, winning a couple of unsanctioned races at Magnolia Motor Speedway and 411 Motor Speedway in mid-May. We won at the Lucas Oil "reopening tour" at Brunswick, Georgia on May 19 and finished on the podium in the other two races at Brunswick.

In June we really got going, closing out the month with four consecutive Lucas Oil wins. Everywhere we went, we were contending for wins, and we were consistent.

In August we scored our biggest win of the season at the Topless 100 at Batesville, winning $40k.

By this time we had a pretty good lead in the Lucas Oil series points. We started getting lots of questions about winning another Lucas Oil title, but I kept reminding everybody that our main focus was winning races. As I've always said, if you win races the points will take care of themselves.

Somebody started saying, "2020…it's the year of the 20!" I will admit, I liked the sound of that. As the season went on I had my sights set on 20 wins for the year. That would make for a nice, round, meaningful number.

We reached win No. 18 at I-80 Speedway in Nebraska on September 18. But our consistency fell off a little bit down the stretch, and we lost several races to rain in late September and through October.

Somewhere along the way we clinched the Lucas Oil series title, and it was nice to not have to worry about points anymore.

As our super late model season closed out we were stuck at 18 wins. But I was offered a chance to run a crate late model at Bulls Gap on November 14, and we won $15k. We finished our season with a win just up the road at 411 Motor Speedway on November 28, the Iron Man race.

20 wins in 2020. Not bad.

We had a great year, but we were helped by the fact that several top teams struggled a little bit in 2020. That's part of points racing, of course. Not only do you benefit from your own good performance, but you can benefit when others have bad luck. You don't wish that on anybody but

Our association with Vic Hill Racing Engines has been good, and it meant a lot to have Vic on hand at Portsmouth to celebrate our 2020 championship. (Heath Lawson photo)

Our championship crew in 2020: Kurt Owens, Cody Mallory, and Jeff "Mullet" Strope. I'm proud of everything we accomplished—TOGETHER! (Heath Lawson photo)

that's the way it works. Several strong guys had tough stretches where they didn't run well or had bad luck, and that worked in our favor.

And sometimes if works the other way; they benefit when *you* struggle. We had a couple of years there where we were the ones struggling.

But in 2020 we didn't tear up our car and we were able to heat up and stay consistent at the right time, and that's how you win a title. We avoided the roller coaster; we didn't have huge highs and lows.

Our number one goal was to go out and finish races and we were able to do that. When our consistency fell off a little bit down the stretch we could withstand it because we had built a pretty good cushion in points.

I will admit, the whole points thing was a little distracting there toward the end.

We lost a couple of races down the stretch because of yellow flags. The North/South 100 at Florence, for example. We had a nice lead and were running a good rhythm, but a late caution shuffled the deck and we ended up third.

My driving style helps me on long runs. I'm able to keep my tires under me, and in that scenario—long runs under green—I've always done well. Whatever I'm doing as a driver definitely suits those conditions.

Tim McCreadie, on the other hand, is obviously doing something different that benefits him when there is a late caution that bunches the field. If you give McCreadie a caution, somehow he finds a way to benefit.

There were also races where we had a straightaway lead and somehow we started to slow down. I have not yet figured out what I'm doing that could cause that. Maybe I become too cautious, you know what I mean? That goes back to the old school idea that "slower is faster," but I'm not sure that holds true anymore. Nowadays it seems like slower is just slower.

When it comes to figuring out ways to be better behind the wheel, we've always taken that real serious. We're always looking for ways to improve; I figure you're never good enough, especially now when things are so competitive.

We've watched a lot of videos, studying what I am doing, and what the car is doing. The key is figuring out how to make changes as a driver to better take advantage of what the car is doing. Or *not* doing, depending on the situation.

One example came many years ago at Virginia Motor Speedway. Chris Fox kept telling me I wasn't turning in early enough, but I wasn't sure about that. It *felt* like I was turning in when everybody else was. But I watched a video, and could see exactly when the other guys were turning in compared to me. Sure enough, I was turning in a tiny bit later than everybody else. The video proved it beyond a doubt.

I'm open-minded on making adjustments, and I try to never be stubborn. Many times, though, the driver can't see what is happening or can't feel it properly. In the case of Virginia Motor Speedway, we put a quicker steering box in the car and that solved our problem. It wasn't that I was turning later; it was because the steering was too slow. We had always been two-tenths off there, and when we put the new steering box in we immediately gained back those two tenths.

So we will continue to study how we're doing on those long runs, continue to try to get better as a driver.

The 2020 Lucas Oil Late Model Dirt Series championship was our fourth title with the series, tying us with Earl Pearson Jr. as the only four-time champions.

The championship meant a lot to our team, especially when we knew some people had written us off as "over the hill." It felt good to prove those people wrong.

Even though we won the title, when it was all over it felt like something was missing. I think that was because, with the COVID situation, we didn't have a chance to celebrate at the end of the season. I don't normally care much for racing banquets, but when we weren't able to have a post-season banquet I wondered if maybe people might not notice our winning the title.

A lot of people will look back at 2020 and be glad to put the year behind them, but for us it was a great year. But people will probably be eager to forget about 2020 and I understand that.

That kind of lights a fire in us to go out and win another championship.

It was special to think about joining Earl Pearson Jr. as the only four-time series champion. I've been friends with Earl as much as anybody out there, and we've had some good times traveling together. Earl has been with the series since the beginning and he's like the "King" of the Lucas Oil series.

It was also pretty cool to beat the younger guys to four titles. That felt pretty good! To be honest, I figured somebody would have scored four long before we did.

It would be awesome to be the first one to five series titles. We'll see how that plays out but it sure would be a great accomplishment!

25

The Crew

Immediately after our 2020 season ended, as we were celebrating our fourth Lucas Oil Late Model Dirt Series championship, we made a big change. Soon after our final race I let two of our crew guys—Cody Mallory and Jeff "Mullet" Strope—know that they wouldn't be back with the team in 2021.

That was a shock to a few people outside our team, and I suspect they were trying to read some things into what was happening. But there wasn't anything dramatic going on…it was just a bunch of guys who had pretty much worn each other out.

Dirt late model racing—probably every form of short track racing—is not nearly the big-dollar enterprise people might think. Basically we race for a hobby, because it's highly unlikely anyone is making a lot of money. At the end of the year when you total up your winnings and total up all your expenses, the expenses are almost always way more than the winnings. Even when you've had a great year and won a bunch of races!

What kind of a crazy business is that, never being profitable?

Sponsors make up the difference. The money you get from various sponsorships helps offset your expenses and keeps your team afloat. Many of the top teams get a deal on various products—engines, shocks, body panels, fuel—and that helps, but you have many other expense items in your budget. Diesel fuel, maintenance on the truck and trailer, insurance, utilities at the shop, it adds up pretty fast.

A big cost for every team is the crew. And, sad to say, there probably isn't a team out there today that is paying their guys what they're worth. The money just isn't there.

If you want to see guys work hard, come to the race track. Guys on every crew—and most of the drivers—are out in the hot weather, cold weather, early in the day, late at night, sweating, freezing, dirty, dusty, and

Our crew guys work hard, in tough conditions. Kier "Big Snack" Hoover is giving us signals at Florence in 2014. (Rick Schwallie photo)

Chris Fox has never been far away, and anytime he's able to come racing with us I am smiling! (Heath Lawson photo)

lonely. They leave their home and family every weekend—or sometimes for weeks at a time. It's not an easy life.

You've heard that expression: "A labor of love." Well, that describes the guys who work on a racing crew. If these guys were paid what they're worth the teams wouldn't make it to the end of the season because they'd run out of funds.

I don't like it but that's the way it is. If I could change it, I would. But it ain't within my power to change.

That's one of the reasons it's so hard to find people willing to work on a racing crew. Every team struggles with this issue, probably more now than ever before. Very few people have such a passion for racing that they're willing to endure the tough conditions and circumstances.

The people on a team—the driver and the crew—are married to each other. In fact, during racing season you'll spend more time with your crew than you'll spend with your wife and children. And, just like in a marriage, personalities are a factor.

Our chemistry in 2020 was average. Not great, and not terrible. We hung together and got our work done and our overall performance was very good.

A lot of us hear this in interviews: "You guys are running real well, you and your crew must have good chemistry." And, of course, we nod and talk about how well everybody is working together.

Well, that ain't always reality. There have been many nights throughout my career where we've actually won the race, but afterwards me and my guys were so sick of each other that we were fussing and feuding and dang near ready to fight. The slightest little thing can set people off and they're yelling and cussing. You might like somebody as a friend, but spend too much time together and their ways and their habits begin to rub you the wrong way.

There are many nights when people don't especially want to be there. But you have to push on. There are no timeouts, and no breaks.

A racing crew spends too much time in the same space, for way too long. You leave the shop and ride together in a box for six, eight, 10 hours. You sleep in the truck, you go to the bathroom in the truck, and you eat your meals in the truck. When you get to the race track you unload the car and get busy, usually working until late into the night. Then you load up and pile into the truck and get on the road and do it all over again.

It ain't hard to see the obvious friction that can come from that setup. Sounds real glamorous, right?

By the time we got to the end of the season in 2020, me and my guys were just worn out with each other. I felt like we needed a fresh start—all of us. No hard feelings in any way. We wished Cody and Mullet well and we plan on staying friends with both of them.

All of us—together—had a great year and we should share that satisfaction. None of us were perfect, including me. But we were good enough to win. In my opinion, we made each other look good. And we can all still learn and apply it going forward, wherever we are.

Mullet and I had worked together for a long time, and we were pretty much like family. Jeff had done our tires for many years. But I am 100 percent sincere when I say that a change was good for both of us.

When we hired Cody I had heard various stories that he was a controversial person, but we had no problems. He brought some good things to the team and I appreciated his help. I really liked Cody's signaling during a race—he does a great job with that. And he was good with seeing what the car was doing.

Cody loves to push the boundaries on things like bodywork. We'd be working in the shop, scrambling to get on the road, and I'd look at the way Cody had our body and shake my head.

"They're gonna make us change that," I'd say.

"No they ain't!" he'd insist. "That's legal!"

Sure enough, we'd unload the car and here comes Steve Francis, the tech director with the Lucas Oil series. He'd look at our body and wave Cody over and explain that he needed to change this or that. Cody would argue, but I don't believe he ever once changed Steve's mind. Steve would explain that the body needed changed before we presented for hot laps and he'd walk away. Cody would cuss…and grab his tools.

We'd just laugh. "I told you!" we'd say. And Cody would cuss some more.

The one crew member that stayed on after our 2020 season was Kurt. I know; blood is thicker than water. That's true. But it's also true that Kurt does a great job. He's always willing to step in when we need help, in any area. He's a great team player and he's always there for us.

People say I'm laid back, but Kurt is twice as easygoing as me. Nothing gets him worried. He just keeps his head down and does his job. He doesn't have big highs or lows and that's very important. Highs and lows are the problem; when a guy can keep himself centered he's generally pretty easy to work with. And Kurt keeps himself centered.

But those danged dogs…well, I guess we'll just have to put up with ol' Oscar and Turbo.

One thing I appreciate about Kurt is that business has never affected our relationship as brothers. Actually, my whole family is that way. Nothing has ever come between me and Kurt and our sister Tammy. We are very fortunate.

Cory Fostvedt joined our team at the beginning of the 2021 season and we've had a good experience together. Cory is from South Dakota and has a lot of experience. It's been a good match so far.

I said it here a minute ago, but dang, it's hard to find people willing to work on these cars. It's a ton of work and sacrifice and not just anybody can do it.

There have been a couple of times where I've worked so hard on the car that I thought I was going to die. One night Chris Fox and I were racing the modified, and it was one of those ridiculous hot nights at the track. We crashed and had to hustle to fix the car and it was just unbearable. I just about keeled over on that one.

Another night at Wheatland I set fast time on my first qualifying lap then tried to knock the wall down on our second lap. The car was all torn up, and me and Chris had to get it back together before the first heat race. We worked like maniacs and when I got back into the car I was so lightheaded I thought I was going to faint. We got a wet towel to put around my neck to try and get my senses back before the heat race. Man, it was tough.

Those are the things guys need to be aware of before they sign up for this deal. It ain't all fun and games, that's for sure.

But we've been so lucky to have good people around us, especially in those early years when it was just a bunch of kids running up and down the road together.

There have been many different faces, definitely too many to name them all. Chris Fox played such a huge role through so many of those years. A lot of guys worked with us on-and-off, several different times. Buddy Fox, Jeff "Mullet" Strope, Darrell "Hammer" Pack, Shannon Green, Kier "Big Snack" Hoover, Justin Talley, Gary "Bumper" Williams, Gordy Nelson, Glen Benson (our Canadian friend), Kelly "Trucker" Raynor.

Mullet spent a lot of time with us. He first arrived in the early 2010's timeframe, then went to Clint Bowyer's team for a while. Eventually Mullet was ready for something different, and I'll never forget that phone call. "Jimmy, can I come home?" he said. It was great. For quite a while Mullet handled the Loose Gruff modified chassis we were building, and he was a natural at that. He's such a people person, he could meet someone brand new and in just a few seconds they're talking like they've known each other for years. I wish I had that ability!

Cory Fostvedt had his family with us when we won at Smoky Mountain in 2022. (Heath Lawson photo)

When you crash and go off on the hook, it means a ton of extra work for everybody—myself included. (Heath Lawson photo)

Mullet is a loyal, good friend and if I'm ever in trouble I know he'd be right there, ready to scrap with somebody if that's what it takes.

Darrell Pack is a local guy. Hammer is a great worker; you never have to help find him something to do. He keeps his head down and keeps to himself and he is low maintenance.

Sometimes people are more than crew members. Chuck and Stacy Hickman fit that description, as well as Jerry "Smoke" Bridges and his wife Cheryl. Always there to help in any way they can, always supportive. Just great friends! They're willing to take on different things at different times, and it's been a huge help. They are dear friends and racing wouldn't be nearly as much fun without those folks.

I've always called my own setups, and I want to continue to do that. Part of it is control; I can feel what the car is doing and that puts us in the best position to read what's happening. Of course input from our guys is important, because they can see things from a different angle. But I want final say on any changes or adjustments.

A driver's confidence is a key part of winning races, and you never want to start believing you can't win without so-and-so. It's important to develop the confidence that, even if your crew all went home and you had to hire new people, you could still win. That sounds kinda snobby but I don't mean it like that. It ain't about being snobby; it's about putting yourself in a place where you believe you can win—no matter what. Hey, it works both ways: a good mechanic can win races with many different drivers, after all.

I need my crew and they need me. We have to pull together or we ain't going to be successful.

Throughout this book I've said this: I don't like being in charge. If I had a job outside of racing, I would come to work, keep my head down and do my job, and go home at quitting time. I'm not management material, I don't think. But racing doesn't give you that luxury; if we want to travel and race professionally, I have to step up and be a leader of our team. That's part of my job and there's no getting around it.

I have tried to learn and get better.

One thing I have recognized is how ego can affect how a crew functions. If you have a "crew chief" who believes washing the car or sweeping the floor is below him, you're going to have problems. I've tried to cultivate the idea that we are all equals—including me. I'll lie on my back in the mud to change a transmission, and I'll empty the trash can at the shop if needed. That's why I hesitate to call anyone on our team "crew chief." My experience is that putting that title on a guy can cause trouble.

Sometimes it's hard for crew guys to understande what is expected of them, especially younger guys. I'm not talking about the technical work: guys know their job and they know what needs to be done. But it's the stuff in the gray area that can be a problem. For example, people have to understand that you come to the track to race, period. It's not about hanging out with your friends, it's not about gossiping about the other teams, it's not about partying. You are there to win the race.

And when you get somebody on your crew who wants to tell the world how smart they are, that's a real problem. It's funny what happens then… they want to brag about how they figured out a certain thing on the car to make it go faster, and the next thing you know they are sharing key secrets and information that should never leave your shop. The ego drives a man to do foolish things sometimes.

I tend to want a good night's sleep. I get up earlier nowadays, sending Nathan off to school. On the road I'm up before everybody by about three hours. I mean everybody! I'm usually sitting outside the truck early in the morning, having a cup of coffee with only a few stragglers coming by. It's pretty pleasant, actually. I enjoy a nice, quiet morning.

I totally understand that not everybody is like that, especially some of the younger guys who like to stay up late and have fun. I don't tell my guys how to behave. But we do have some boundaries, some limits. I don't mind if they drink; just don't get stupid. And don't let it interfere with our racing. We're around each other for a lot of hours, so I want to give them as much space as possible. You've got to let people be themselves and relax. But like I said…there are boundaries.

I don't like loud and obnoxious people, especially when they've been drinking. So, obviously, I don't like it if somebody on our crew fits that description.

Here's another thing: our work days are hard and long. If your guys stay up until sunrise drinking and partying and they're gassed the next day working in the heat and it hurts your performance…well, that ain't cool, is it?

As we go forward I am going to try harder to be a better manager and leader. I'll keep trying!

We *have* figured out one team rule that we absolutely believe in: No bitching allowed. If you want to bitch, call your wife and bitch at her. Around here, just smile and pretend you're happy.

It goes a lot easier that way.

26

Changing Ideas

One of the things that has surprised me is how my thoughts of the future have shifted and changed as we went along. For example, one of the ideas I always carried in my head was that when I stepped away from driving someday I would go into the business of building racing chassis. After all, I've had a lot of experience with building cars, and spent a good bit of time building cars at Performance Chassis. That's been many years ago, but I always figured that's what I'd fall back on someday.

But I don't think so. In fact, I'm almost sure now that I don't want to pursue that idea.

In a way, I've already tried it. After I left Performance Chassis all those years ago, David Prizer and I started building a few modified cars at our shop. Not a big quantity, but enough to keep us busy and make a few bucks. It was fun, actually. I enjoyed the work, a lot.

The chassis was called Loose Gruff, and we got a lot of questions about that name. Back in the modified days we were racing somewhere and I was driving like a crazy man. I spun off the track all by myself, and after the race one of Chris's friends was joking with us and he wrote "Loose gruff" on the side of our car. Somehow that silly name stuck. I'm not one to fuss over a name anyway, so when they said we needed a name for our chassis that's what we came up with.

My idea with the business was to avoid carrying an inventory of the bolt-on stuff. The chassis business is more than just building a frame; you've got to develop and build the bolt-on pieces as well, and that becomes complicated.

As my driving career went along we had a lot of dealings with various chassis companies. Rayburn, MasterSbilt, Rocket, Bloomquist, Club 29, Barry Wright, Longhorn...and probably a couple more I can't recall. As I watched and learned, I discovered that to compete in the chassis business you have to be all-in. And if you're all-in, it's a huge amount of effort and energy. That level of effort and energy and headaches is huge. I'm not kidding…huge.

One day I suddenly realized: Man, there is surely an easier way to make a living than building race cars.

The construction part I would be eager to do: I love bending and welding and stuff like that. But the other part—dealing with the people—I wouldn't enjoy.

Hang around a big chassis builder for a while and you'll discover that poor guy is on the phone almost the entire day, every day, talking to customers. Answering their questions, listening to their feedback, the whole deal.

When I thought about it, I knew I'd never enjoy that role. Talking on the phone all day…that's not my definition of happiness. But if you're in that business, there is no getting around it.

Another challenge for me is paperwork, and paying the bills. Administrative stuff. I'm dyslexic as shit, and when I write a check I have to look over the invoice and the check five or six times to make sure I get it right. I just don't have the patience for that kind of work and I don't like it much anyways.

Something else you discover is that when you build a race car and sell it to somebody, you are now the cause of all his problems. He paid you good money, and now he ain't running any good and it's all because of your race car. Of course!

That's a whole new level of "dealing with people." I've been on both ends of that deal and it is complicated, to say the least.

And there's this: When a guy gets into a brand new race car and turns some laps, just once I'd like to hear a driver say something like, "I like the way this front end feels, it's so much better than before." But you probably won't hear that, because he will be focused on is what the car is *not* doing right. Racers—humans—are wired that way.

So as a chassis builder, the only thing people are focused on—and telling you about—is what your car is doing wrong. There ain't much "positive reinforcement" in that business.

Very few racers are confident enough to say, "I don't know." When they're asked what a car is doing, they tend to try too hard and that leads them to reach. This is a problem, because reaching can lead to bad information, bad feedback. Any car builder would tell you right quick, they'd rather have no feedback than wrong feedback. Wrong feedback can take you down the wrong path and pretty soon you're lost.

But I must say, our experience building the Loose Gruff cars had some good parts also. We met a lot of great people—including Leon Ramirez and his family, who we eventually went racing with—and it was a great experience to see racers have success in our chassis.

We met many young racers who ran our chassis, and it was exciting when they'd report back after having a great weekend.

And we made some great friendships, people like Bo and Wayne Hammond of Florida. Bo purchased a couple of our cars, and we came to be great friends. Shoot, we could write a whole other chapter just with our dealings with Bo! Bo and Wayne are great people. Bo put Kyle Bronson in his modified some years ago, giving Kyle's career a major boost. Wayne has continued that tradition yet today, and he and Kyle are still racing together. Wayne's business, Brandon Ford, is heavily involved in the Lucas Oil series as a sponsor.

Those were all the upsides, meeting great people like that. I guess you could say that our experience with Loose Gruff chassis gave us a true insight into how the chassis business works. The good, the bad, and the ugly.

Up until the end of the 2020 season, Mullet handled most of the stuff related to the Loose Gruff business. When he left our team that pretty much ended the deal.

Would I ever reconsider and get back into the chassis business? I suppose I could, but I doubt it. We've started and stopped the process so many times I'm not sure it would take off again. Plus, finding good help is very difficult at the moment, and that's a key part of that business.

Honestly, my phone isn't ringing all that much these days with people asking about buying a modified chassis. So it's definitely not a priority.

One of the hardest things about racing today—late models or modified racing, either one—is the vast amount of information and opinions that are out there. When it comes to setup and performance, everybody is an expert…just ask 'em!

That makes it difficult for all of us, especially the younger guys who are trying to learn how to drive or work on these cars. You have a bunch of different people in your ear with strong ideas about the right solution to different problems, and that can easily lead you astray.

What's the best answer to a handling problem? Depends on who you ask.

Fact is, it's complex. Usually, there ain't just one answer. These cars have become so complicated and tricky, we're operating in a very tight window of excellence.

Some time back I read a comment from Dale McDowell where he mentioned that the cars have changed a lot in recent years; he's had to adjust his driving style to make it work. That's exactly right, because I've had to change, too.

Today's car requires you to be way more aggressive. And you have to process a lot of information to understand how to set the car up properly to race aggressively. The chassis guys—builders and their representatives—often insist there is only one way to do this, but I don't necessarily agree.

We've gotten into a bad habit of thinking the aggressive style fits everybody. Actually, it doesn't.

What we've found is that it's become way more difficult to predict exactly what a certain setup—and a certain chassis—is going to do under different conditions.

Here's what I mean: In 2020 our Rocket chassis started off awesome at Volusia, and we won three straight nights against top competition. That was one of the best-handling cars I've ever driven. It was excellent and way fast! The car was a chassis we had ran quite a bit, one of our favorite cars.

A couple of weeks later we took a new car—a copy of that same brand of chassis, and nearly identical—to Smoky Mountain and we were terrible. We chased it and chased it and couldn't hit our butt with both hands. Over the next few weeks we kept working and working, trying different things. Finally we got it back and started winning races again.

That's what I mean when I say the cars are not as predictable. You can get a car really, really good, but man, it's hard to keep it there.

I reckon the chassis starts to flex and bend a little, and maybe you bang the car up a little bit. It feels like these cars can fall off real quick when that happens.

There again, it depends on who you ask. When you get right down to it, we're talking about a hunk of metal and you'd think it would do what you tell it to do. But that doesn't always work.

Either way, that's what keeps everybody jumping these days. Late model racing has never been simple—not really—but it's more complicated and tricky today than ever before.

27

Life...and more

Just as we were finishing this book, our dear friend and team owner Leon Ramirez passed away after a long fight with cancer. I can't begin to describe how much his loss hurt me. Just broke my heart. Leon was a great guy, a great person, a great team owner. It was a terrible loss to everyone, and my heart went out to Leon's family—especially Becky and their sons.

People often say racing is a business, and that's it. Well…I don't know about anybody else, but it's way more than that to me. Leon was not just the owner of our team; he was a friend, a mentor, a coach, an advisor, a cheerleader…all that and more. He was family.

His passing hit me very hard. I'm not one to easily express my emotions, but I was a wreck for several days. Right now—several weeks after his passing—I still find myself tearing up when I think about Leon not being here.

I can't dial that number and hear his voice. I can't go to him with a question or a concern. We aren't able to celebrate the highs together. Leon was a sarcastic guy with a sharp sense of humor, and he loved to bust on you; that's how he showed that he liked you. I will miss having him dog on me and razz me for this or that.

Man, that's such an empty feeling.

Leon's passing naturally left some questions about continuing the team, that sort of thing. Honestly, I'm not ready yet to fully think through all that. It doesn't seem important, not compared to Leon's passing.

Whatever happens, it will work out. It always does.

I can't ever repay Leon and his family for all he did for us. I am so grateful to have him in my life. I wish we could have had many more years together, but that's not how it worked out.

I probably haven't been this torn up since my mama passed away back in December 2014. When we lost her I was a mess, and it took quite some time to get through the grieving process.

Losing our parents is a tough thing for any of us. It seems like the healing process takes a long time, and you never heal up fully.

In February 2020 we had a great outing at Volusia and won three straight nights. After the races that final night I was so excited, so happy. We were calling people and sharing the good news, and everybody was celebrating.

I had this flash of an idea: I need to call Mama and tell her! She's gonna be so excited!

Of course, after just a moment I knew I couldn't do that. And just then it felt like an arrow went right into my heart, and I felt all that pain, all that grief, like it had happened yesterday.

I walked out of our hauler and went up into the empty grandstands and sat there, all by myself, crying like a kid.

Mama had been gone for more than six years, but not really. She'll never really be gone, not in my heart and in my mind.

That's how I feel about Leon. In my heart, in my mind, he'll never truly be gone.

The only way I know to deal with loss like this is to keep going. For us, that means to keep racing.

As we began the 2022 season, we continued to experience the conflict that racing naturally brings out. Do I want to be out on the road, away from home, racing? Or do I want to be home with my family and my friends?

It's the same thing I've wrestled with for many years. I love racing, and I love what we do. But I also love being home.

As I'm sitting here telling you all this, I'm thinking about a typical Thursday afternoon on New Cave Church Road. The truck is nearly loaded, and we're finishing up our tires. The car is almost ready, with Cory and Kurt getting set to get 'er loaded up. It's a sunny day and later tonight—or maybe first thing in the morning—we're looking at an eight-hour ride.

Once again I look at the hauler and a brief thought crosses my mind: I'm not sure I want to go.

Once we get on the road I'm fine. My mind clicks into gear and all my thoughts are focused on this weekend's racing. But sure as anything, on the return trip as we roll to the Newport exit on I-40—whether it's morning or night or whatever time—it feels great, knowing we're almost home. Home is great—wonderful.

Through the years there have been many nights when we're rolling up on that I-40 exit and my mind shifts to a different place, a different process. It's usually in the odd hours of the morning—3 a.m., 5 a.m., 7 a.m.—when we're flicking on the signal for the exit. I'll start thinking about the rest of the day...after I get a nap, maybe me and Nathan can do something. Or maybe Melissa and Nathan will hop in our Jeep and we'll go for a ride. By evening time I'm ready to sink back on the couch and flip on the TV.

With Nathan and Melissa traveling with me more and more, there is no real reason why it should feel so good to get home—after all, the things I love the most are with me. But for some reason I still feel a sense of joy, and relief, when we get home.

A few years ago we built a house up on the side of the mountain, and it's been a great home. I don't just mean a great house; I mean a great *home.*

When we're home we ride our ATV up the mountain, having a good time. We like sitting on our porch, overlooking the nearby valley.

Home. Ain't noplace like it.

We'll watch TV and hang out and it's great. Our dog—a white Siberian Husky mix named Nova—will be right there in the middle of everything.

Nova is a funny 'ol dog. She's kinda like a teen-ager, stubborn and temperamental. Sometimes when she's mad at us she'll walk over to the side of the room and sit there staring at the wall, throwing her fit.

She likes to go outside and scout around, and she'll stand at the door to let us know it's time to go out. We have several black bears roaming around our area now and then, coming down off the mountain. If there are any bears in the vicinity, Nova will take a step through the door and stop in her tracks. Her ol' nose will twitch a couple of times and she'll back right up. No thank you! We'll go outside a little later, maybe.

Nova knows: the sniffer never lies.

Having Nathan and Melissa travel with us has been a great thing in recent years. Fact is, it's renewed much of my excitement for racing, because I don't feel disconnected with my family every weekend.

If they are with us, it's better. Simple as that.

So many times in the past, I've missed out on things while on the road. Football games, graduations, plays, everything. Tons of things I didn't get to see. But when my family is out there with me, I don't have to worry about missing anything.

Nathan has pretty much grown up around this deal. He understands the process, and he's figured out how to inch his way into the picture when we're interviewed on TV. I laugh when he does that and it's been lots of fun.

Having Nathan and Melissa travel with us has made a huge difference in how I've come to love racing once again. (Dave Argabright photo)

See this right here? This is what it's all about. (Rick Schwallie photo)

Nathan has said that it's pretty cool to have a race car dad. Well, that's an awesome thing to hear.

There was a time a few years ago, when I was feeling burned out on racing, I honestly thought about quitting. I started to feel like I was missing Nathan growing up, missing home, just…missing too much.

Finally, I asked Nathan one day, "Son, do you want Daddy to quit racing?"

He stopped and looked at me.

"Don't you need to race, daddy?"

"Well, I don't actually *need* to race, I guess, but racing is how we make money for our groceries and things."

"Well, Daddy, having a race car is pretty cool. You need to keep doing it."

There you go. Question is answered until further notice.

One of the greatest moments of my life was when Nathan was smaller. We were riding in the car to the shop and I looked at him and said, "Boy, you've got to stop growing."

"Why, daddy?"

"Because I want you to stay little forever."

He started to cry.

"Why are you crying, Nathan?"

"Because I want to grow up to be just like you, Daddy. But you said I can't grow up!"

Now we were BOTH crying.

We've had so much fun together. One time when he was quite a bit younger we were out on the road, staying in our bunk in the trailer. We got to laughing about something goofy and pretty soon we were laughing so hard we were both crying. Moments like that are so much fun.

I've tried to explain to Nathan how lucky he is. To be able to travel all over the country at such a young age, to experience the things he has, it's wonderful. I hope he appreciates it. Sometimes I think he does. He's very good about accepting mom and dad's authority. He's just a good boy all around and me and Melissa are very grateful for him.

So what would I do if I ever quit racing? I'm not sure. I have thought about it some, but not a lot. As the years have passed I have learned some things I enjoy, and things I don't enjoy. I've been a little bit surprised about that, actually. There were things that I was sure I'd want to do at some point—such as building race chassis—but now that some time has passed I've discovered that I don't have much of an appetite for it after all. And there are other things that I never dreamed I'd be interested in, but I am.

I'm grateful for the impact David and Norma Prizer had on my life. I'm not sure where I'd be without them. David still comes by our shop every day, and it means a lot to have him nearby. (Dave Argabright photo)

I've enjoyed learning about SolidWorks, a 3-D CAD design software. I'm fascinated by this stuff! I was interested enough that I purchased the system and through trial and error taught myself how to use it. My ability right now is elementary, but I'm learning. I love the concept of envisioning a piece and designing it on the computer and then building it. That is something I hope to pursue a little more. Exactly how I would use it I don't know, but I'm excited about learning more.

I enjoy taking our Jeep out and riding around. That's probably my best hobby right now, tooling around in our Jeep. We've had two or three and I like this one a lot, a 2012 model we bought locally. We'll go off-road, but also highway riding. You can ride all day around our house and never hit pavement. But mostly we just cruise around, enjoying the day. It's a nice release and a fun way for our family to spend time together.

When I think back to my early years in super late models, a lot of the guys we raced against in the beginning have retired and left the sport. Taking their place has been a lot of young racers, some of 'em not even born yet when we started.

I never dreamed we'd race this long, yet here we are.

I remember being the young guy who was eager to learn what was going on. Now things are different, with me being the veteran going up against those younger racers.

Many of the younger guys today are respectful. Some aren't. Either way, I haven't had any specific problems with anybody. When you're in the heat of the battle with somebody younger, it isn't the same as with a veteran guy. You expect to get doored now and then, at that age we did it too.

It's been good to see so many talented young racers come into our sport. That's good for everybody, all around.

When we won the 2020 Lucas Oil Late Model Dirt Series title the MAVTV guys put together a video of many of the series drivers commenting about racing with me. It was nice hearing them say good things, I admit. It felt good. I am glad they respect me and I appreciate them saying they want to race me cleanly. Although I think some of 'em fibbed a little bit about that…they might rub on us a little more than they admit to!

I am who I am…I don't race just to get people to say nice things. But when others talk about their respect for me—not just as a driver, but as a person—it makes me realize the impact people like David and Norma Prizer had on my life. David and Norma are truly good people and they would do anything for anybody. As a very young man I saw this, watched how they treated people, and that's the way I wanted to be. No doubt about it, David and Norma were a huge influence on the person I am today. Huge!

I see people as good. And I want to be good, too, and treat people right. Leon Ramirez and Mike Reece—and several others—put me in their race car because they cared about me and wanted to help me. If it wasn't for people like that, I wouldn't be anywhere.

A while back we were at Fairbury, Illinois, hanging out and talking with a few people. I mentioned that I've been on both sides of this thing, and I'm happy seeing other people succeed. I understand how much a racer wants to make their way in our sport, to make a living and be successful. It means so much, especially to a younger guy who is trying to get there. Man, I understand. I want to see their dreams come true, just like mine came true.

Jonathan Davenport spoke up and thanked me for saying that. His wife Rachel looked at me and said, "Man, why are you so damned nice?"

We had a lot of fun with that comment. But I'm not the jealous type, honestly. We work hard to kick their ass, and I WANT to kick their ass. But if they beat us, I'm happy for them.

When people say nice things about me, it's humbling. Still—I don't think of myself as anything special.

A few years ago I started to hear this question: "How long are you going to keep doing this?"

I turned 50 in early 2022, and at this moment I don't ever plan on quitting. From the beginning, I've always figured I'd do this until they threw me out. However, hearing that question came a little earlier than I wanted it to!

I still enjoy racing, a lot. Nothing—and nobody—is pushing me to quit. We're still running good and every time we roll the car out I feel like we can win.

If all the team owners pulled out, that would quickly determine how much I still want to race. That would be a game changer, at least for me. I am not going to race on my money, because late model racing has grown beyond that. I have no problem admitting it.

One thing I have realized over the past couple of years is this: With the growth of racing, with the different things we've done and experienced, we have somehow lost a certain element of fun. Pure, pure fun. That's what racing was for us in the beginning, and I'm sorry the sport has somehow strayed from that.

I'll bet I'm not the only racer who feels that way.

A couple of years ago we were at Columbus, Mississippi for the Cotton Pickin' race, and they always run the street stock race after our race. The street stock racing at Columbus is awesome, and we always stay and watch.

A guy offered me to drive his car and I said, "Heck yes!" We qualified quick time, and started on the pole. We took off and I had a comfortable lead, and suddenly the car got loose and wasn't quite as good. The rear end had slipped on the leaf spring, and was moving back and forth. The guys behind me caught up and got alongside us, and the caution came out.

I put the car on the bottom for the restart and said to myself, "They're gonna have to go around me on the outside."

We ended up winning and it was super, super fun. I'm sure we were in their way, but we won. My late model crew was hooting and hollering, having a great time.

After the race another driver came over and shook my hand.

"It was a pleasure racing with you," he said.

"I guess I was in your way a little," I admitted.

"Well…yeah, you were in my way a LOT!"

"You butthole!" I said. "You weren't supposed to agree with me!"

We laughed and laughed, and it was great. The whole deal was great. I have no idea what the race paid, but that didn't matter. It was pure, fun racing.

How'd our sport drift away from when it was just plain fun?

Here's another story: We were racing a while back—I believe it was in Georgia but I'm not sure—and were parked next to a local late model racer. Just as their heat race finished a lady came running into their pit, all torn up with emotion, crying and shouting. She was all excited because they had made a transfer spot and were in tonight's Lucas Oil series feature.

That stopped me in my tracks. What a great perspective for me…I've raced long enough at this level that just making the feature is expected. Taken for granted, pretty much.

Yet here was this lady, this team, crying and celebrating and filled with joy because they made the show.

Listen…I totally remember that feeling. But it seems that too often I forget that perspective.

I'm grateful for experiences like watching that team celebrate. It's important we never lose that perspective. Never.

That's a good way to finish our book, and close things out. With gratitude.

I'm grateful that so many good things happened in my life. David and Norma Prizer taking me under their wing, discovering racing, Melissa and Nathan and my family, so many friends I couldn't possibly count 'em all… many good things.

I'm grateful for all the good things in my life...everything that's happened in racing, and for my family. Melissa and I are accepting the 2020 championship hardware from Lucas Oil Series Director Rick Schwallie. (Heath Lawson photo)

With Larry Moore at Knoxville in 2014. (Dave Argabright photo)

In a lot of ways I'm still that kid from Newport, shy and backward. As I said at the beginning, I've traveled far and wide but always came home to Tennessee. Yet some amazing things happened along the way. Wonderful things, things I'll never forget.

I am humbled just thinking about my life experience.

I've been asked in interviews about what I'm most proud of in my life. Obviously, I want to do right by my family—a good man, a good dad, that kind of thing. I've been fortunate enough to win races and some championships, and that's nice also. That's important.

But some of the things that happened, it's hard to put into words how it has made me feel.

I've had babies named after me—and they weren't even my kid!

I've heard from people who tell me about their relative who recently passed away after requesting to be buried in their favorite Jimmy Owens t-shirt. To think that our racing has touched and excited people to that point, it's pretty amazing.

I've had occasion to become a hero—to those who were my heroes! Early in our career during a trip to Florida we were invited to stay at the home of Larry Moore, a dirt racing legend. Larry Moore was my hero and for years afterwards we were excited to tell people we stayed with him for a few nights. Then one day a couple of years ago we ran into Larry and he explained that he brags to people about the time Jimmy Owens and his guys stayed with *him*.

"Oh man," he said to me, "you're waaayyyyy cool, Jimmy! You're my hero!"

I do not have the words to explain what it meant to hear him say that.

Something happened to me recently that helped me understand some of this, and put it into perspective. It brought some things into focus, just as we were figuring out what we wanted to say at the ending of this book.

We were racing at Smoky Mountain Speedway, a favorite local track just down the road from Newport. After the races we were visiting with people at the back of our trailer when a middle-aged couple approached us.

"You saved my life, Jimmy," the man said.

I kind of laughed at first, because I thought the man was joking. But he had a serious expression and when he spoke again his voice started to crack a little bit.

"Your racing keeps me going," he said. "I get in a real dark spot sometimes…real dark. I get to feeling like I don't want to go on. But I love following your racing, and it helps me get up out of that dark spot and keep going."

Life is good...very, very good! (Heath Lawson photo)

I was just about speechless. I had no idea what I was supposed to say, other than I was very happy that he's able to get out of that dark spot. If I've helped in the slightest way, I'm glad. And grateful.

Here's the thing: for years we've all recognized that in the big picture, there are many things more important than racing. It's just cars going in circles, right?

But we're wrong about that. To countless people, racing brings joy. And happiness. And pleasure. And, in many cases, inspiration and hope.

Ain't that something?

Celebrate the joy, man. That's what life is all about.

I've had fun writing this book. It's a lot of work, but I'm glad we did it. It has kept my thoughts coming back again and again to all the good times, the good things, and the good people.

Thanks for riding along, and sticking with us to the finish. We'll be appearing at a dirt track near you, sometime soon. I hope you'll come by our pit and say hello. I'll be looking for you.

JIMMY OWENS

NOTABLE ACCOMPLISHMENTS

590+ Open Wheel Modified and Dirt Late Model Career Victories
Won First Ever Race Entered - Street Stock in 1991 at Kingsport (TN) Speedway
4-Time UMP National Modified Champion (1998, 2000, 2001, 2002)
Won 49 Feature Events in 65 Starts in 1999

2007
$40,000 'World 100' Winner at Eldora (OH) Speedway
$50,000 'North/South 100' Winner at Florence (KY) Speedway
$20,000 'RaceFest World Championship' Winner at West Virginia Mtr. Speedway
$10,000 'Blue/Gray 100' Winner at Cherokee (SC) Speedway
17 Dirt Late Model Victories

2008
Dart Winternationals Point Champion at Golden Isles (GA) Speedway (3 Wins)
$40,000 'Hillbilly 100' Winner at Tyler County (WV) Speedway
$10,000 'Scorcher' Winner at Volunteer (TN) Speedway
$10,000 'Ralph Latham Memorial' Winner at Florence (KY) Speedway
$10,000 'Bluegrass Classic' Winner at Bluegrass (KY) Speedway
$10,000 'March Madness' Winner at Cherokee (SC) Speedway
$10,000 Advance Auto Parts Thunder Series Winner at Volunteer (TN) Speedway
14 Dirt Late Model Victories

2009
$100,000 'Dirt Late Model Dream' Winner at Eldora (OH) Speedway
$40,000 'Topless 100' Winner at Batesville (AR) Motor Speedway
$10,000 'Ralph Latham Memorial' Winner at Florence (KY) Speedway
$10,000 Lucas Oil Late Model Dirt Series Winner at Tazewell (TN) Speedway
$10,000 Lucas Oil Late Model Dirt Series Winner at Portsmouth (OH) Raceway Park
$10,000 World of Outlaws Series Winner at Lowe's (NC) Motor Speedway
Finished Second in Lucas Oil Late Model Dirt Series Point Standings
7 Dirt Late Model Victories

2010
$50,000 'North/South 100' Winner at Florence (KY) Speedway
$10,000 Lucas Oil Late Model Dirt Series Winner at Brownstown (IN) Speedway
$10,000 Lucas Oil Late Model Dirt Series Winner at Bedford (PA) Speedway
$10,000 Lucas Oil Late Model Dirt Series Winner at Wythe (VA) Raceway
$10,000 Lucas Oil Late Model Dirt Series Winner at Cleveland (TN) Speedway
$10,000 Lucas Oil Late Model Dirt Series Winner at Volunteer (TN) Speedway
$10,000 Lucas Oil Late Model Dirt Series Winner at Lucas Oil (MO) Speedway
$10,000 Lucas Oil Late Model Dirt Series Winner at Fonda (NY) Speedway
$10,000 World of Outlaws Series Winner at Bluegrass (KY) Speedway
$10,000 World of Outlaws Series Winner at Dirt Track (NC) at Charlotte
Finished Second in Lucas Oil Late Model Dirt Series Point Standings
10 Dirt Late Model Victories

2011
Lucas Oil Late Model Dirt Series National Champion
$50,000 'North/South 100' Winner at Florence (KY) Speedway
$44,000 'World 100' Winner at Eldora (OH) Speedway
$30,000 'Show-Me 100' Winner at Lucas Oil (MO) Speedway
$10,000 Lucas Oil Late Model Dirt Series Winner at Rome (GA) Speedway
$10,000 Lucas Oil Late Model Dirt Series Winner at Volunteer (TN) Speedway
$10,000 Lucas Oil Late Model Dirt Series Winner at Fonda (NY) Speedway
$10,000 Lucas Oil Late Model Dirt Series Winner at Cleveland (TN) Speedway
$10,000 Lucas Oil Late Model Dirt Series Winner at East Bay (FL) Raceway Park
$10,000 Ultimate Super Late Model Series Winner at Volunteer (TN) Speedway
$10,000 World of Outlaws Series Winner at Dirt Track (NC) at Charlotte
$7,000 Lucas Oil Late Model Dirt Series Winner at Knoxville (IA) Raceway
13 Dirt Late Model Victories

2012
Lucas Oil Late Model Dirt Series National Champion
$50,000 'Dirt Track World Championship' Winner at Portsmouth (OH) Raceway Park
$30,000 'Show-Me 100' Winner at Lucas Oil (MO) Speedway
$21,800 'National 100' Winner at East Alabama Motor Speedway
$20,000 'Jackson 100' Winner at Brownstown (IN) Speedway
$15,000 'Cotton Pickin' 100' Winner at Magnolia (MS) Motor Speedway
$10,000 + Car 'Bad Boy 98' Winner at Batesville (AR) Motor Speedway
$10,000 Southern All Star Series Winner at Cleveland (TN) Speedway
$10,000 Lucas Oil Late Model Dirt Series Winner at Lucas Oil (MO) Speedway
$10,000 Lucas Oil Late Model Dirt Series Winner at Lawrenceburg (IN) Speedway
$10,000 Lucas Oil Late Model Dirt Series Winner at Dixie (GA) Speedway
(2) $10,000 World of Outlaws Series Wins at Dirt Track (NC) at Charlotte
12 Dirt Late Model Victories

2013
Lucas Oil Late Model Dirt Series National Champion
$30,000 'Show-Me 100' Winner at Lucas Oil (MO) Speedway
$27,000 'Silver Dollar Nationals' Winner at I-80 (NE) Speedway
$25,000 'Hillbilly 100' Winner at I-77 (WV) Raceway Park
$20,000 'Cotton Pickin' 100' Winner at Magnolia (MS) Motor Speedway
$10,000 Lucas Oil Late Model Dirt Series Winner at Attica (OH) Raceway Park
$10,000 Lucas Oil Late Model Dirt Series Winner at Roaring Knob (PA) Motorsports
$10,000 Lucas Oil Late Model Dirt Series Winner at Hagerstown (MD) Speedway
$10,000 Lucas Oil Late Model Dirt Series Winner at Lonestar (TX) Speedway
$7,000 Lucas Oil Late Model Dirt Series Winner at East Bay (FL) Raceway Park
$5,000 Lucas Oil MLRA Series Winner at Lucas Oil (MO) Speedway
10 Dirt Late Model Victories

2014
$50,000 'USA Nationals' Winner at Cedar Lake (WI) Speedway
$40,000 'Topless 100' Winner at Batesville (AR) Motor Speedway
$12,000 World of Outlaws Series Winner at Dirt Track (NC) at Charlotte
$10,000 Lucas Oil Late Model Dirt Series Winner at LaSalle (IL) Speedway
$10,000 Lucas Oil Late Model Dirt Series Winner at Tazewell (TN) Speedway
$10,000 Lucas Oil Late Model Dirt Series Winner at Florence (KY) Speedway
$10,000 Lucas Oil Late Model Dirt Series Winner at Muskingum Co. (OH) Speedway
$10,000 Lucas Oil Late Model Dirt Series Winner at 201 (KY) Speedway
$10,000 Lucas Oil Late Model Dirt Series Winner at Lucas Oil (MO) Speedway
$10,000 Lucas Oil Late Model Dirt Series Winner at Lakeside (KS) Speedway
$10,000 Unsanctioned Winner at Volunteer (TN) Speedway
$6,000 World of Outlaws Series Winner at Lernerville (PA) Speedway
$5,000 'World 100' Twin 25 Winner at Eldora (OH) Speedway
$4,000 Spring Nationals Series Winner at Volunteer (TN) Speedway
$2,500 'DLM Dream' Twin 25 Winner at Eldora (OH) Speedway
Finished Second in Lucas Oil Late Model Dirt Series Point Standings
15 Dirt Late Model Victories

2015
$25,000 'National 100' Winner at East Alabama Motor Speedway
$12,000 Lucas Oil Late Model Dirt Series Winner at Macon (IL) Speedway
$10,000 'Wild West Shootout' Finale Winner at USA (AZ) Raceway
$3,000 'Wild West Shootout' Winner at USA (AZ) Raceway
Finished Third in Lucas Oil Late Model Dirt Series Point Standings
4 Dirt Late Model Victories

2016
$30,000 'Show-Me 100' Winner at Lucas Oil (MO) Speedway
Finished Ninth in Lucas Oil Late Model Dirt Series Point Standings

2017
$12,000 Lucas Oil Late Model Dirt Series Winner at Smoky Mtn. (TN) Speedway
$10,000 Lucas Oil Late Model Dirt Series Winner at Tazewell (TN) Speedway
$10,000 Lucas Oil Late Model Dirt Series Winner at Florence (KY) Speedway
$7,000 Lucas Oil Late Model Dirt Series Winner at Brownstown (IN) Speedway
2x $5,000 'National 100' Prelim Winner at East Alabama Motor Speedway
Finished Fifth in Lucas Oil Late Model Dirt Series Point Standings
6 Dirt Late Model Victories

2018
$40,000 'Knoxville Late Model Nationals' Winner at Knoxville (IA) Raceway
$25,001 'First in Flight 100' Winner at Fayetteville (NC) Motor Speedway
$10,000 World of Outlaws Series Winner at Volunteer (TN) Speedway
$10,000 'World 100' Twin 25 Winner at Eldora (OH) Speedway
$6,000 Lucas Oil Late Model Dirt Series Winner at Lucas Oil (MO) Speedway
Finished Fifth in Lucas Oil Late Model Dirt Series Point Standings
69 Races Entered, 5 Victories, 24 Top Fives, & 43 Top Tens

2019
$40,000 'Knoxville Late Model Nationals' Winner at Knoxville (IA) Raceway
$15,000 'Diamond Nationals' Winner at Lucas Oil (MO) Speedway
$12,000 'World Finals' Winner at Dirt Track (NC) at Charlotte
$12,000 Lucas Oil Late Model Dirt Series Winner at Tri-City (IL) Speedway
$12,000 Lucas Oil Late Model Dirt Series Winner at Atomic (OH) Speedway
$12,000 World of Outlaws Series Winner at Smoky Mtn. (TN) Speedway
$10,052 'Scott Sexton Memorial' Winner at 411 (TN) Motor Speedway
$10,000 World of Outlaws Series Winner at Davenport (IA) Speedway
Finished Fifth in Lucas Oil Late Model Dirt Series Point Standings
78 Races Entered, 8 Victories, 36 Top Fives, & 45 Top Tens

2020
Lucas Oil Late Model Dirt Series National Champion
$40,000 'Topless 100' Winner at Batesville (AR) Motor Speedway
$15,000 Lucas Oil Late Model Dirt Series Winner at Magnolia (MS) Mtr. Speedway
$15,000 Crate Late Model Winner at Volunteer (TN) Speedway
$12,000 Lucas Oil Late Model Dirt Series Winner at Florence (KY) Speedway
$12,000 Lucas Oil Late Model Dirt Series Winner at I-80 (NE) Speedway
$12,000 Lucas Oil Late Model Dirt Series Winner at Portsmouth (OH) Raceway Park
$12,000 Lucas Oil Late Model Dirt Series Winner at Talladega (AL) Short Track
$12,000 Lucas Oil Late Model Dirt Series Winner at 411 (TN) Motor Speedway
$10,000 World of Outlaws Series Winner at Beaver Dam (WI) Raceway

3x $10,000 World of Outlaws Series Winner at Volusia (FL) Speedway Park
77 Races Entered, 20 Victories, 44 Top Fives, & 53 Top Tens

2021
$26,000 'Powell Memorial' Crate Winner at All-Tech (FL) Raceway
$20,000 'Jackson 100' Winner at Brownstown (IN) Speedway
$20,000 FloRacing Night in America Winner at 411 (TN) Motor Speedway
$10,053 Spring Nationals Series Winner at Smoky Mountain (TN) Speedway
$10,052 Spring Nationals Series Winner at 411 (TN) Motor Speedway
$5,000 Lucas Oil Late Model Dirt Series Winner at Batesville (AR) Mtr. Speedway
$5,000 Iron-Man Series Winner at Lake Cumberland (KY) Speedway
$5,000 World of Outlaws Series Winner at Cherokee (SC) Speedway
Finished Fourth in Lucas Oil Late Model Dirt Series Point Standings
85 Races Entered, 8 Victories, 31 Top Fives, & 54 Top Tens

Index

Special thanks...

Heath Lawson (L) and Rick Schwallie (R) kindly opened their photo archives to us and provided many of the images in this book.
Thank you Heath and Rick!
(Dave Argabright photo)

Their images are available for purchase at these websites:

Rick: https://www.latemodelphotos.com/
Heath: https://www.heathlawsonphotos.com/

Dave Argabright has worked in motorsports media since 1980 in print, broadcast, and digital coverage. He has covered nearly every aspect of American oval racing in a variety of roles and publications including *NATIONAL SPEED SPORT NEWS*, *SprintCar and Midget Magazine*, *OPEN WHEEL Magazine, PRI Magazine, Car and Driver,* and *Road & Track*. His broadcast experience includes MAVTV, TNN, CBS Sports, ESPN, SPEED TV, and the Indianapolis 500 Radio Network.

Dave is a 2014 inductee in the National Sprint Car Hall of Fame. His professional honors include the "Mike Swims Award of Excellence" and the "Frank Blunk Award for Journalism" among others. A Hoosier native, Dave and his family reside in Noblesville, Indiana.

OTHER BOOKS BY DAVE ARGABRIGHT

STILL WIDE OPEN - with Brad Doty
AMERICAN SCENE - A COLLECTION
HEWITT'S LAW - with Jack Hewitt
EARL! - with Earl Baltes
LET 'EM ALL GO! - with Chris Economaki
LONE WOLF - with Doug Wolfgang
FAST COMPANY - with Speedy Bill Smith
LET'S GO RACING! - with Rex Robbins
ON TOP OF THE WORLD - with Larry Moore
MODERN THUNDER - with
John Mahoney and Pat Sullivan
LIFE WITH LUKE - with Jimmy Sills

The Jimmy Wilson Collection
SPRINT CAR SALVATION
FAST AND FEARLESS
SPRINT CAR SHOWDOWN
SPRINT CAR CHALLENGE
SPRINT CAR LEGEND
SPRINT CAR COURAGE

Book reorder information:

American Scene Press LLC
P.O. Box 34
Noblesville, IN 46061
(317) 219-5716
orders@daveargabright.com

www.daveargabright.com

www.jimmyowens20.com